Intersecting Pathways

AMERICAN ACADEMY OF RELIGION
CULTURAL CRITICISM SERIES

SERIES EDITOR
Bjorn Krondorfer, St. Mary's College of Maryland

A Publication Series of
The American Academy of Religion and
Oxford University Press

AAR
Intersecting Pathways

Modern Jewish Theologians
in Conversation
with Christianity

MARC A. KRELL

OXFORD
UNIVERSITY PRESS

2003

OXFORD
UNIVERSITY PRESS

Oxford   New York
Auckland   Bangkok   Buenos Aires   Cape Town   Chennai
Dar es Salaam   Delhi   Hong Kong   Istanbul   Karachi   Kolkata
Kuala Lumpur   Madrid   Melbourne   Mexico City   Mumbai   Nairobi
São Paulo   Shanghai   Taipei   Tokyo   Toronto

Copyright © 2003 by The American Academy of Religion

Published by Oxford University Press, Inc.
198 Madison Avenue, New York, New York, 10016
www.oup.com

Oxford is a registered trademark of Oxford University Press

Library of Congress Cataloging-in-Publication Data
Krell, Marc A. (Marc Aaron), 1967–
Intersecting pathways : modern Jewish theologians in conversation
with Christianity / Marc A. Krell.
p.   cm.—(American Academy of Religion cultural criticism series)
Includes bibliographical references and index.
ISBN 0-19-515935-7
1. Judaism—Relations—Christianity.   2. Christianity
and other religions—Judaism.   3. Jews—Identity.
4. Judaism—Doctrines—Comparative studies.
5. Theology, Doctrinal—Comparative studies.
I. Title.   II. Series.
BM535 .K74 2003
296.3'96—dc21   2002008643

9 8 7 6 5 4 3 2 1

Printed in the United States of America
on acid-free paper

To Julie

Acknowledgments

The following journals have allowed me to reprint material from my published articles: brief selections from the introduction and epilogue were published in "Decentering Judaism and Christianity: Using Feminist Theory to Construct a Postmodern Jewish-Christian Theology," *Cross Currents* 50, no. 4 (winter 2000–2001): 474–87; portions of chapters 1 and 2 in this book were published in "Schoeps vs. Rosenzweig: Transcending Religious Borders," *Zeitschrift für Religions-und Geistesgeschichte* 52, no. 1 (2000): 25–37; a brief selection from chapter 3 was published in "Eliezer Berkovits's Post-Holocaust Theology: A Dialectic Between Polemics and Reception," *Journal of Ecumenical Studies* 37, no. 1 (winter 2000): 28–45.

In completing this book, I owe many thanks to the following people: George Griener, Elliot Dorff, Claude Welch, Gary Lease, and Stephan Kienberger. In particular, I want to acknowledge Arnold Eisen and David Biale, who supervised the writing of this manuscript in its original form as a dissertation. Professor Eisen was instrumental in helping me to shape my argument in a concise, clear fashion that showcases my own contribution to the field. I have been profoundly influenced by the historiography of David Biale, whose pointed comments enabled me to focus on my overall argument without arguing against those whom I discuss. In addition, my personal discussion with Richard Rubenstein provided me with valuable insight into his work.

I would also like to express my special appreciation for the recent guidance of my colleagues J. Edward Wright, Lawrence Baron, Randi Rashkover, James Moore, and Zachary Braiterman, who have helped me transform the dissertation into a book. Their suggestions regarding both content and structure led me to tighten this work considerably and weave it together much more smoothly. I especially wish to thank Zachary Braiterman for his comprehensive chapter-by-chapter commentary. His critical remarks forced me to be more consistent in my portrayal of the fluid boundaries between Judaism and Christianity, by encouraging me to focus more on the conversation between Jewish theologians and Christian figures rather than on who was influenced by whom.

On a personal note, I would like to thank my mother, Florie Krell, for her ongoing emotional support and friendship. Finally, I want to thank my part-time editor, best friend and wife, Julie Schaefer Krell, who has been my strongest supporter and source of inspiration. Through her companionship and love, she has made me realize what is truly important in life. Together, we brought into the world our greatest sources of joy, our sons Alexander Micah and Jonah Evan.

Contents

Intersecting Pathways

Introduction

Uncovering Jewish-Christian
Dialectic in History

When speaking at his first political rally as the United States Democratic candidate for vice president in 2000, Senator Joseph Lieberman of Connecticut stated, "There are some people who might actually call Al Gore's selection of me an act of chutzpah!"[1] Regardless of the eventual election outcome, Vice President Gore clearly made a bold decision to break down religious and cultural barriers that had prevented American Jews from seeking the highest public offices in a Christian-dominated country. In fact, rather than focusing on Lieberman's centrist political positions as a reason for his choice, Gore seized the moment to showcase Lieberman's religious affiliation and to emphasize the fact that Lieberman was the first Jew to be the vice presidential candidate of any major party, comparing it to the election of the first Catholic president in 1960, John F. Kennedy. Moreover, Lieberman himself invoked the African American political and religious leader the Reverend Jesse Jackson, who said upon hearing of the choice that when one cultural barrier is lifted, the walls fall down for everyone in American society.

It is ironic, however, that while Jackson praised the choice of Lieberman as a vice presidential candidate, other members of the African American community began to question Lieberman's loyalty to them and his willingness to fight for their rights. At issue was his supposed support for California Proposition 309, which would outlaw affirmative action as discriminatory. The growing Jewish opposition to affirmative action along with the political and economic gains made by Jews like Lieberman provide African Americans with evidence of the increasingly insider status of the Jews in

American society.[2] While numerically a minority, American Jews are now perceived as part of the Judeo-Christian majority by African Americans as well as by underprivileged Chicano and Latino groups.[3] In light of the terrorist attacks against the United States on 11 September 2001 and the ongoing Palestinian-Israeli conflict, an increasing number of Americans perceive the Jews as having too much political and economic power in the United States today. More specifically, in a post September 11th survey of one thousand people of different ethnic, religious, age, and regional backgrounds, the most antisemitic Americans were four times as likely as those holding no antisemitic views to believe that American Jewish leaders have too much influence over United States foreign policy. While 35 percent of the African American respondents to the survey possessed these strongly antisemitic views, an even more alarming 44 percent of foreign born Hispanic Americans voiced similar opinions.[4]

Ultimately, this cultural ambiguity has produced a contradictory American Jewish self-consciousness, wherein Jews' identification and integration with the Christian majority directly conflict with their equal desire to preserve their minority status as outsiders in relation to a hegemonic Christian culture.[5] This ambivalence between security and vulnerability that Jews possess was most clearly evident in their somewhat mixed reaction to the choice of Joseph Lieberman as a vice presidential candidate. His candidacy appeared to be a transparent symbol of the simultaneity of Jewish insider and outsider status in a predominantly Christian America, and it is a symbol with which some Jews are uncomfortable.

The culturally ambiguous status of contemporary American Jewry in relation to Christian society can be traced to a parallel Jewish-Christian liminality occurring on the religious or theological level in the twentieth century. In this way, theology may be understood as a cultural activity in the sense that human beings construct it in the context of sociocultural interaction, and like cultural identity, it too is forged out of an ambiguous power dynamic. Instead of being an indisputable and normative discourse, theology is socially and historically conditioned just like all other human activities. Moreover, from a postmodern perspective, theology does not arise within a self-contained and self-originating culture but rather is constructed situationally amid a host of cultural alternatives. In fact, one could argue that theological statements are produced not within enclosed cultural boundaries but at the constantly fluctuating boundaries with other cultures.[6]

This book explores a pattern of Jewish theological and cultural boundary construction in the twentieth century in which certain Jewish thinkers have been developing Jewish theologies based on a theological and cultural interchange with Christianity. This shared discourse with Christianity arises out of a history in which both Christian and Jewish identities have been constructed to some extent symbiotically in relation to each other. Moreover, this symbiosis has been generated by a dialectic between attraction to and repulsion by one culture for the other that has been visible in theological texts of both communities since antiquity.

I use the term "symbiosis" in its dialectical sense as it is described by Steven Wasserstrom in *Between Muslim and Jew: The Problem of Symbiosis under Early Islam*. He states that symbiosis involves "genuine mutuality and authentic benefit both, only if it is allowed its delusions and its dominations, its manipulations and exploitations, its half-baked altruisms and its full-blown fusions."[7] Wasserstrom discusses the original transposition of the term from biology to the study of Jewish history, and he further clarifies its usage with regard to the Jewish-Muslim relationship. He points out that it was first used by Martin Buber and other German intellectuals to define what Hermann Cohen portrayed as the relationship between "Germanism and Judaism."[8]

In his book, Wasserstrom discusses the term "creative symbiosis" in its application to early medieval Jewish-Muslim relations as described by Shlomo Dov Goitein in *Jews and Arabs* (1974). Wasserstrom argues that Goitein and his successors have assumed only the positive connotation of symbiosis when discussing early medieval Jewish-Muslim encounter, without examining its dialectical nature. He calls this "the 'problem' of symbiosis" and refers to it in the following passage:

> By means of (usually unacknowledged) commonalities—self-legitimation, delegitimation of the other, distanced constructions of the other, esoteric intimacies—otherness could be implemented as an agent of self-construction. The irritant could be interiorized; opposition could be domesticated; the other could be used to present the self.[9]

While I agree with the dialectical nature of symbiosis, the term "dialectic" applies more accurately to Jewish-Christian encounter throughout history. When discussing the medieval relationship between Judaism and Christianity, the historian Amos Funkenstein stated that the "conscious rejection of values and claims of the other religion was and remained a constitutive element in the ongoing construction" of Jewish and Christian identities. Funkenstein claimed that there are "no other two religions tied to each other with such strong mutual bonds of aversion and fascination, attraction and repulsion." In fact, he argued that Judaism and Islam were much less interested in each other and thus produced an insubstantial number of anti-Jewish polemics in contrast to the hundreds of Jewish-Christian polemical treatises. Unlike the confrontational cultures of Judaism and Christianity, Judaism and Islam harbored indifference for each other bordering on contempt, and Islamic opposition toward Jews "never translated into hostility towards Judaism."[10] In light of Wasserstrom's work, it could be argued that Funkenstein was somewhat inaccurate in his assessment of the Jewish-Muslim relationship.

However, as we examine the history of Jewish-Christian encounter, there is clearly a dialectical symbiosis at work in the construction of Jewish and Christian identities. This dialectical, yet constructive, force for identity has appeared in significant textual intersections between Judaism and Christianity all along their historical pathways toward self-definition in the form of polemics, apologetics, disputations, and dialogue. Just as their biblical, ancestral twins Jacob and Esau jostled each other in their mother Rebecca's womb, Jews and Christians have continued to define themselves in relation to each other while never forming completely separate identities. As Daniel Boyarin states in his analysis of early Jewish and Christian co-emergence, "Like closely related siblings, they rivaled each other, learned from each other, fought with each other, perhaps even sometimes loved each other."[11] Yet the metaphor is clearly contradictory in the sense that both siblings, Jews and Christians, have claimed to be the younger one who supplants the older one, thus contributing to the ambiguous and contradictory nature of their relationship throughout history. From a Jewish perspective, the midrashic implications of Gen. 25:23 actually suggest that rabbinic Judaism was born slightly after its older brother, the Church. This "temporal paradox" leads Boyarin to produce "a midrash that never was" by exploring how rabbinic Judaism was influenced by its slightly older brother, Christianity.[12]

In the following chapters, I analyze the theologies of four twentieth-century Jewish thinkers, Franz Rosenzweig, Hans Joachim Schoeps, Richard Rubenstein, and Irving Greenberg, who clearly defined themselves in relation to their "elder" Christian sibling. Their works reflect a common attempt to understand the impact of Christian culture on the historical events that befell the Jews prior to and following the Holocaust, and to reassess the relationship between the two religions. Yet, in their efforts to better conceptualize Jewish identity in relation to Christianity, these Jewish thinkers reveal previously blurred boundaries. They not only reflect upon the relationship between Judaism and Christianity, but their engagement with Christian thought and culture leads to a reconstruction of Jewish theology. Ironically, these modern philosophers attempt to reify Jewish identity in conversation with Christianity, thus traversing cultural boundaries in order to erect them anew.

These modern Jewish thinkers have participated in the ongoing construction of what Susannah Heschel calls a "counterhistory" of Christian scholarship developed by the nineteenth-century scholars of the Wissenschaft des Judentums (Science of Judaism), and which I would argue goes back to Moses Mendelssohn's effort at rapprochement with German Christian culture in his book *Jerusalem* (1783). Counterhistory is a genre of literature actually dating back to antiquity that exploits the literary sources of one's adversary "against their grain," consequently replacing one's self-image with a "pejorative counter-image."[13] Yet Amos Funkenstein pointed out the potential for mutual destruction resulting from dueling counterhistories "if only because the forger of a counteridentity of the other renders his own identity to depend on it." He based his conclusion on the dialectical paradigm of the nineteenth-century philosopher Hegel, who provided the first philosophical analysis of identity construction as a social phenomenon in which one must define oneself by negating the identity of an "other" in order to be recognized as a legitimate self.[14]

Throughout history, there have been repeated instances of both Jews and Christians exploiting each other's narratives to construct their own identities. Beginning with Augustine's *City of God* in the fourth century, Christian thinkers turned the Hebrew Bible on its head to promote the Christian supersession of Judaism, while Jewish thinkers composed polemical tracts like *Toldot Yeshu* (Generations of Jesus) in late antiquity and *Nitzachon Yashan* (Old Book of Polemic) in the medieval period that inverted stories of Jesus in the New Testament and church ritual in order to malign Christianity.[15]

When we arrive at Mendelssohn's *Jerusalem*, we discover a modern continuation of counterhistory emerging that "demonstrates a Jewish desire to enter the Christian myth, become its hero, and claim the power inherent in it."[16] Mendelssohn was really the first Jew to embody the cultural hybridity of German Judaism in his attempt to create a dual identity as a Jew and a German *Aufklärer* (follower of the Enlightenment). While promoting the intellectual and spiritual affinity of the Jew as a "human being" with German enlightened culture, Mendelssohn tried to appeal to German Christians for tolerance of Jewish ritual observance and religious particularity by reclaiming the Jewishness of Jesus as an example of a Jew who observed God's commandments while respecting the laws of the land.[17] Yet, as Franz Rosenzweig would later note, this radical bifurcation of Jewish religious praxis and German cognitive culture left in its wake a Judaism devoid of intellectual and spiritual guidance for the average Jew.[18]

The scholars of the Wissenschaft des Judentums and proponents of Reform Judaism sought to fill the perceived intellectual and spiritual void for Jews left by Mendelssohn's portrayal of the German-Jewish relationship by presenting a dual history of Judaism and German Christian culture in Jewish terms that demonstrated their common conceptions of humanity and ethical behavior.[19] Yet they argued that Judaism had already planted the seeds of ethical monotheism in the West and possessed this idea throughout history, whereas Christianity came to it gradually through a long religious struggle against paganism. This Jewish account of history ran counter to the historical Christian construction of Judaism as a degenerate and fossilized religion that had been superseded by Christianity. These scholars not only attempted to set the Jewish record straight but also reconfigured Christian history by portraying Christianity as a "paganized version of Judaism which betrayed the message of its Jewish founder" and persecuted Jews throughout history. In this Jewish version of history, Judaism would be at the center of Western civilization, with its Hebrew Bible and rabbinic literature replacing classical Greek literature and the New Testament as the fundamental sources of Western thought.[20]

The German Jewish philosopher Hermann Cohen developed the counter-history of the Wissenschaft des Judentums further yet without the polemical overtones In his last book, *Religion of Reason Out of the Sources of Judaism*, pub lished posthumously in 1921. In that work, he stated that "Christ was truly the Messiah of the nations" because in his name, Christians would convert the nations to Jewish monotheism by making concessions to pagan culture.[21] Funkenstein notes that Cohen described the development of German Christianity from the medieval period through the Reformation to German idealism "as a progressive history of de-Teutonization—as a road leading from German paganism through Protestantism to rational ethics, that is Judaism."[22]

While respecting his effort to restore the metaphysical importance to Judaism vis-à-vis German Christian culture, Cohen's disciple Franz Rosenzweig criticized his teacher for portraying an idealized harmony between Judaism and German culture based on a false "spiritual affinity." Whereas Mendelssohn had mistakenly separated the Jewish people from their spiritual affinity with German Christendom, Cohen tried too hard to harmonize Jewish spirituality with German Christian culture at the expense of the Jewish people. Rosenzweig accused Cohen and other liberal Jews of trying to translate Jewish theology into the idiom of world history and culture, while failing to realize that Judaism remains ontologically distinct from them. Instead, Rosenzweig envisioned a creative tension existing for Jews between the living, metahistorical reality of Judaism and German Christian culture.[23]

Throughout his work and especially in *The Star of Redemption* (1921), Rosenzweig demonstrated this dialectic between Jewish and Christian cultures. Initially repulsed by the secularization and historicism of religion leading up to World War I, Rosenzweig was attracted to Christianity as a foundation for faith based on revelation. However, after deciding to convert to Christianity, Rosenzweig had an epiphany in a Yom Kippur service: He realized that Jews do not have to come to the Father through Jesus because God has already redeemed them through the covenant of circumcision. The two themes of revelation and Israel's eternality became constituent elements in Rosenzweig's construction of a Jewish theology in relation to Christianity. He accomplished this by inverting Augustine's dualistic historiosophy of the "City of God" and the "City of Man" to portray Jews as occupying a metaphysical position in contrast to Christians who dwell in earthly history. In addition, Rosenzweig turned Christian anti-Jewish images on their heads to reaffirm Jewish uniqueness. His ambivalence toward Christianity was clearly demonstrated in his portrayal of Judaism and Christianity as having mutually incompatible yet reinforcing roles in the process of redemption.

In the years leading up to the Holocaust in Nazi Germany, Hans Joachim Schoeps tried to move from the creative tension forecast by Rosenzweig between Jews and Christians to a truly dialogical relationship. However, like the cultural German-Jewish symbiosis, this dialogue was really only an inner Jewish dialogue that did not prevent the systematic annihilation of the Jews in Europe. In *Jüdischer*

Glaube in dieser Zeit (1932), Schoeps observed that the political and religious climate was deteriorating as a result of mounting secularism and faithlessness rooted in both Christian and Jewish cultures. Schoeps foresaw a common solution to this mutual problem in the shared redemptive task of Judaism and Christianity. He illustrated this integration of Jewish and Christian elements by proposing a "Critical Protestant" Judaism that appropriated the Protestant proclamation to return to the concrete Word of God in opposition to liberal historicism and orthodox ritualism. Schoeps's work can be compared to that of Rosenzweig because they both constructed existential Jewish theologies in "conversation" with Christianity. Whereas both Jews and Christians often see Rosenzweig's theology as a model for dialogue, Schoeps actually went further than Rosenzweig in breaking down the barriers between Judaism and Christianity. While Rosenzweig and Schoeps both gave Christianity an unprecedented role in redemption, Schoeps actually recognized Christian uniqueness and placed Christianity on a more equal level with Judaism.

Following the Holocaust, the American thinkers Richard Rubenstein and Irving Greenberg both explored the level of Christian involvement in the tragedy and perceived the need to reposition the Jew in relation to Christianity. These Jewish scholars actually followed in the footsteps of a Jewish scholar (Jules Isaac) and a Christian scholar (James Parkes) who had already begun to reexamine the role of Christianity in creating the climate for the Holocaust. In *Jésus et Israël* (1948), the French Jewish historian Jules Isaac asserted that the Christian "teaching of contempt" was a necessary precondition for the Holocaust. Isaac argued specifically that the Christian charge of deicide against the Jewish people was the justification for a history of violence against the Jews culminating in the Holocaust.[24] Already in 1934, the Christian scholar James Parkes had linked modern antisemitism to the theological anti-Judaism of the Church in antiquity in *The Conflict of the Church and the Synagogue*.[25] In *Judaism and Christianity* (1948), Parkes established a direct connection between the Holocaust and Christian anti-Jewish teachings in the New Testament.[26] Finally, in his *Antisemitism* (1964), he described an "unbroken line" of moral and theological continuity between the formative period of the Church in the fourth century to the Nazis in the twentieth.[27]

Richard Rubenstein would go even further than Isaac and Parkes in his radical rejection of Western theism by blaming both Judaism and Christianity for creating and perpetuating the myth of an omnipotent male God of covenant and election that produced the sibling rivalry leading to the Holocaust. Rubenstein challenged both communities to demythologize their religious traditions as a foundation for dialogue, while at the same time approximating Christian motifs and anti-Jewish myths when constructing his critique of rabbinic Judaism. Through psychoanalysis, he projected his own sense of impotence and guilt regarding the fulfillment of Jewish law onto the rabbis and, in the process, confirmed pre-Holocaust, German Protestant portrayals of a legalistic and self-punitive rabbinic culture whose members worship an angry, transcendent God.

Next, in his attempt to construct a panentheistic theology with feminine divine imagery, Rubenstein perpetuated the Jewish-Christian dialectic by blaming Judaism for patriarchy. Additionally, he found Pauline Christianity to be more psychologically advanced than rabbinic Judaism because of its recovery of latent pagan motifs demonstrating the reunification of God and humanity that he claimed were repressed by the Rabbis. Ironically, in his effort to break down the myths separating Judaism and Christianity after the Holocaust, Rubenstein actually resurrected them in his post-Holocaust critique of rabbinic Judaism.

Irving Greenberg was influenced by the ecumenical climate in the United States following Vatican II, when many Christian theologians responded to the work of Jules Isaac and James Parkes regarding Christian theological culpability for the Holocaust by redefining theologically their own identities in relation to Judaism.[28] While condemning Christian antisemitism throughout history as a major factor leading to the Holocaust, Greenberg also recognized the objectification of Christianity as part of the very formation of Jewish identity and warned against using the Holocaust as an excuse for further antagonism. Instead, he viewed the Holocaust and the establishment of the State of Israel as "orientating events" that have revelatory significance for both Judaism and Christianity in that they reorient Jews and Christians toward God and each other. In dialogue with Christian thinkers A. Roy Eckardt and Paul van Buren, Greenberg portrayed a "new organic model" of the Jewish-Christian relationship based on a single yet pluralistic covenant that is constantly unfolding. However, Greenberg reclaimed for Jews theological motifs such as the crucifixion and resurrection, usually articulated by Christians, to describe the Holocaust and the establishment of the State of Israel, consequently diluting their Christological symbolism in a Jewish framework. Hence, while recognizing Jewish-Christian interrelatedness, Greenberg failed to allow for Christian difference.

What brings these theologians together and makes them worthy of special consideration is their ambiguous relationship with Christianity and the resulting impact that their encounters with Christian thought and culture had on the construction of their Jewish theologies. The theologies discussed here reveal a uniquely diverse set of circumstances in which modern Jewish scholars have moved further than many of their contemporaries toward dialogue with Christians while inadvertently, at times, promoting Jewish-Christian opposition in different ways.[29] These Jewish intellectuals went as far as they could in their respective eras to reach across Jewish and Christian boundaries, yet they each ended up in one way or another reviving traditional polemical or apologetic positions of either Jewish or Christian origin when constructing their theologies. Regardless, in every case these Jewish thinkers responded to the historical events leading up to and following the Holocaust by constructing theologies in conversation with Christianity. These particular theological writings reveal for us how different encounters with Christian thought and culture have led Jewish thinkers not only to reexamine their relationship with Christians but also to reconstruct their own identities in relation to their fellow Jews and to God in the twentieth century.

From turn-of-the-century Germany leading up to the Holocaust, Rosenzweig and Schoeps both expressed an unprecedented appreciation for Christianity based on a perceived Jewish-German symbiosis, yet each was forced to reevaluate the Jewish-Christian relationship in light of a burgeoning anti-Judaism and antisemitism. Rosenzweig contributed to this ambiguous Jewish-Christian dynamic by granting Christians an important albeit inferior role in the redemptive process because they lack the divine truth that Jews already possess. Schoeps reacted to Christian antisemitic charges by both attacking and identifying with them to a certain extent. On the one hand, he engaged in an anti-Christian polemic over the predisposed redemptive status of Jews versus Christians in relation to God; on the other hand, he reformulated Christian anti-Jewish polemics in his own critique of rabbinic legalism.

Following the Holocaust, Rubenstein and Greenberg perpetuated a Jewish-Christian ambiguity by condemning European Christendom for its complicity in the Nazi genocide, on the one hand, while on the other hand viewing the Holocaust as a tragic wake-up call to reconstruct Jewish as well as Christian theologies in relation to each other. While Rubenstein urged Jews and Christians to abandon their mutually destructive religious myths after the Holocaust, various Christian myths against Jews actually resurfaced in his own intra-Jewish critique. In his effort to promote mutual reconciliation after the Holocaust, Greenberg reconceived the Jewish-Christian relationship as an ongoing interconnection, while at the same time subsuming Christian theology in a Jewish framework. In all these cases, modern Jewish theologies are ambiguously formed along the porous boundaries between Jewish and Christian cultures. These Jewish theologies emerge out of the complex negotiations between Jewish thinkers and their Christian milieu. Assembled together, the works of these four thinkers provide us with an exceptional snapshot of the multiple and often contradictory constructions of modern Jewish identity out of the cauldron of modern Jewish-Christian dialectic.

Ultimately, the works of these four Jewish-Christian interlopers demonstrate that modern Jewish identity is predicated in some way upon its ambivalent encounter with Christianity. While these thinkers may have gone further than many of their modern Jewish contemporaries in their engagement with Christianity, their writings are especially instructive because they point to a more general Jewish-Christian theological liminality emerging in the modern period that corresponds to a parallel cultural liminality. In the work of these theologians, Jewish and Christian theologies intersect with one another, as the two religious communities move along their own pathways toward self-definition. In their theological responses to events prior to and following the Holocaust, these Jewish thinkers define themselves in relation to Christian culture. When examined in comparison with their Christian counterparts, these theologies reflect a common language that is the source for both antagonism and dialogue. Together, these Jewish-Christian intersections constitute a Jewish identity that has been dialectically constructed in relation to Christian culture, yet which remains uniquely Jewish. Moreover, one could argue that these theological intersections are both an impetus for and a reflection of the parallel cultural intersections that occurred for these two religious communities in the twentieth century.

Cultural Studies as a Methodology for Studying Jewish-Christian Relations

Cultural studies provides a possible tool to bridge the apparent gap between the theological and cultural formulations of Jewish identity, ultimately portraying a more complete historical picture of Jewish self-definition in relation to Christianity. Moreover, this methodology sheds new light on how the power relations between Jews and Christians have impacted the construction of Jewish theologies in this century. Using the tools of cultural studies, we may be able to subvert the essential categories of Judaism as the victimized minority versus Christianity as the victorious majority culture. Instead of viewing Jewish theologies as either reflections of passive internalization or active resistance of Christian culture, one can understand modern Jewish theologies to be products of intercultural conversations between Jewish thinkers and their Christian counterparts past and present.[30] This would counteract the traditional social-scientific portrayal of Jewish culture as a monolithic and unchanging essence. Frederic Jameson describes culture in the following way:

> Culture is not a "substance" or a phenomenon in its own right; it is an objective mirage that arises out of the relationship between at least two groups. This is to say that no group "has" a culture all by itself: culture is the nimbus perceived by one group when it comes into contact with and observes another one. It is the objectification of everything alien and strange about the contact group.[31]

With this perspective, one can better understand the unique dialectic between Judaism and Christianity that has generated to some degree the ongoing construction of Jewish and Christian identities. At different times throughout Jewish history, either elite or popular members of the Jewish community have defined themselves in relation to a Christian "Other," whether it is a concrete individual or a mythical creation. Hence, we have seen an appropriation of various genres, motifs, terms, institutions, and rituals traditionally associated with Christianity either in the writings of the intellectual few or in the customs of the populace, which is accomplished in a polemical, parodic, or neutralized fashion.[32]

The rubric of cultural studies loosely consists of six characteristics that appear in one way or another throughout this analysis of Jewish-Christian relations. First, cultural studies is a rigorously intellectual practice that is disciplined in the sense that it attempts to preserve the discipline of cultural authority while at the same time seeking new forms and articulations of this authority. These reconfigurations of authority are based on new discoveries of knowledge rather than the continuing historical status of the producers of that knowledge.[33] Instead of tracing the historical development of preexisting cultural identities, cultural studies offers a more spatialized approach in which subjects are mapped according to the varying social, political, and cultural positions they occupy that constitute practices of both authority and resistance.[34]

Based on this premise, my work examines the construction of twentieth-century Jewish theologies in light of an accepted intellectual tradition of biblical and rabbinic interpretation marked by either Jewish resistance or capitulation to Christian culture. At the same time, this analysis uncovers alternative patterns of this theological development that arise out of Jewish conversations with Christianity and throw into question the status of the Jew as victimized outsider. Like Lawrence Silberstein, Daniel Boyarin, and other cultural critics, I am engaged in a critique of the normalizing discourse of Jewish identity that tends to simplify the complex processes through which Jewish identities are produced, inhibits alternative modes of thinking, and occludes relations of power among Jews and between Jews and others. Instead, I am attempting to map the multiple locations in which one identifies Jewishly as a result of cross-cultural encounters with Christianity.[35]

Next, and perhaps most significantly, the practice of cultural studies is considered "radically contextualist" in the sense that cultural events, practices, and texts cannot exist apart from the conditions that constitute them. Three main consequences arise out of this contextualism: First, proponents of cultural studies are antireductionist in the sense that they refuse to reduce reality to any single element, be it culture, biology, or economics. Although they do link cultural identity construction to power relations, cultural theorists view power as complex and contradictory, consisting of multiple foundations that cannot be reduced to one another.

Second, cultural studies assumes that no cultural or discursive practice exists on its own but can be examined only as a set of discursive alliances in which different texts, symbols, or discourses converge with one another at a point of cultural intersection or negotiation.[36] In this contextual framework, identities are viewed as "contradictory and multiple, produced rather than given, and are both taken up and received within particular social and historical circumstances."[37] Moreover, in his discussion of identity in relation to culture, Etienne Balibar states "that every identity that is *proclaimed* (with fanfare or in secret) is elaborated as a function of the Other, in response to his desire, his power and his discourse." Hence, he radically decenters the notion of cultural identity, shifting the origin of group identity from the collective self to the Other. In effect, Balibar transforms the notion of belonging to "a culture" into "belonging to a network, to an intersection of cultures."[38]

Yet these cultural intersections are not merely haphazard; they illustrate what cultural theorists posit as certain patterns or trajectories known as "articulations," the third consequence of contextualism. An articulation refers to the attempt by scholars of cultural studies not just to deconstruct the power relations between cultures but also to reconstruct or redefine these relations in order to better understand them. In a sense, these scholars are constantly rearticulating new relationships between cultures that affirm their identities in light of their ever-changing historical contexts.[39] This analysis disarticulates the boundaries between Jews and Christians in the twentieth century while rearticulating their identities in relation to each other. By constructing Jewish theologies in conversation with Christian culture, the four Jewish thinkers whom I portray in the following pages appear to stand, whether knowingly or not, on the border between Judaism and Christianity. Yet this intermediate zone has not been the basis for a dilution of Jewish identity; it has been rather, the location for a pattern of Jewish identity construction in relation to Christianity in the twentieth century. In this scenario, the essence of insider and outsider roles diminishes, and one is neither "the Same" nor "the Other." Instead, one "stands in that undetermined threshold place where she constantly drifts in and out."[40] These twentieth-century Jewish theologians participate in an organic process of displacing and realigning the borders of Jewish and Christian identities.

My work is based on what Henry Giroux calls "border pedagogy" because of its "acknowledgement of the shifting borders that both undermine and reterritorialize different configurations of culture, power, and knowledge." In fact, my proposed texts are read "against, within, and outside their established boundaries."[41] Ultimately, when exploring these texts, the reader herself becomes a "border crosser" after becoming aware of the common ground that these Jewish and Christian thinkers share.[42] In this study, texts commonly described as central or marginal are viewed in relation to one another as equally valid representations of Jewish thought in the twentieth century. David Biale argues that this "dialectical interaction of marginal and master narratives" illustrates "the very oddity of the Jewish experience," which "may shed light on the nature of canonical literatures in general."[43]

The methodology of cultural studies is also theoretical and political in ways that interrelate with each other. Theories associated with cultural studies are not supposed to be a priori assumptions but rather responses to specific societal and cultural questions or contexts. The truth and validity of cultural theories must be judged by their ability to provide a better understanding of the context and the possibilities for seeing it differently. This attempt to challenge

the perceived structures of power and suggest an alternative theory of relationships is what makes cultural studies political.[44] According to Lawrence
Grossberg, "For cultural studies the world is a field of struggle, a balance of
forces, and intellectual work must understand the balance and find ways of
challenging and changing it."[45]

Another characteristic of cultural studies is its interdisciplinarity. It reaches
across various academic disciplines while recognizing its own partiality.[46] It is
this self-conscious sense of partiality or limitation that constitutes the final characteristic of cultural studies. The methods of cultural studies are self-reflective
in the sense that "the analyst is a participant in the very practices, formations,
and contexts he or she is analyzing." Thus, when engaging in cultural studies,
theorists must reflect on their own relationship to the theoretical, political, cultural, and institutional contexts that they study and the various connections that
they establish through their research.[47]

This book takes up the theoretical and political agenda of cultural studies
in the sense that it responds to the current Jewish cultural context in the United
States vis-à-vis Christianity and the questions it raises, by offering a new theoretical paradigm for understanding the relationship between the two cultures.
Moreover, this analysis wrests theology from its theoretical moorings and
places it under a cultural microscope in an attempt to reveal its discursive
messiness. Instead of affirming Jewish theology as an indisputable meta-
discourse, this study posits the intersection of theological and cultural disciplines that come together to form the larger discursive totality of a religious
community. The feminist poststructuralist Mary McClintock Fulkerson goes
so far as to assert that theological principles have no meaning except in an
"intertextual" or dialogical relation with other discourses.[48] Finally, the following discussion of twentieth-century Jewish-Christian relations demonstrates the
self-reflexive nature of cultural studies in the sense that this analysis grows out
of my ambiguous position as an American Jew vis à vis Christian culture. In
this multicultural society, Jewish theologians can no longer engage in traditional
apologetics with Christianity that characterize the Jewish people as a persecuted
minority surrounded by a fixed boundary with Christian culture.

Alternatively, contemporary Jewish thinkers must affirm Jewish identity in
the face of continuing antisemitism from those who either perceive Jews as a
demonic minority or view them as the power behind the hegemonic majority.
An important group of Jewish scholars led by David Novak, among others, has
recently begun to move away from this type of apologetic position with their
genuine efforts to reaffirm Jewish theology in dialogue with Christianity. Novak
formulated his approach to Jewish-Christian dialogue with his groundbreaking
Jewish-Christian Dialogue: A Jewish Justification (1989), where he presented a
history of Jewish ambivalence toward Christianity in which Jews evaluate and
ultimately engage their Christian Other while largely maintaining a position of
superiority. This is reflected in the rabbinic discussion of the Noachide laws,

medieval *chidushim*, nineteenth-century historicism of Jesus, and the twentieth-century systematic theology of Franz Rosenzweig. Following his historical study of Jewish encounters with Christianity, Novak concluded that while Jews and Christians lack a shared theological tradition, they jointly possess a "Judeo-Christian ethic" based on a "theonomous morality." Thus, both religious communities share a common scriptural morality conceived by a God of creation and covenant.[49]

Novak, along with Tikva Frymer-Kensky, Peter Ochs, and Michael Signer, continue that line of reasoning in their unprecedented public statement of Jewish support for theological dialogue with Christians in "Dabru Emet: A Jewish Statement on Christians and Christianity" and in their follow-up book, *Christianity in Jewish Terms* (2000), also edited by David Sandmel. "Dabru Emet" makes the following theological claims: First it promotes a God jointly worshiped by Christians and Jews whose words appear in a mutually revered Hebrew Bible with a shared set of moral principles. Second, this document acknowledges that while this God has been revealed differently to Jews and Christians, they should respect each other's revelatory claims and ultimately work together in a common divine mission of world redemption, at which point only will their "humanly irreconcilable" differences be resolved. Third, the authors of this document assert that Christians should support the Jewish State of Israel in the divinely promised land recorded in the Hebrew Scriptures. Fourth, this document condemns Christian anti-Judaism throughout history leading up to the Holocaust, yet it refuses to equate Nazi antisemitism with Christianity. Finally, the authors affirm that a newly improved relationship with Christianity will not weaken or subsume Jewish identity in a homogenized Judeo-Christian religion or culture.[50]

Christianity in Jewish Terms concretizes the earlier document by examining various theological concepts centering around God, scripture, commandment, Israel, worship, suffering, embodiment, redemption, sin, repentance, and the image of God from a Jewish perspective based on classical sources. The authors then compare these theological interpretations to a corresponding set of Christian interpretations in order to gain a better understanding of them in relation to Judaism. The Jewish contributors to this volume examine not only Christian writings from antiquity to the modern period but also those progressive post-Holocaust reformulations undertaken by both Catholic and Protestant scholars in an effort to root out fundamental anti-Jewish elements and to recognize the rightful place of Judaism in the cosmos. These essays are followed by Christian responses in which the scholars attempt to validate these Jewish portrayals of Christianity from their own perspectives and in turn to examine the significance of Judaism for their own understandings of Christianity.[51] With this dialogical exploration, the editors of this volume hope to enable Jews "to rediscover the basic categories of rabbinic Judaism and to hear what the basic categories of Christian belief sound like when they are taught in terms of this rabbinic Judaism."[52] In the process, Jews not only can strengthen their understanding and appreciation of Judaism after the Holocaust but also can become more aware of Christian theology in general and the recent efforts of Christian scholars in particular to rescue it from its anti-Jewish past.[53]

In the context of this introduction, it is impossible to provide a fully adequate analysis of these significant texts, yet it is important to make some general observations about these dialogical efforts in light of this project: First, when reading the public statement "Dabru Emet," one is struck by the extraordinary collaboration of an interdenominational group of Jewish scholars and rabbis to produce a joint statement recognizing recent Catholic and Protestant attempts at reconciliation with Judaism and offering its own perspective on Christianity in light of these efforts. Moreover, the parallel academic book, *Christianity in Jewish Terms*, represents possibly the first formal gathering in history of Jewish scholars to construct a Jewish theology of Christianity. Next, when one analyzes these texts more closely, they both corroborate and potentially conflict with my thesis regarding Jewish-Christian relations in the twentieth century. On the one hand, the authors of these texts have clearly abandoned traditional apologetic approaches toward Christianity in the sense that they recognize the new complex reality that Jews now face with their Christian neighbors in which the power dynamic has shifted. Despite the Holocaust, Jews have increased their political power in Western democracies and have created their own Western style democracy in the State of Israel. At the same time, Christian influence has shrunk to some degree, bringing the two cultures more closely together then ever before and creating a new dynamic for dialogue.[54]

In addition, the authors of "Dabru Emet" and more particularly *Christianity in Jewish Terms* self-consciously present theological positions "about and in response to Christian theologies that themselves arose from within, about, and in response to Judaism."[55] Peter Ochs and David Sandmel even go so far as to describe an "almost symbiotic relationship between the two traditions" that has existed since antiquity, while "these mutual influences have been obscured by a rhetoric of rejection."[56] These statements seem to reflect a certain degree of Jewish-Christian convergence based on a shared theological discourse that has contributed and continues to contribute to the formation of Jewish and Christian identities in relation to each other. In other words, these scholars seem to recognize that they are participating in an ongoing process of aligning and realigning Jewish and Christian borders in response to the construction of theologies by members of their neighboring religious tradition. Thus, through theological dialogue, Jews and Christians experience, as Sandmel describes it, "a deepening of our own religious experience and self-understanding."[57]

At the same time, however, David Novak sets a precondition for Jewish-Christian dialogue in the book that preserves more essential boundaries between the two religions, proclaiming that the vision of each participant in the dialogue of the other's religion "must not lead to any distortion of what each tradition, itself separately, teaches as the truth."[58] This statement reflects a more traditional apologetic stance that fails to recognize the more fluid theological bound-aries between Judaism and Christianity acknowledged previously. However, Novak warns against disputation, triumphalism, and proselytization when en-tering religious dialogue because these methods all seek to negate the other par-ticipant by either ignoring religious commonalities to preserve opposition and hierarchy or ignoring religious difference in order to promote a higher agenda of conversion. At the same time, he states that participants in the dialogue should avoid syncretistic statements because they would replace the ultimate character of Jewish and Christian revelatory claims with "a new religious reality" that would be considered idolatry. He also warns Jews and Christians to avoid relativistic claims because this would deny the utter uniqueness and mutually exclusive nature of Jewish and Christian truth claims.[59]

In his assessment of Jewish-Christian dialogue, Novak ultimately urges the reader to walk a fine line between theological absolutism and relativism by try-ing to find religious common ground while preserving the indisputable nature of theological claims until God can resolve them in a messianic future. This is a praiseworthy attempt to bring together Jews and Christians from both ends of the religious spectrum for a potentially meaningful dialogue; it enables all participants, especially the Jews, to feel comfortable, knowing that they are not compromising their identities in the process. However, Novak's pronounce-ments on dialogue also elevate and bracket out theology from its historical in-teraction with other cultural discourses. This position appears at the very least to dispute the claim that twentieth-century Jewish theologies have been con-structed in conversation with Christian culture, and it goes against the more sweeping idea seemingly endorsed by Ochs and Sandmel of a type of Jewish-Christian symbiosis dating back to the dawn of Christianity. While Novak dis-agrees with the construction of "a new religious reality" in contemporary Jewish-Christian dialogue, one could argue that Jews and Christians have been constructing new religious realities in response to one another's theological claims at different times throughout history, yet in a dialectical rather than a dialogical manner.

Hence, the authors of *Christianity in Jewish Terms* appear to be ambivalent in their approach toward dialogue with Christians. On the one hand, they want to move beyond traditional apologetics by claiming to perpetuate the dialogical construction of Jewish and Christian theologies throughout history; on the other hand, they want to promote, as the title of their book may imply, a conversation between Jews and Christians from behind more classically defined borders. One of the stated goals of *Christianity in Jewish Terms* is to "contribute to the revi-talization of Judaism after the Shoah and in the face of modern secularism and postmodern doubt."[60] To accomplish this, these scholars want to reestablish a clear definition of Judaism in relation to Christianity through its classical sources while using modern hermeneutical tools. In their efforts to combat secularism and alleviate postmodern doubt, they are perhaps understandably ambivalent about engaging in a cultural critique of Judaism in relation to Christianity that would deconstruct the boundaries between the two religions and potentially reveal a more cross-cultural construction of Jewish theology.

While many Jewish scholars have been reluctant to engage in cultural criticism at the expense of Jewish particularity, a new type of apologetics has emerged which David Biale calls "deconstructive apologetics." He argues that this type of scholarship is best illustrated by Jewish feminists who are engaged in a double polemic, one internally waged against the exponents of the patriarchal rabbinic framework, and one externally enacted against those anti-Jewish feminists who attribute the origin of patriarchy to biblical and rabbinic Judaism. He states that this new type of apologetic is "an attempt to mobilize the Jewish tradition to subvert or challenge those contemporary theories which tend to exclude Jews."[61]

To illustrate his point, Biale cites Daniel Boyarin's book *Carnal Israel* as an example of one of the most systematic presentations of apologetics and cultural criticism. Boyarin was accused of constructing an apologetic by the two audiences he intended to address: the feminists to whom he offers Talmudic culture as a generally positive model of gender relations in contrast to the Greco-Roman or Christian world, and the proponents of rabbinic Judaism which he criticized in certain areas for being misogynistic. However, he anticipates the criticism of those who would call his work apologetic by referring to Franz Rosenzweig's "apology for apologetics" in his essay, "Apologetisches Denken (1923)." There Rosenzweig defended the construction of apologetics as the "noblest of human occupations" when they do not embellish or avoid areas of vulnerability in "one's own province."[62] Following that admonition, Boyarin attempts to protect his "own province," rabbinic Judaism, by accounting for historical "truth," while at the same time maintaining his "ethical commitment to changing the present gender practices of that culture." Yet, instead of calling his work apologetic, Boyarin adopts an approach that he calls "generous critique": "a practice that seeks to criticize the practices of the Other from the perspective of the desires and needs of here and now, without reifying that Other or placing myself in judgment over him or her."[63]

David Biale argues that despite his claims to the contrary, Boyarin at times tends to reify the Greco-Roman or Christian Other by portraying it monolithically with regard to patriarchy. However, Biale credits Boyarin with frequently subverting "some of the cherished dichotomies of the contemporary humanities by setting them against the tradition of rabbinic Judaism."[64] Like Boyarin, Jewish scholars can recover their marginalized voice in the history of cultures, while at the same time dealing with the problems associated with their integration into the hegemonic majority.[65] Yet Boyarin is not merely deconstructing rabbinic discourse but also reconstructing what he considers to be a "usable past" by acknowledging those areas in the culture that are beneficial for today while also contextualizing the "recalcitrant and unpalatable aspects of the culture" that are inappropriate. However, he is careful not to devalue prior or contemporaneous readings of rabbinic Judaism in favor of his own but merely claims to open the possibility for other interpretations of the same texts.[66] In fact, Boyarin argues, "Since our cultural situation is different from that of the medieval Rab-bis, it is incumbent on us, as scholars and as cultural critics, to discover other faces in the same texts—faces that can be more useful for us in re-constructing our own versions of culture and gender practices."[67]

In light of Boyarin's cultural critique, I propose an apologetics for Jewish identity in relation to Christianity that is not "deconstructive" but "reconstruc-tive." This approach deconstructs the master narratives that have maintained closed borders between Jews and Christians, while reconstructing Jewish iden-tities that develop in opposition to and ultimately in dialogue with Christianity. This work therefore shifts the focus from opposing truth claims to contradic-tory and multiple identity construction. In this book, I am attempting to fulfill one of the primary goals set by the emerging Jewish cultural studies, to un-cover a space of common discourse between Jews and non-Jews based on a "critical approach to the politics of culture." While exploring and articulating identities in the context of history, this approach simultaneously remakes that same history.[68]

Although this book deconstructs the boundaries between Judaism and Christianity, Jewish identities are not subsumed in a homogeneous and ahistorical "Judeo-Christian" totality; instead, Jews are continually reestablish-ing their difference through their historical encounter with Christian theology and culture. This demonstrates another contention of Jewish cultural studies, that "differences can be enriching and nonexclusive rather than constraining and competitive."[69] I would argue that in light of the currently ambiguous Jew-ish-Christian cultural milieu, it is essential that we acknowledge the "faces" of Christian thinkers that have previously been undiscovered or ignored in mod-ern Jewish theological texts. Such a discovery may be used to reconstruct a con-temporary version of Jewish culture vis-à-vis Christianity in a multicultural context. My use of cultural studies to describe the Jewish-Christian relationship is similar to that of Boyarin in *Dying for God*, where he portrays the co-emergence of rabbinic Judaism and Christianity in late antiquity as two intertwining cul-tures. Boyarin draws upon the cultural theorist Homi Bhabha's notion of "cul-tural hybridity" to describe what he perceives as "the shared and crisscrossing lines" of Jewish and Christian histories and religious development.[70]

Although he initially relies on family metaphors to describe the Jewish-Christian relationship, Boyarin then turns to a semantic model as a foundation for a "wave theory" of Jewish and Christian histories. According to this theory, Jewish and Christian languages stem from a common "protolanguage" that pro-duces initial similarities between the languages. Despite geographic divergence of Jewish and Christian groups, an innovation in the languages of one group spreads like a wave to other groups in other locations because the languages are still in contact with one another. Thus, while both rabbis and church fathers of late antiquity distinguished Jewish from Christian languages to constitute their orthodox canons, "one could travel metaphorically, from rabbinic Jew to Christian along a continuum where one hardly would know where one stopped and the other began." This model points to one heterogeneous Jewish-Christian "circulatory system" in which discursive elements periodically converge and diverge from one another. Moreover, according to this theory, there appears to be a gap between the claims of certain texts that groups are distinct from another and the actual blurriness of the religious boundaries "on the ground," suggesting a greater possibility of religious and cultural convergence than previously thought.[71]

While the modern boundaries between Judaism and Christianity are clearly more defined than those of late antiquity, there continues to be a simultaneous convergence and divergence of religious and cultural discourse. This study uncovers a period of history in which certain modern Jewish thinkers have knowingly or unknowingly utilized a shared theological vocabulary with their Christian colleagues. However, as we have seen in the past, there is a "double discursive" process at work in Jewish history. To one degree or another, these modern Jewish thinkers continue to reify Jewish culture as a unified, fixed entity. However, their essentialist rhetoric conflicts with a "processual discourse" that reflects the ongoing construction of cultural identities as part of a dialogical process in which there is "an elastic and crisscrossing web of multiple identifications." In fact, their attempts to reaffirm absolute differences between the two religious cultures actually reflect the creative process of remaking cultures in relation to one another.[72]

In this work, I suggest that we challenge the potentially totalizing metanarrative of modern Jewish historiography and reconceptualize twentieth-century Jewish identity as being constructed to some extent out of a process of intercultural identification with Christianity. Using the nonessentializing discourse of cultural studies, none of the Jewish thinkers I discuss can be simply "stitched" into a place of authority in the Jewish, sociocultural patchwork. Instead, they articulate the diversity of cross-cultural experiences, meanings, and ideas that come together in the ongoing construction of Jewish identities in history.

I

From the Outside Looking In

*Franz Rosenzweig's Construction of a
Jewish Theology in Light of His Ambivalent
Encounter with Christianity*

Franz Rosenzweig's theology emerged out of the intersection of
Judaism, Christianity, and secular philosophy at the beginning of
the twentieth century and was a clear reflection of the historical
situation of German Jewry at the close of the nineteenth century.
At that time, German Jewish scholars of the Wissenschaft des
Judentums (Science of Judaism) had attempted to unite Jewish and
German Christian cultures through the medium of secular or
historical knowledge. A century earlier, the eighteenth century-
Jewish philosopher Moses Mendelssohn had also attempted to
integrate *Judentum* and *Deutschtum* by carving out a neutral zone of
universal, natural reason to which Jews could contribute as human
beings in the street while preserving their particularity through
home ritual observance. However, the Wissenschaft des Judentums
shunned that bifurcated identity in favor of a Jewish-German
symbiosis based on a self-perceived intellectual and spiritual affinity.
In their attempt to identify with their environment, these Jewish
thinkers saw themselves as quintessentially German in the sense of
committing even more genuinely than any native Saxonian, Prussian, or Bavarian to the idea of a homogeneous culture. As a result,
the scholars of the Wissenschaft des Judentums perhaps unwittingly, began to view Judaism as if from the outside looking in,
creating a unique German-Jewish subculture that was neither fully
German nor Jewish.[1]

Rosenzweig's Circuitous Route toward Jewish Identity:
A Biographical Sketch

Franz Rosenzweig was raised in the shadow of the Wissenschaft des Judentums, destined to inherit its aspirations while rebelling against its complacency. His own family's development proved to be a perfect indicator of the mixed direction that the Wissenschaft des Judentums would take at the beginning of the twentieth century. His great-grandfather Samuel Meyer Ehrenberg was the headmaster of the Samsonschule, the Jewish Free School of Wolfenbüttel that replaced traditional Torah study with secular education. Ehrenberg was also the teacher of the two founders of the Wissenschaft des Judentums, Isaac Marcus Jost and Leopold Zunz, who initiated the study of Jewish sources with the methods of modern, academic scholarship if only to ensure Jewish culture received a proper burial. Ironically, Rosenzweig's uncle Victor Ehrenberg converted to Christianity after marrying a Gentile woman who was a direct descendant of Martin Luther. Subsequently, Rosenzweig's first cousin and confidant, Rudolf Ehrenberg, was baptized and ultimately identified himself as a Christian.[2]

Rosenzweig was born in 1886 in Cassel to assimilated Jewish parents for whom Judaism was a basically superficial component of an otherwise German national identity. After studying at the Gymnasium, Rosenzweig pursued medicine and later attained a doctorate in philosophy in Freiburg under the tutelage of Friedrich Meinecke in 1912. His doctoral dissertation, "Hegel and the State," examining Hegel's political philosophy, was later published in 1920 and became an indispensable work in the field. In 1913, following years of estrangement from Jewish tradition, Rosenzweig developed the perception that Judaism consisted of an anachronistic set of rituals that could not provide him with a living relationship to God. After powerful persuasion by his close friend Eugen Rosenstock (later Rosenstock-Huessy), a Christian historian and convert from Judaism, Rosenzweig seriously considered converting to Christianity. Yet, after intense discussions with friends and perhaps a religious epiphany at a Day of Atonement service, Rosenzweig decided to "remain a Jew."[3] He would later reexamine intellectually and spiritually his Jewish identity in Marburg under the influence of the Jewish philosopher Hermann Cohen, who had pioneered the Marburg school of neo-Kantianism, and would rediscover his own Jewish identity in his last work, *The Religion of Reason out of the Sources of Judaism*, published posthumously in 1921.[4]

After being drafted into the German army during World War I, Rosenzweig began to write his magnum opus, *The Star of Redemption*, in 1916 while in the Balkan trenches, and it was later published in 1921. This was not a book about Jewish theology per se but rather a fundamental critique of Hegel's closed system of Being in which human history is subsumed and ultimately collapses in the arbitrariness of violence and war. For Rosenzweig, this existential dilemma finds its resolution in the absolute irreducibility of Judaism and individual Jewish existence to the totalizing consciousness of Western Christian civilization.[5] In this monumental work, Rosenzweig was perpetuating the tendency toward philosophical self-reflection of the Wissenschaft des Judentums, while trying not to let Jewish identity be submerged into German Christian culture.[6]

In order to recenter the Jew in *Judentum* and *Deutschtum* following the war, Rosenzweig passed up an academic career and instead, in 1920, established a center for adult Jewish education at the Frankfurt Free Jewish School where German Jews could "know Judaism as Judaism" without surrendering their German cultural sensibilities.[7] In 1921, shortly after his marriage to Edith Hahn, he began to suffer the first signs of amyotrophic lateral sclerosis (Lou Gehrig's disease) that would ultimately lead to his untimely death eight years later. Despite his ensuing paralysis, Rosenzweig continued to communicate with the help of a special typewriter that he could operate with the slight movement of his finger, the only movement he could still perform. Yet he not only communicated but also, quite remarkably, continued to write, translating the Hebrew Bible into German with Martin Buber, while individually translating the medieval poetry of the Jewish philosopher Yehuda Halevi.[8] Ultimately Rosenzweig's life and work as a Jew were deeply interdependent and remained that way until his intellectual power finally succumbed to his physical debilitation.

Rosenzweig's Love-Hate Relationship with Christianity

Because of his circuitous route to Jewish identity through secular, historical knowledge and Christian thought, Rosenzweig's Jewish theology was subsequently idiosyncratic. To a large extent, his portrayal of the Jews as an eternal people corresponded with the historical Jewish self-perception of Israel's eternity based on the metahistorical premise of a divine promise. However, Rosenzweig's theology corresponded fully with neither rabbinic nor liberal Judaism. His metahistorical portrayal of Judaism clashed with traditional Jewish self-consciousness in the following ways: First, Rosenzweig's extratemporal and extraterritorial framework does not explicitly correspond to the daily Orthodox prayer for an eschatological return to Jewish sovereignty in the land of Israel as historical agents. Second, in his existential reinterpretation of *Halakhah*, Rosenzweig refused to submit to a traditional notion of an all-encompassing law, but rather desired to transform the law into "commandments" that can only be observed based on the ability of the individual to fulfill them in the spontaneous encounter with God.[9] Yet, despite his rejection of the traditional notion of *Halakhah*, Rosenzweig also rejected liberal Jewish attempts to historicize Judaism by viewing it as a historical discipline that must be studied scientifically or empirically and associated with universal, rational ideas.[10]

When examining Rosenzweig's views on Jewish history and destiny that are not consistent with either traditional or liberal Jewish self-perception, one could argue that these ideas emerge out of his dialectical encounter with Christian thought throughout his brief career. On the one hand, Rosenzweig shared a general antipathy to historicism and relativism with his Protestant colleagues Franz Overbeck and Karl Barth and his close friend Rosenstock. In his response to this mutual dilemma, Rosenzweig drew upon a shared cultural and theological discourse with these Christian thinkers who attempted to restore the absolute distinction between God and humanity and the otherworldly nature of religion.

Yet while Rosenzweig was attracted to the same ideas expressed by his Christian contemporaries regarding divine revelation and eternality, he also came to the realization that it was these theological motifs that would invariably distinguish Judaism from Christianity and necessitate their opposition to each other. This was reflected in his attempt to reclassify Judaism as metaphysical and metacultural as opposed to Christianity, which he considered a historical phenomenon. In doing this, Rosenzweig was actually inverting the Augustinian theological categories of the "City of God" and the "City of Man." In painting this portrait of Christian temporality, Rosenzweig also drew upon the historiography of the Christian philosopher Schelling, who had envisioned a greater worldly presence for Christianity. Finally, Rosenzweig accepted Christian caricatures of Jews as carnal, stubborn, and blind, but he provided each of these terms with a positive valence to explain the persistent survival of the Jews as God's chosen people through their biological continuity.

Thus, throughout his brief career, Rosenzweig demonstrated a tension between fascination for and aversion to theological discourse articulated by Christian thinkers and often constructed his Jewish identity from a Christian vantage point. Rosenzweig demonstrated this dialectic between attraction and repulsion in his portrayal of Judaism and Christianity as having mutually incompatible, yet reinforcing roles in the process of redemption. Funkenstein observed that Rosenzweig went further than the Jewish philosopher Hermann Cohen in recognizing the legitimate status of Christianity. Whereas Cohen called Christ "the messiah to the nations," Rosenzweig perceived in Christianity "an expression of revelation *sui generis*." However, Rosenzweig clearly viewed the Jews as having the exclusive status as God's chosen people until the end of time, possessing the eternal truth that the rest of the world will ultimately possess. This dialectical position "allowed him to view Judaism and Christianity as being at the same time incompatible, necessary, and, to a measure, interdependent."[11]

Revelation and Jewish Eternality vis-à-vis Christianity

In response to what German Protestant thinkers like Franz Overbeck and Karl Barth perceived as a crisis of secularization and historicism of religion at the turn of the century, Rosenzweig turned to Rosenstock, a Christian historian and convert from Judaism, for theological direction in 1913. During his early years as a college student from 1905 to 1908, Rosenzweig had been influenced by the philosophers Nietzsche and Kant, causing him to doubt the belief in objective truth based on reason and leading him to conclude that all truths are subjective. Then, in a 1910 letter, he began to criticize Hegel for raising the study of history to the level of divinity and defending it as though he were constructing a theodicy, a defense of divine justice.[12] Rosenzweig writes that for Hegel,

> every act becomes guilty as soon as it enters history . . . this is why God must save man not through history but genuinely as the "God of religion." Hegel considers history as divine, as a theodicy, while for him action is naturally profane. . . . For us religion is the only authentic theodicy. The struggle against history in the nineteenth century sense is for us identical to the struggle for religion in the twentieth century sense.[13]

In this letter, Rosenzweig already begins to raise objections to Hegel's totalizing philosophy of history in which human actions are absorbed into the conceptual paradigm of history. Here Rosenzweig raises an argument that will later become the foundation of *The Star*, that the "All" of philosophy breaks apart with the individual's concrete experiences of suffering or fear of death, and the historical encounter with a God who is beyond history through revelation.[14] Yet, as Stephane Moses argues, "this declaration of faith is purely intellectual," in the sense that it was based only on a rational argument and not on a personal testimony of faith. That would come later in response to Eugen Rosenstock's affirmation of faith in Christ.[15]

Through his dialogue with Rosenstock in 1913, Rosenzweig came to an understanding of faith based on revelation as a historical fact and an ever-renewed possibility based on the "simple confession of faith" by Rosenstock, forcing Rosenzweig to abandon any form of historical relativism. According to Rosenstock, in order to avoid self-oriented, philosophical, and historical relativism without self-destruction, one must have faith in the revelation of the incarnate Logos of Christ. In this experience, God spoke to humanity in the "word become flesh," which can never become a stagnant human concept. This event provides an absolute orientation in terms of space and time. Instead of defining the human subject as the center and origin of thought, the event of divine revelation affirms an oriented universe in which there is an origin of time and a central space from which the revelation emanates. In the case of Christianity, the origin is Christ and the central space is the land of Israel, the place of his birth. Moses points out that for "each individual, belief in the Revelation means situating himself within this absolute history and geography."[16]

Rosenzweig accepted this idea of the individual who experiences revelation as being "at the center of a necessary universe" possessing an "irrefutable truth," and this would form the central idea around which *The Star* would revolve. Yet, following his discussion with Rosenstock, Rosenzweig thought that this event of revelation could only logically have taken form in Christianity, the preeminent, living religion of the West.[17] Rosenzweig was overwhelmed by the fact that an objective scholar like Rosenstock could affirm religion as the most reliable answer to his philosophical questions about the world. This demonstrated the living strength of Christianity for Rosenzweig more compellingly than any philosophical argument regarding the relationship between reason and faith. Moreover, in Rosenzweig's world at the time, "there was no room for Judaism." Rosenstock described Rosenzweig's superficial observance of Judaism as "a personal idiosyncrasy, or at best a pious romantic relic" that could not provide him with a necessary orientation in the world. Subsequently, from the months of June to September following their encounter, Rosenzweig resolved to become a Christian in order to experience the revealed, living God.[18]

However, he wanted to become Christian while remaining a Jew, as did the founders of Christianity, and not through the intermediate stage of paganism. Hence, he actually decided to attend High Holiday services in September 1913, in order to remain faithful to the Torah up until the moment of his baptism. Yet it appears that the Day of Atonement service strongly influenced him to return to Judaism. Later he would write that Yom Kippur "is a testimony to the reality of God that cannot be controverted."[19] In the days following that service, Rosenzweig wrote a letter to his mother asserting that "the development of Judaism has by-passed Jesus, whom the pagans call Lord and through whom they reach the Father; it does not pass through him."[20] A week later, he informed his friend Rudolf Ehrenberg that after a complete self-examination, his conversion to Christianity was no longer necessary and no longer possible, because he remained a Jew. Rosenzweig concluded that the people Israel do not have to come to the Father because they are already with him. Hence, Jews stand apart from world history, already anticipating the eschaton by their very nature as an eternal people chosen by God.[21]

These two themes, divine revelation and Israel's eternality, became constitutive elements in the construction of his Jewish identity in relation to Christianity. He dealt with the first theme in his essay "Atheistic Theology" (1914), comparing the crisis of Protestant identity generated by the quest for the historical Jesus to the failure of Jewish theology to account for supernatural revelation. The Swiss Protestant philosopher Franz Overbeck had criticized nineteenth-century German Protestant scholars for equating Christianity with culture, and portrayed a crisis of Protestantism resulting from the paradoxical, historical realization that there is no way back to the original form of Christianity as a world-renouncing Jewish, apocalyptic sect. Overbeck denounced the historicism and secularization of Christianity by Protestant theologians who borrowed methods of historical and philosophical criticism from the secular sciences, transforming the otherworldly message of Christianity into a social, cultural, and political movement within history.[22]

Just as Overbeck opposed Hegel's perception of Christianity as the progressive realization of an idea, Rosenzweig criticizes Jewish and Christian liberal theologians for portraying God in a Hegelian manner as an immanent factor of human evolution. According to Rosenzweig, theology becomes atheistic when it fails to account for the dialectic between the divine and the human. He argues that just as the liberal Protestants replaced the incarnation of God with the idea of the humanness of God in Jesus, liberal Jews replaced the divine descent at Sinai with the autonomy of the ethical law. Hence, while the language of God and humanity is retained, the dialectic between the divine and the human becomes an inner human dialectic that ultimately leads to a mythologization of revelation.[23] Here Rosenzweig uses language similar to that of Karl Barth, asserting that the problem with Jewish and Christian theologies is that "the distinctiveness of God and humanity . . . seems to be eliminated." He goes on to criticize the current perception of revelation, arguing at one point that "the plunging of a higher content into an unworthy vessel is quieted," and that there is no longer a sense of the "breaking of the active divine into the resting human."[24] While in "Atheistic Theology," Rosenzweig maintains the Barthian dialectical distinction between God and humanity, he later portrays revelation in more dialogical terms, describing an I-Thou encounter through language, based on biblical models.[25]

Rosenzweig's portrayal of the Jewish people as eternal was analogous to Barth's dehistoricized, eschatological portrayal of the Church presented most clearly in the second edition of his commentary on the Epistle to the Romans. Barth viewed Christianity to be an unhistorical phenomenon which actually belongs to an *Urgeschichte*, a prehistory that is both protological and eschatological. According to Bruce McCormack, Barth agrees with Overbeck that a historical existence of Christianity is absurd because of its original eschatological expectations, yet instead makes the eschatological characteristic of Christianity into its highest virtue.[26] Similarly, Rosenzweig viewed the Jewish people as eternal because of the fact that they anticipate the eschaton by their already established status as a redeemed nation. Consequently, the Jews cannot grow as a people in the context of history because that would imply that their perfection has not yet been attained in time. For Rosenzweig, "Eternity is just this: that time no longer has a right to a place between the present moment and consummation and that whole future is to be grasped today."[27]

Moreover, just as Barth rejected Protestant attempts to equate Christianity with cultural progress, Rosenzweig rejected Zionism as a secular movement that equated the Jews' eternal longing to return to their holy land with a political movement like all others. In fact, he argued that the political movement of Zionism deified the nation, representing the culmination of the development of what he perceived to be an "atheistic theology."[28] Because Jews can realize the eternal peace of redemption in every moment through their immediacy to God, they do not have to strive for it politically, like all the other nations in history.

Hence, for Rosenzweig, an apolitical, exilic existence is actually appropriate to ensure Israel's eternal status outside of history.[29]

However it may be argued that In his later years, Rosenzweig perceived that Zionism was not like other nationalisms because Zionists did not completely desire a state in and of itself.[30] In his analysis of Rosenzweig's last diaries, Stephane Moses even goes so far as to say that Rosenzweig actually conceived of an abstract messianism that, although completely passive, allowed for the possibility of a historical event triggering it. Moreover, he argues that Rosenzweig does not necessarily exclude the possibility of Zionism being a messianic movement. Finally, according to Moses, Rosenzweig grants a historic dimension to Jewish faith illustrated in the prayer for return to the land of Israel.[31]

Rosenzweig further developed his metahistorical portrayal of Israel in response to the crisis of historicism that he observed to be culminating in World War I. In 1917, influenced by his teacher Friedrich Meinecke, Rosenzweig had envisioned a dialectic of history in which the world would be actually transformed into a purely ecumenical, political order through the seemingly contradictory imperialistic politics exhibited in World War I.[32] In his essay "Realpolitik," written at the Macedonian front, he argued that in order to realize the world-historical destiny of the war, Germany must abandon the approach to Realpolitik as an end in and of itself.[33] Rosenzweig was suspicious that the Prussian nation-state, although motivated by the desire to protect its ethnic diaspora and irredenta, actually engaged in the self-centered imperialism and domination that led to World War I. Subsequently, he abandoned Fichte's position that Prussia represents the concept of the ideal nation-state because of its service to world history. Eventually, by May 1918, Rosenzweig grew disenchanted with the war as a dialectical event in history when the German Military High Command took over and engaged in Realpolitik without the awareness of its dialectical contribution to a new world order.[34]

Already in April 1918, Rosenzweig had written to Hans Ehrenberg that the Christian-led *Zwischenreich* (interim kingdom of history) was problematic for him as a Jew whose only reality is God and the divine kingdom. In that letter, Rosenzweig claims that he belongs to the interim kingdom "only because of the coercion of nature (which equals history there)—this is not my own free choice."[35] It may be argued that Rosenzweig's portrayal of Israel as ontologically distinct from the warring states of world history grew out of his disappointment with the imperialism of the Prussian state in World War I. In *The Star*, he observes that the nations of the world claim to achieve eternity through the historical destiny of their states. However, when encountering the Jewish people, they are forced to realize that eternity does not result from the latest conquest of the historical moment but rather is present in the very existence of the Jewish people that lies beyond history and is preserved through procreation.[36]

Rosenzweig's portrayal of the Jews as eternal was consistent with historical Jewish self-perception based on the idea that "the uniqueness and the eternity of Israel were a transcendental, metahistorical premise and promise, not the outcome of history."[37] This perception can already be seen in the Talmud and is accentuated by medieval philosopher Yehuda Halevi and early modern rabbi Yehuda Loew of Prague, who, like Rosenzweig, attributed to the Jews a genetic, divine predisposition.[38] In *The Star*, Rosenzweig identifies explicitly with Halevi's portrayal of the Jews as carrying the seeds of the *amr ilahi* (divine logos) among the nations. Like a seed transforming the earth and water into its own substance in order to form one tree, the Torah dispenses the divine influence to the nations who do not realize and even reject it until the coming of Messiah.[39]

However, Rosenzweig appeared to approximate the Augustinian categories of the "City of God," and the "City of Man" as models for a dualistic historiosophy in which Judaism occupies a sacred ahistorical realm in contrast to Christianity, which dwells in profane history. Like Augustine, Rosenzweig had become disgusted with the historical idealization of the "nation-state" and the lust for power that characterized it.[40] Both thinkers revolted against the literature and philosophy in the pagan culture of their day to which they each had once been attracted. In both cases, this revolt led to a dialectic between history and metahistory.[41]

In response to anti-Christian propaganda following the defeat of Rome by the Goths in 410, Augustine wrote a "counterhistory" of Rome in which he turned Cicero's *Republic* on its head to portray Roman history not as a gradual unfolding of justice but as a history of an earthly "City of Man" based on power and greed. Augustine juxtaposed this city with a heavenly "City of God" built on faith in Christ. In contrast to the Roman inhabitants of the "City of Man," Christians do not have a conflict between *salus*, self-preservation and *fides*, a pledge to a higher being, because their identities are bound up with that of God.[42] For Augustine, the prototypical inhabitants of the "City of Man" were the Jews, whose ancestor Cain committed the most grievous act of power and greed, the killing of his brother Abel, the prefiguration of Christ and representative of the heavenly "City of God."[43]

The individuals who convert to Christianity join a community of sojourners or "resident aliens" that makes up the earthly constituency of the "City of God" in conjunction with its heavenly representation.[44] Those who wish to join the church can become members in the "City of God" on earth through faith, yet they are not guaranteed a membership in the eternal city. They remain strangers in this world until the end of time, when they may be elected to the eternal city by divine grace. At that time, the two constituencies will be united in one eternal city. Augustine refers to Noah's ark during the Flood as a typological prefiguration of the "city of God sojourning in this world; that is to say, of the church, which is rescued by the wood on which hung the Mediator of God and men, the man Christ Jesus." Augustine later refers to the "suffering servant" status of Christ by saying that his suffering for the remission of sins demonstrates what Christians "ought to suffer for the truth."[45]

Furthermore, Augustine portrays the "pilgrims" of the "City of God" on earth as being exiled from their heavenly city of Jerusalem that is allegorically prefigured by its earthly type in the Hebrew Scriptures.[46] Augustine states that while in mortal captivity throughout the nations, the Christian pilgrim "makes no scruple to obey the laws of the earthly city, whereby the things necessary for mortal life are administered." Ultimately, this accommodation is the source of a "temporal peace," yet it does not represent enjoyment, but merely "solace" for earthly misery. The peace that truly represents enjoyment for the earthly sojourners of the "City of God" is based on faith in a hidden presence that will become visible in the world to come.[47]

Because the Jews fail to atone for their crime of deicide and refuse to convert to Christianity, they remain in the "City of Man." Augustine must justify their continued existence as Jews by developing a "witness people myth," which expresses a tension between reprobationist and preservationist elements that continues in Christian portrayals of Judaism throughout history. On the one hand, Augustine describes the destruction of the Temple and subsequent dispersion of the Jews as a punishment for their crime of deicide.[48] Like Cain, they should wander the earth powerlessly with a sign of their crime, yet they should not be killed.[49] Alternatively, Jews also carry a sign of God's providence that they are to be witnesses of the authenticity of the New Testament. He explains that because of their carnal status, Jews continue to adhere to the literal meaning of the Hebrew Scriptures, and when they read the Old Testament, a veil covers their eyes. Thus, they do not even realize that they are blind to the spiritual meaning of their own Scriptures that testify to Christ.[50] Moreover, according to Augustine, God dispersed the Jews in order that they would spread the gospel of Christ to all the nations, and therefore should be preserved until their final conversion in the eschaton, when the "City of Man" will be destroyed and the righteous souls will be resurrected in the eternal city of Christ.[51]

Rosenzweig clearly refers to Augustine's *City of God* in *The Star* when he describes the Jewish people as being beyond the contradiction between *salus*, and *fides*. He states that in his "clever refutation of Cicero," Augustine argued that "the Church cannot fall into such conflict between its own welfare and the faith pledged to a higher being; for the Church *salus* and *fides* are one and the same thing." Yet Rosenzweig later claims that the Jewish people already have the "inner unity between faith and life" for which all the nations are still striving. In fact, "while Augustine may ascribe it to the Church in the form of the unity between *fides* and *salus*," this unity "is still no more than a dream to the nations within the church."[52] In contrast, Jewish unity of faith and life is manifest in blood that enables Jews to guarantee their eternity merely through "the natural propagation of the body."[53] Because the Jews have already reached the goal of eternal truth toward which the other nations are moving, they must now wait with hopeful anticipation for the others to catch up.[54] Hence, the Jewish people "must deny itself active and full participation in the life of this world with its daily, apparently conclusive solving of all contradictions," in order that it will not become "disloyal to the hope of a final solution." Unlike the other nations that work toward overcoming temporality through the functioning of the state, the Jewish people have already achieved an eternal status "even in the midst of time!"[55]

In this case, Rosenzweig's dialectic between history and metahistory differs from that of Augustine in that Rosenzweig does not divide his version of the "City of God" into two constituencies, one in heaven and one on earth. Funkenstein points out that Rosenzweig's "City of God is here on earth, already eternal in that it will be ever present. . . . Judaism will not change even in the world to come."[56] In contrast, Augustine's *peregrinus* is a temporary resident on earth who must realize his dependence on the surrounding environment and appreciate its favorable conditions. Like the Jews, the Christians are now in exile in Babylon but await their liberation in Jerusalem.[57] For Rosenzweig, exile is almost completely an ontological category. In *System and Revelation*, Stephane Moses explains that in Rosenzweig's eyes, "exile is separation itself, that is a standing aside in relation to the world and its history."[58] Moreover, Rosenzweig turns the notion of exile on its head, viewing it as a signifier for eternal life in this world. Because the Jews are already one with their heavenly Father, they may be separated from the world, yet they are never separated from their eternal source.[59]

Yet while Judaism must remain outside of the world, it is divinely ordained that the world must ultimately become eternal. Just as the Christians depend on the earthly Jews to spread the gospel of Christ in Augustine's *City of God*, Rosenzweig describes the Jews as depending on Christians to eternalize or redeem the world through proselytization. According to him, the Jewish people cannot universalize itself or assimilate among the nations of the world for fear of losing its particular relationship with God and resorting to apologetics to define itself.[60] Paul Mendes-Flohr states that the role of the Church in Rosenzweig's framework is to enter into history "in order to transform and elevate pagan sensibility, most refinely expressed in philosophical culture, by infusing it with the Word of God."[61]

Rosenzweig's envisioned role for Christianity is really a secularized version of the typological doctrine of the three churches that portrays three ages of the church: the Petrine, Pauline, and Johannine. This idea was first conceived by Joachim of Fiore in the twelfth century and then later developed by the German idealist philosophers Lessing, Fichte, Hegel, and Schelling. Rosenzweig appropriated this Christian view of history from the writings of Schelling and applied it to his dialectic between history and metahistory. Specifically, he endorsed Schelling's view that during his lifetime, the Church was on the threshold of the Johannine eschatological age of "a free undogmatic Christianity." In this upcoming age, the Church will no longer be a material presence but rather will spiritually blend with the secular world of science, philosophy, and knowledge.

Rosenzweig interpreted this to mean that the Church would now transform or convert the pagan world to monotheism.[62]

Specifically, Rosenzweig valued Christian images like the cross because they embody the recognition of universal human suffering and enable all of humanity to find consolation in it. When discussing Rosenzweig's portrayal of Christian images, Leora Batnitzky argues that by structuring passion from a communal as well as an individual perspective, Christianity depicts "both the possibility of universal community (and thus the possibility of redemption) and the tragic fate of the finite human being."[63] For Rosenzweig, Christian belief forever begins with imagery, and Christians are thus always at the beginning of the "eternal way" toward redemption. However, Christians also have an inherent propensity toward idolatry because of their continual insistence that their revelation is complete and that they have no reason to begin anew their path toward redemption. According to Rosenzweig, this idolatrous belief in the completeness of Christian revelation arises out of Christian antisemitism constituted by hatred and resentment toward Jews because of their competing claim for a complete revelation. Here he explicitly inverts the doctrine of Christian supersessionism by arguing that Jewish revelation is already complete and that Christians cannot help but to covet it. Ultimately, Rosenzweig demonstrates his ongoing ambivalence toward Christianity by promoting Christian symbolic worship as being potentially redemptive and therefore necessary, while at the same time arguing that it inevitably leads to idolatry and antisemitism.[64]

David Novak claims that in his portrayal of the Christian role in redemption, Rosenzweig apparently overestimated Christian power while underestimating Christian uniqueness. Novak observes that by using the terms "Christendom" and "Christianity" interchangeably, Rosenzweig mistakenly elevated Christian influence at a time when the world was actually becoming less Christian, and secularism was beginning to threaten Christianity as well as Judaism. He points out that Rosenstock observed this problem in 1916, disagreeing with Rosenzweig for equating Christianity with the imperialism of the nations and arguing that paganism, in the form of scientism, was becoming dominant in all the churches.[65] Novak concludes that for Rosenzweig, what appears to be a Christian-led redemption is really a Judaicization of the world because the world will become redeemed only when it becomes like the Jews, possessing eternal truth.[66] Novak argues that this demonstrates the opposite of ecumenicism by giving Christianity no legitimate messianic role in and of itself. He adds that no "religion can maintain itself very long, demanding as it must the absolute loyalty of its adherents, and at the same time regard itself as in any way subordinate to another religion."[67] This dilemma is illustrated in a letter from Rosenstock to Rosenzweig, in which Rosenstock rejected Rosenzweig's assignment of Christianity to Judaize the pagans. Rosenstock claimed that it is exactly "this naïve pride of the Jew" from which Christ redeemed the world.[68] According to Novak, Rosenzweig's theological framework implicitly encourages Christians to convert to Judaism to achieve individually what they attempt to achieve as a religion on behalf of humanity at the end of time.

Yet Richard Cohen disagrees with this type of logic and adds that according to Novak's argument, "Jews bent on missionizing might find their vocation in Christianity."[69] Moreover, Cohen argues that for Rosenzweig, the Jewish exclusive election in this world is only a vessel for the eternal truth that will be revealed at the end of time, and this is an all-inclusive divine totality that will be neither Jewish nor Christian.[70] Even while granting Christianity the primary task for this-worldly redemption, Rosenzweig recognizes the danger of Jews being too inwardly directed and ignoring the outside world. Hence he describes three ways that Jews are responsible to the unredeemed non-Jewish world: First, Jews should pray for the messiah to come. This traditional messianic approach is ironically the most ecumenical way of bringing about redemption for Rosenzweig because it allows the Jews to remain self-absorbed and provides the most credibility for Christianity's historical mission.[71] Second, Jews save the world through their suffering. Here Rosenzweig draws upon the interpretation of the "suffering servant" motif in Isaiah 53 traditionally articulated by Christians. This approach to redemption actually requires a greater Jewish contribution while maintaining the Christian responsibility for depaganizing the world.[72] Third, Jews need to promote ethical behavior illustrated "in the love of one's neighbor and anonymous works of justice."[73] Hence, this task applies not only to their fellow Jews but also, and more important, to the rest of the world. However, this mode of redemption is the least ecumenical, because it would actually overtake the Christian mission, negating any sense of Christian difference. In this case, the best option for Christians would be to convert to Judaism.[74]

While inverting Augustinian categories of the "City of God" and the "City of Man," in his dualistic historiosophy, Rosenzweig appeared to reject the polemical model of Augustine by trying to portray Judaism and Christianity as representing two legitimate paths toward redemption. This description of Jewish-Christian correlation is also demonstrated in Rosenzweig's dialogue with Hans Ehrenberg.[75] Rosenzweig's discussion of the common redemptive task of Judaism and Christianity illustrates what some scholars argue is the foundation for a post-Holocaust "two-covenant" theology that allows for the credibility of both religious communities in relation to each other. This type of theology appears in the writings of the post-Holocaust Christian thinkers Paul van Buren and A. Roy Eckardt and the Jewish thinker Irving Greenberg.[76]

However, Leora Batnitzky points out that while van Buren defines dialogue as a serious attempt to understand the other on the other's terms, Rosenzweig argues that this is impossible for Jews and Christians whose very identities are constituted by a judgment against the other.[77] Yet Batnitzky claims that Rosenzweig's portrayal of the Jewish judgment against Christianity does not compromise Christian difference, "and even allows Christians to intensify their identity as different from Jews. While Christians modify their perceptions of themselves, Christians remain Christian."[78] The question then arises as to how Christians can retain their difference when they are circumscribed in an exclusively Jewish framework that will apparently become inclusive in the messianic age. Ultimately, one could argue that in *The Star*, Rosenzweig totalizes Christianity by defining the Christian redemptive task on his own terms and carving out its role in relation to Judaism. Ironically, by following Rosenzweig's model, van Buren, Eckardt, and Greenberg ultimately perpetuate this Judaicization of the world by failing to fully allow for Christian difference and constructing what John Pawlikowski has called a "Judaism for the Gentiles."[79]

Rosenzweig clearly illustrated the dialectic between attraction and repulsion by Jews and Christians for each other when admitting that there is a "formal relation" between Judaism and Christianity while also maintaining that there is no "living relation" between Jewish and Christian theologies.[80] Moreover, in *The Star*, he portrayed Judaism and Christianity as being intimately bound together by God, while at the same time claiming that God "has set enmity between the two for all time."[81] He illustrated this enmity in a 1916 letter to Rosenstock in which he promoted essential differences between the two religions. Rosenzweig stated that three articles separate the Jew from the Christian: First, Jews have the truth; second, they are already at the goal; and third,

> that any and every Jew feels in the depths of his soul that the Christian relation to God, and so in a sense their religion, is particularly and extremely pitiful, poverty-stricken, and ceremonious; namely, that as a Christian one has to learn from someone else, whoever he may be, to call God "our Father." To the Jew, that God is our Father is the first and most self-evident fact—and what need is there for a third person between me and my father in Heaven?[82]

Yet Rosenzweig illustrates an ambivalence toward Christianity when inverting Augustinian portrayals of Judaism. Rosenzweig constructed three fundamental elements of Jewish identity out of Christian caricatures of the Jews. First, he accepted the Pauline premise that Jews are a carnal people yet rejected its Christian conclusion that Jews have no spiritual connection to God. Rosenzweig inverted the word "carnal" to refer to the preservation of Jewish "eternal life" based on physical procreation. He contrasted this with Christian self-preservation on the "eternal way" based on proselytization.[83] Second, Rosenzweig accepted the Christian characterization of Jews as stubborn yet inverted its negative associations. Traditionally, Jews are portrayed as stubborn because of their refusal to accept Christ and, as a result, have been rejected by God. Ultimately, they have been separated from their Christian neighbors and forced to wander endlessly away from their land. Rosenzweig accepted the perception of Jewish stubbornness, separation from Christianity, and exilic wandering, yet he turned these characterizations into an affirmation of Jewish survival and closeness to God.[84]

Specifically, he claimed that what appears to Christians as stubbornness to accept Christian conversion actually signifies Jewish fidelity to God. In a letter to Rudolf Ehrenberg in 1913, Rosenzweig argued, "To us, our 'stubbornness' is fidelity and our "infidelity towards God" is remedied—just because it is infidelity and not an original primeval estrangement ('Adam's' fall into sin!)—only by repentance and return, not by a transformation of conversion."[85] Hence, for Rosenzweig Jews have been stubborn, yet only by remaining faithful to God, despite repeated infidelity. However, Christians have misunderstood the nature of that infidelity and its remedy. Because the infidelity is not an inherited sin, Jews do not require a spiritual transformation by converting to Christianity but rather remain in the covenant by virtue of repentance and return.

Moreover, in his 1916 letter to Rosenstock, Rosenzweig elaborates on the issue of Jewish stubbornness and even views it as a necessary component of Jewish election. Rosenzweig raises the following question:

> But could this dogma of the stubbornness of the Jews be likewise a Jewish dogma? It not only could be; it is. But the awareness of being rejected has quite a different place in Jewish dogmatics and is the very counterpart to a Christian awareness of being elected to rulership, an awareness that exists beyond the vestige of a doubt. Jewish religious evaluation of the destruction of the Temple in the year 70 is tuned to this concept.[86]

Here Rosenzweig explicitly accepts the idea of Jewish rejection by God espoused by Christians and turns it on its head to represent Jewish election. Richard Cohen describes Rosenzweig's inverted formulation as "the dual Jewish consciousness of election," based on a collective sense of separation and affirmation.[87] Rosenzweig himself alludes to this in his commentary on Yehuda Halevi's poem "Out of My Straits" when he states that the "whole world asserts that the Jewish people is outcast and elect, both; and the Jewish people does not itself . . . refute this dictum, but instead merely confirms it."[88] In this instance, Rosenzweig affirms the *Unheimlichkeit*, or uncanny nature, of Judaism as perceived by the non-Jewish world and transvalues it, associating the unnatural separation of Jews from the Christian majority with their eternal status. Batnitzky points out further that Rosenzweig agrees with Richard Wagner's antisemitic portrayal of the Jew who "has a God all to himself—in ordinary life strikes us primarily by his outward appearance, which, no matter to what European nationality we belong, has something disagreeably foreign to that nationality."[89] Yet, of course Rosenzweig associates that foreignness with "true eternity" that must always be seen as "alien and vexing to the state, and to the history of the world."[90] Ultimately for Rosenzweig, Jewish election signifies an otherworldly distinctiveness that unfortunately brings with it a disturbance to the "normality" of the Gentile world. Hence, Jews are eternally removed from the world by God and are essentially made abnormal for the sake of the world. Because Jews represent God's presence, they should be absent from the everyday routine of human life, but they are not. Batnitzky considers that for this very reason they illustrate Wittengstein's definition of "uncanny" according to G. F. Bearn, "the presence of what ought to be absent."[91]

As a Jew, Rosenzweig agreed with Christians that Jewish separation and exilic wandering following the destruction of the Second Temple represented a divinely ordained punishment, but he disagreed regarding the nature of the sin and its implications. While Christians traditionally argued that the destruction of the Second Temple and dispersion were punishments for Jewish rejection of Christ and deicide, the Rabbis saw their primary sins as senseless internal hatred, social injustice, and lack of leadership. However, they also saw their exile as the historical manifestation of a cathartic, spiritual process of expiation and purification.[92]

Later in the sixteenth century, arguably in response to the expulsion of the Jews from Spain, the Lurianic Kabbalists developed this cathartic theodicy further by arguing that along with the people Israel, there is actually a process of self-purification occurring within God through self-alienation. In order to remove the "roots of sternness," *Ein Sof*, the primordial, infinite God, contracted to create an "empty space" of nondivinity in which divine light was poured. However, the receiving "vessels" could not contain God's light and broke, causing the sparks of divine light to be concealed by the vessel shards. Through the fulfillment of commandments, Jews can retrieve God's light and gradually achieve a *tikkun olam*, a restoration of the world and ultimate redemption.[93]

In addition to the cathartic theodicy, Jews constructed two other major types of theodicy throughout history to justify their dispersion: the missionary and the soteriologic. The missionary theodicy affirmed that Jews had to be dispersed in order to spread the Word of God to the nations. This theodicy was constructed in eras of Jewish-Gentile cooperation by Jewish philosophers such as Philo in Hellenistic Roman Alexandria and Yehuda Halevi in medieval Muslim Spain. The soteriologic theodicy was developed by the medieval rabbinic commentator Rashi, who interpreted the suffering servant motif in Isaiah 53 to refer not to the Messiah but to the people Israel. While rejecting the idea that Christ was the suffering servant, Rashi accepted the Christian idea of vicarious suffering for the sins of the world.[94]

In *The Star*, Rosenzweig drew upon the soteriologic theodicy and, like Rashi, appropriated the Christian interpretation of the suffering servant in Isaiah 53 to provide a justification for Jewish suffering throughout its wandering in history. Specifically, he stated that Israel's election by God is predicated on its tenacious suffering not only for its own sins but also for the sins of the world. In fact, the eternal vitality of the Jews is proven by the very hatred against them. According to Rosenzweig, God "afflicts Israel with disease so that those other peoples may be healed." As Richard Cohen explains, this can be interpreted to mean either that the non-Jewish world will persecute the Jews until they realize their own injustice or that God will react to Israel's affliction by purging the evil from the world.[95]

Yet, according to Rosenzweig, it is not the non-Jewish world in its Christian character that oppresses the Jews, but rather in its pagan character. Christians are part pagan because they can only impart love and not receive it. Through its mission, the Church spreads the love of divine revelation to the pagans and thereby depaganizes the world. Hence, Christian missionizing actually leads to a decrease in oppression of the Jews and ultimately saves Christians from their own pagan impulses toward hatred and destruction. However, Rosenzweig perceived this method of redemption as less desirable in the eyes of God than the methods of prayer and acts of love and justice.[96]

Finally, Rosenzweig accepted Augustine's portrayal of the Jews as blind, but not because they are unaware of the spiritual meaning of their own Scriptures which point to Christ. Instead, Rosenzweig portrayed the Jews as standing at the center of the star, eternal flame of truth, that causes them to be blinded to the rays of its light penetrating the world.[97] In a letter to Rosenstock in 1916, Rosenzweig writes, "Is not part of the price that the synagogue must pay for the blessing in the enjoyment of which she anticipates the whole world, namely, of being already in the Father's presence, that she must wear the bandages of unconsciousness over her eyes?"[98] In this letter, Rosenzweig explicitly inverts the Augustinian supersessionist claim by stating that Jews are blinded not because they are ignorant of God's revelation but because they already possess too great a knowledge of it. While Rosenzweig promotes the redemptive potential of Christian visual imagery, he seems to argue that Israel does not require, let alone possess, such a vision of God because it is by its very existence the true image of God's revelation that the Christian world is yet to receive.[99] In addition, because of their proximity and direct connection to eternal truth, the Jews are to some degree oblivious to its effects in the world. Because Jews are at the center of the star with their backs to the world, they are blind not only to its rays but also to the place of their own identity as a people in relation to the world. Funkenstein explains Rosenzweig's conception of Judaism as "a form of existence that, in order to reflect upon itself, would have to transgress beyond itself and see itself in Christian eyes."[100]

In contrast, Christianity is blind to the real image of the truth possessed by the Jews and must pursue the rays of that inflamed truth into the world.[101] Here, Rosenzweig implicitly accepts the Augustinian notion of Jews as the "witness people," yet not merely as the continuation of a monotheistic idea and referent for Christian truth. Rosenzweig inverts the valence of the "witness people" motif by portraying it as a reference to the endurance of Israel as an eternal, living people "whose glow provides invisible nourishment to the rays" of Christianity. In other words, Jews possess divine truth by their very existence, and Christians must recognize this through their continual attestation to the Jewish "witness" of divine truth.[102]

Thus, by converting Christian anti-Jewish images into symbols of Jewish eternality, Rosenzweig was able to transform accusations of Jewish abnormality into affirmations of Jewish superiority. Consequently, he perpetuated the Jewish-Christian dialectic by reversing the fortunes of Judaism and Christianity. Yet, in his construction of Jewish identity in relation to Christianity, Rosenzweig explicitly illustrated a sense of interdependence between the two religions that really had not been expressed before by a Jewish thinker. While he opposed the apologetic efforts of liberal, German Jews to assimilate into German Christian culture, Rosenzweig was nonetheless often at pains to establish Jewish uniqueness by understanding it from within the Christian culture. In fact, for Rosenzweig, defining identity from an outside perspective is an essential quality of the Jewish people. In another excerpt from his commentary to Yehuda Halevi's poem "Out of My Straits," Rosenzweig makes the following statement about the Jewish people: "The unique characteristic of the people is this: that it looks at itself in about the same way as the outside world looks at it."[103] Thus Rosenzweig cites the necessity of sharing a cultural discourse with Christianity if only to confirm the notion of Jewish difference. As Funkenstein described it, Rosenzweig felt that he had "to buy his right to be different by showing how well, how much from the inside, he grasped the point of view of 'the other'. . . . In order to become 'himself' he had to be first 'the other.'"[104]

Indeed, Rosenzweig described what he believed to be the contradiction of Jewish existence: living outside of the general culture while at the same time participating in it. Batnitzky explains that for Rosenzweig, the Jewish people "is not a nation among nations, but a nation for the nations. In being a nation for the nations, Judaism remains a nation separate from the nations *for the sake of* the nations."[105] Hence, as the eternal people, Jews live outside of the general culture of the nations for the sake of redeeming them. However, as individuals, Jews participate in the profane cultures in which they live. In coming to this conclusion, Rosenzweig drew upon the aesthetic theory of the German Christian philosopher Schelling, who defined an idea in the following way: "Every idea has two unities: the one through which it exists within itself and is absolute . . . and the one through which it is taken up as a particular into the absolute as into its own center."[106] Rosenzweig incorporates Schelling's notion of the idea into his understanding of Jewish identity by arguing that because of their unique theological status, the Jewish people "must not close itself off within borders, but include within itself such borders as would through their double function, tend to make it one individual people among others."[107] While attempting to maintain an ontological Jewish uniqueness, Rosenzweig allows for the blurring of cultural borders, thus portraying the dual nature of Jewish identity.

However, by constructing his Jewish theology in conversation with Christianity, Rosenzweig demonstrates the prior existence of overlapping theological as well as cultural borders. While claiming to preserve the absolute nature of Jewish identity in relation to Christianity, Rosenzweig demonstrates a more dynamic construction of a Jewish identity that is produced rather than given and enunciated at specific historical intersections between Judaism and Christianity.[108] He does not reaffirm preexisting theological boundaries with Christianity but rather appears to realign those that are already shifting. In this way, he sets the stage for the work of Hans Joachim Schoeps, who would go even further by acknowledging the blurred boundaries between Judaism and Christianity and actively crossing over them to construct his Jewish-Christian theology. Whereas Rosenzweig tried to carve out Jewish theological difference from within Christian culture, Schoeps would take the radical step of conjoining Jewish and Christian theologies in his own work and in his portrayal of the Jewish-Christian relationship. Yet, despite their differences, both of these Jewish thinkers demonstrated a fascination for Christian motifs that transcends theological borders.

2

Hans Joachim Schoeps's "Critical-Protestant" Theology

A Jewish-Christian Amalgamation

Like his older contemporary Rosenzweig, the German Jewish theologian Hans Joachim Schoeps constructed a systematic Jewish theology in conversation with Christianity that was supposed to preserve Jewish uniqueness while at the same time recognizing its contiguity with German, Christian culture. Similar to Rosenzweig, Schoeps grew up in an assimilated Jewish home yet later rebelled against bourgeois Jewish liberalism, arguing that it had changed Judaism from a theocentric religion into a historical, anthropological discipline. He disagreed with the effort to make God into a projection of either natural-cosmic forces or ethical-political ideals by historicizing revelation.[1] Moreover, like Rosenzweig, Schoeps constructed a theological response to this religious dilemma out of a cultural discourse shaped to some extent by the early writings of the Protestant thinker Karl Barth. Additionally, in his attempt to recover faith in a transcendent God, Schoeps also became attracted to the theological writings of Martin Luther as interpreted by the Lutheran scholar Karl Holl.

Using Lutheran and early Barthian lenses, Schoeps viewed both Jews and Christians as having fallen away from God in sin through secularization and historicization of religion. He charged that they had forgotten that faith in God cannot be proven rationally but rather is "dialectically determinable as having and at the same time not-having, as knowledge and equally non-knowledge."[2] Therefore, Jews and Christians must realize their creaturely status and decide to respond to the divine command through faith in an irrational, unmediated revelation.[3] Whereas Rosenzweig would eventually utilize this shared cultural discourse to draw essential theological distinctions between Judaism and Christianity, Schoeps would embrace this common language and create a theological hybrid, radically exposing the fuzzy boundaries between Judaism and Christianity that Rosenzweig had unwittingly demonstrated in his work.

While both Jews and Christians often see Rosenzweig's theology as a model for dialogue, Schoeps actually went further than Rosenzweig in reconstructing a mutually reinforcing Jewish-Christian relationship. Both Rosenzweig and Schoeps gave Christianity an unprecedented role in redemption, yet Rosenzweig portrayed it as subordinate to Judaism.[4] In contrast, Schoeps tended to recognize Christian uniqueness to a greater extent and at times even placed Christianity on equal footing with Judaism. Yet, because of his apparent construction of a Jewish-Christian hybrid, his detractors in the two religious communities considered Schoeps to be neither Jewish nor Christian enough.[5] This demonstrates his unique positionlessness on the border between Judaism and Christianity. Schoeps's seemingly contradictory and multiple Jewish subjectivity demonstrates a Jewish-Christian heterogeneous totality in which Jewish and Christian identities are intertwined yet not melded together. While attempting to retain Jewish difference, Schoeps's model of Jewish-Christian interconnection was misunderstood and subsequently marginalized in the master narratives of Jewish intellectual history.

Schoeps's Ambiguous Relationship with German Christian Culture: A Biographical Sketch

Throughout his life, Schoeps often found himself in a cultural and religious "no-man's-land" because his theological and political positions transcended Jewish and German Christian boundaries. He was born in Berlin in 1909 to a comfortable middle-class family, and by his teenage years, he yearned to identify with a movement larger than himself that rejected bourgeois values and embraced an inner spiritual passion lacking in his own life. Because he was too young to serve in World War I, Schoeps and his Jewish contemporaries became envious of the camaraderie of the German veterans who had been involved in the middle-class Wandervogel movement that promoted the "romantic transcendence of the everyday world" through the shared experience of wandering in nature, leading to a new sense of community (*Gemeinschaft*) based on brotherly love.[6] While originally enthralled by the comradeship achieved in battle, the members of the movement who survived the war began to reject petty nationalism and became convinced of the need for deeper human ties beyond politics and the "society" (*Gesellschaft*) created by bourgeois civilization.[7]

Yet, by 1912, the mainly Protestant Wandervogel became increasingly antisemitic, promoting an Aryan superiority that excluded Jews. In response to this change, many assimilated Jewish youths tried to find a Jewish alternative for the shared inner experience of the Wandervogel community in opposition to bourgeois rationalism.[8] That year, a group of young Zionists established the Blau-Weiss movement in order to perpetuate this universal intuitive experience of community albeit in a nationalist form, following the leadership of the German-Jewish philosopher Martin Buber. He argued that by seeking to establish a state in Palestine, Zionists were attempting to create a true human community governed not by the "need for power" but by spirit.[9]

In *Bound upon a Wheel of Fire*, John Dippel points out that while Schoeps shared Buber's desire for a community based on inwardness, "he welcomed this steadfast Germanic chauvinism, this yearning for a uniquely Teutonic response to the challenges (and evils) of the modern era."[10] Consequently, the young Schoeps disagreed with any youth organization like the Blau-Weiss, communist or socialist groups promoting a cause that would be construed as foreign to the mythical idea of "Germanness" that the Wandervogel espoused. Instead, he aligned himself with politically conservative Jews who defended German cultural heritage and the Prussian monarchy against modernist artistic and political movements. Besides wanting to be accepted as Germans, these Jews who had fought in World War I had developed a genuine patriotism based on the perceived economic, social, and political achievements of their "fatherland." After being shut out of antisemitic right-wing groups, these Jews formed parallel groups like the Reich Association of Jewish War Veterans in 1918 that promoted similar ideas of wartime solidarity and the resurrection of the monarchy, while at the same time championing the military service of Jews.[11]

Schoeps's German-Jewish cultural affiliation was directly linked to his ambiguous relationship to Christianity. In October 1926, he became influenced by the Christian thinker Eberhard Arnold's vision for religious reform and wrote his first article for Arnold's journal, *Die Wegwarte*, in which he lamented in Lutheran and early Barthian terms the sinfulness of his generation due to its alienation from God. Subsequently he called for prophetic and political action based on a brotherhood "whose spirit was poured out into the world by Christ."[12] Schoeps believed that it was the Prussian youth who would create this new brotherhood that would transform the German nation and ultimately the world. Three years later, Schoeps attempted to fulfill his vision by establishing the Freideutsche Kameradeschaft (Free German Comradeship) in the forest of Thuringia. Schoeps described the members of this organization to be the "shock troops" for the spiritual revolution that he envisioned because they would be able to "turn from the tumult of the world into the depths of the self, and to return from this self with renewed strength into that world."[13] Through its brotherhood, this organization would demonstrate that in order to succeed, any German national movement must stem from the common realization of createdness and dependence upon a transcendent God.[14]

By 1932, Schoeps began to realize that the National Socialist movement, which promoted a race-based national identity, had failed to recognize this universal sense of creatureliness and thus did not fulfill the mission of a true German nation: to preserve societal order that is based on the divine order of creation. In addition, he discovered ironically that only by remaining Jewish could he truly participate in the mission of a German nation. In *"Odd Fellows" in the Politics of Religion*, Gary Lease explains that for Schoeps there were two parts to a genuine German national identity, the theological dimension based on the facts of God, creation, and revelation, and the Prussian nationalist dimension, which consisted of "a 'confession' to the idea of societal order as reflecting the creational order, the state as responsible both to society and to God."[15] At that point, Schoeps came to realize that the theological dimension of his identity was actually rooted in his Jewish heritage, specifically in the idea that God is creator, demonstrated most clearly in the divine revelation at Sinai and ensuing covenant with Israel. In fact, he argued, at least to his Jewish audience, that there was a propensity for experiencing revelation in the very biological makeup of the Jew.[16]

While drawing upon Protestant and Lutheran categories to describe Judaism, Schoeps had found a Jewish model of irrational revelation in the work of the nineteenth-century philosopher Salomon Ludwig Steinheim, who argued that humanity must freely subordinate the rational thought process of cause and effect to the higher truth of revelation, which must be accepted precisely because it contradicts human reason. In fact, Schoeps's book *Jüdischer Glaube in dieser Zeit* (1932) laid the groundwork for a modern Jewish theology that drew extensively on Christian categories but also relied on Steinheim's concept of revelation as a demonstration of the unique singularity of God and divine creation of the world out of nothing.[17] Ultimately, Schoeps uncovered a "subterranean" tradition of suprarational thought in Jewish history that includes the work of Yehuda Halevi, Chasdai Crescas, and Steinheim.[18]

In 1933, Schoeps set out to promote this dual Prussian-Jewish identity by establishing an intellectual organization of Jewish youths called Deutscher Vortrupp (German Vanguard), based on the model of the pre–World War I German youth movement. However, this Jewish intellectual vanguard would not only promote German patriotism but also restore a deeper commitment to Judaism. This conservative Jewish group attacked the Zionist movement for doing exactly what Buber had argued against, trying to create a state "based on power." In contrast, the Vortrupp proclaimed what it considered to be the true historical mission of Judaism, to provide the spiritual foundation for a Prussian identity, and it pursued that mission by representing Jews who wanted to achieve a political rapprochement with the Nazi regime.[19] At the same time, Schoeps disassociated his organization from more radically conservative Jewish groups like the Schwarzes Fahnlein, which called for its members to withdraw from all Jewish organizations that did not promote nationalistic identification with the German race. In his 1934 critique of the Schwarzes Fahnlein,

Schoeps argued that being Jewish is based not on choice but on obligation by virtue of Israel's covenant with God at Sinai, and thus cannot be freely ignored or abandoned. Nonetheless, Schoeps insisted that his loyalty to Germany would not be diminished and in fact could be maintained only by his allegiance to Judaism.[20]

Sadly enough for Schoeps and the other more conservative Jewish groups, their patriotic love for Germany remained unrequited by the Nazis, and eventually Schoeps was forced to disband the Vortrupp after its offer to serve in the German army was rejected in 1935. Despite this defeat, Schoeps continued to hold secret meetings in the winter of 1935–36 with his outlawed group and even planned to distribute its newsletter. However, a Gestapo agent infiltrated these meetings and arrested Schoeps along with his followers on the charge of high treason.[21] As a result, Schoeps was finally forced to flee to Sweden, where he continued to write cultural critiques of Germany under his own name as well as a pseudonym. After the war, Schoeps was one of the very few German Jews to return to Germany immediately, where he accepted a teaching position at the University of Erlangen in 1947. He published his perhaps most popular work on the theology and history of early Jewish Christianity in 1949 and then proceeded to establish a new interdisciplinary approach to historical studies called *Geistesgeschichte*, or "history of consciousness." Despite his prestigious scholarly achievements in areas such as Prussian history, early Christianity, New Testament exegesis, nineteenth and twentieth-century intellectual history, and contemporary cultural criticism, Schoeps would continually be criticized by his fellow Jews until his death in 1980 for his political and religious affinity for German Christian culture.[22] Yet by standing on the threshold of Jewish and German Christian cultures, Schoeps dramatically illustrated the parallel cultural and theological expressions of modern Jewish-Christian liminality.

Schoeps versus Rosenzweig: Promoting Existential Alternatives to Liberalism and Orthodoxy

At first glance, there are many similarities between the theological development of Rosenzweig and Schoeps. While they both rejected the historicism of Jewish liberalism, neither Rosenzweig nor Schoeps fully embraced classical rabbinic Judaism either. While they each agreed with the rabbinic, preemancipatory notion of Jewish eternity based on biological continuity, they also portrayed the Jewish people as extraterritorial, basically rejecting the traditional eschatological expectation that there will be a historical restoration of Jewish sovereignty in the land of Israel. Consequently, Rosenzweig and Schoeps largely rejected Zionism, which they felt had betrayed the unique, religious status of Judaism. For both Rosenzweig and Schoeps, Zionism was associated with secularization and assimilation, a political movement like all others that disconnected the Jews from their unique divine origin and mission. In *Jüdischer Glaube*, Schoeps went so far as to compare Zionists with antisemites who tend to wrongly associate the people Israel with "what one understands as a people in the worldly-political sense." However, just as Rosenzweig would later soften his stance on Zionism, Schoeps acknowledged that Zionism might serve a purpose in rehabilitating a weakened Jewish community in the diaspora. Schoeps even portrayed Zionism as the effort to construct "a home for persecuted and disenfranchised Jews in Palestine to which no person will object."[23]

On the issue of Jewish eternality, Schoeps seemed to replicate Rosenzweig's portrayal of the Jewish people as having an eternal, otherworldly status through the sanctification of their blood, as a result of "the grace of election." Moreover, he argued that the "chosenness of the people Israel signifies the predisposition for an unmediated receiving of revelation which is given as an everlasting reality in the revealed covenant."[24] Schoeps also traced this idea back to Yehuda Halevi's portrayal of God planting this essential, religious predisposition in the soul of the first human, which is then transmitted to the entire people of Israel at Sinai through inheritance and a mystical tradition of their ancestors.[25]

However, unlike Rosenzweig, Schoeps was ambiguous when portraying the essential holiness of Jewish blood and what constitutes the essence of Judaism in general. When describing the "holy nation" of Israel in *Jüdischer Glaube*, Schoeps referred to it as a "revelatory community with a biological center of origin, never sinking down to a mere confession, rather just as the church is the institute of sacrality for Christianity, [the holy nation of Israel] has its sacrality in the blood inheritance."[26] Yet when comparing his theology to that of Halevi, Schoeps argued that Jewish salvation is not found in an inherited substance but in an understanding of revelation that can only be grasped as a potential possibility. He asserted that in this sense, the election of Israel cannot be understood as an essence but rather as a potency.[27] Gary Lease observes that for Schoeps, the Jews only have a divine promise in their blood. The blood did not produce the belief in a divine promise, "but it simply marked the possibility of actualizing that belief. And this actualization is always a human act."[28]

Schoeps was forced to clarify the notion of a Jewish predisposition to revelation based on race in his 1932 dialogue with the German cultural critic Hans Blüher. Blüher was most known for his early writings on the importance of the Wandervogel movement in German culture, and he was working toward a general theory exploring the human creation and preservation of culture. Arguing that religion is a product of human culture, Blüher portrayed in antisemitic terms what he perceived to be the revolt of Israel against Christian purity as an example of how a religion like Judaism is born, grows, and dies in history. Schoeps, who had admired Blüher's work on the Wandervogel movement, felt compelled to write a letter opposing Blüher's position to the CV-Zeitung, the United Association of German Citizens of Jewish faith. This letter led to a debate between Schoeps and Blüher followed by several letters throughout 1932 that were eventually published. Ironically, the two interlocutors developed a friendship that would continue after the war, and Blüher ultimately renounced his antisemitic views, while even considering conversion to Judaism!

However, during their 1932 debate, Blüher stated somewhat ambivalently that while Jews possessed a sacred blood grounded in God's promise, it was for this reason that they must be excluded from other nations and resigned to live in the ghetto. In fact, he argued that based on their holy semen, Jews had excluded themselves from the German people and the Prussian nation. In his response to this argument, Schoeps was forced to explain his earlier conflicting claims about Jewish election to defend his allegiance to the German people and the Prussian nation. In the following statement, he asserts that Israel's election is both an essential biological component and a potential source of holiness to be activated:

> Each Israelite, through his bodiliness, possesses the constitutional predisposition to salvation, the organic disposition to the receiving of revelation, by means of the right attitude of consciousness concerning the Law. . . . This grace of election of the *brit*, [demonstrated by the fact] that the calling to the unmediated following of God is latently submerged in Jewish blood, also gives the reason for the fact that one can recognize the Jewish people physically with almost near certainty 3000 years after their charismatic constitution.[29]

Here Schoeps is clearly portraying a predisposition to salvation that is essentially linked to the biological and physical makeup of the Jew. Yet, at the same time, he links this genetic predisposition to salvation with a potential appropriation of revelation through obedience to the Torah. The question then arises as to how Schoeps can depict the Jews as having an eternal connection to God that is both an essence and a potency to be activated.

This ambiguity may be explained in Schoeps's theological discussion of the perpetual possibility of Jews to return to God after they have sinned. He addressed his contemporary Jews with the urgency of the prophet Micah, asserting, "God forgives sin and overlooks the heinous deed of the remnant of his inheritance" (Mic. 7:18).[30] In contrast to Rosenzweig's portrayal of the Jews as being separated from the profanity of modern historical development, Schoeps identified contemporary Jews with the sinful remnant of God's inheritance who are in a fallen state of godlessness. In fact, he argued that the religious situation of his day was more serious than Rosenzweig had realized because the blood inheritance was no longer a "present self-understanding" for Jews but rather a memory to be recalled. Nonetheless, to those sinful Jews, Schoeps exhorted that salvation is still possible in two ways: First, one can remember "the eternal givenness of the possibility of salvation," which is based on the divine origin of the Jewish people and guaranteed through the historical progenitor, Abraham. Second, one can actualize the possibility of salvation through a return to the fear of God illustrated in faithful observance of the law.[31]

Consistent with traditional Jewish self-perception, Schoeps emphasized the fundamental importance of the Sinaitic revelation and obedience to the demanding Word of God as established in the Torah. Yet, in his opposition to rabbinic tradition, he rejected the "pseudo-authority of formalistic, frozen rituals."[32] Schoeps wondered whether or not tradition had in fact become mere convention and asked if "ritual without transparent content is no more than magic? Magic is not dangerous for the times if the Word is heard and Jewish existence is anchored in the fear of God as creaturely existence."[33] However, he surmised that he and his fellow Jews had lost the God-fearing piety that their ancestors had because of their "so secularized and terribly perverted consciousness."[34]

In his effort to make the hearing of God's Word a present event, Schoeps argued in a Protestant fashion that the Divine Word must be preached as dogma to the world. In *Jüdischer Glaube*, he maintains that just like the church, "the synagogue has . . . the calling in its sermon to the world to validate the fact that God is the Lord and that the world, which flees from his claim of dominion, falls to judgment." Schoeps maintains that this calling can be preached and proclaimed only in "its appropriate form of theological speech."[35] This theological sermon is constituted by "four fundamental clauses under which the entire content of Jewish belief can be subsumed." These four doctrines include the uniqueness of God, creation ex nihilo, the revelation of the law of salvation, and divine retribution. He attempts to justify his dogmatic approach by appealing to the authority of various philosophers throughout Jewish history who have also portrayed Judaism dogmatically: Philo, Maimonides, Joseph Albo, Salomon Ludwig Steinheim, and Hermann Cohen.[36]

However, Gershom Scholem and Alexander Altmann criticized Schoeps for his dogmatic approach, arguing that it was too reductive and not representative of classical Judaism. In his critique of Schoeps's *Jüdischer Glaube*, Scholem argued that by codifying certain dogmas of Judaism, Schoeps was actually twisting essential facts of Jewish tradition and failing to recognize *Kabbalah*, in his perpetuation of an ongoing Jewish apologetic. Specifically, Scholem criticized Schoeps for pinning his entire theology on such a weak foundation as the belief in creation ex nihilo, which received two such completely contradictory interpretations as those of Maimonides and the Kabbalists, and is not even to be found in the Hebrew Bible.[37]

In his essay, "Zur Auseinandersetzung mit der 'dialektische Theologie'" (1935), Alexander Altmann argued against Schoeps that unlike Christianity, Jewish sermons are not dogmatic proclamations that have an independent theological function. In fact, Altmann asks the question, "Is it not all the more so, that Jewish existence documents itself less through preaching to the world than through an inward turning to life under the law of the Torah?" Twenty years later, Altmann contrasted Schoeps's alleged Christian version of revelation as the promise of salvation from sin with that of Rosenzweig, who keeps revelation distinct from redemption.[38]

Schoeps had argued that while Adam's sin did not make humanity inherently sinful, it created a precedent for every individual to freely engage in his or her own sins. Consequently, for Schoeps, revelation becomes "an experience of mercy in which God opens up a possibility for salvation to the fallen ones. Revelation in its narrowest sense . . . is the legalizing declaration of the salvific will of God at Sinai as the law of salvation."[39] He asserted that this potential for sin in the world was demonic and threatened the quality of creation. In response, Altmann argued that for traditional Jewish self-consciousness, the quality of creation could never be lost. Hence, this portrayal of revelation, although occasionally found in rabbinic and kabbalistic thought, is not characteristic of Judaism. He claimed that by portraying revelation dialectically, Schoeps failed to account for the rabbinic understanding of the gracious gift of Torah. Moreover, he argued that whereas Schoeps portrayed revelation as a paradox "uneasily hovering in an historical void," Rosenzweig and Buber portrayed it as "an ever-renewed meeting."[40]

Yet I would suggest that while portraying revelation in a more dialogical manner than Schoeps, both Rosenzweig and Buber presented it in a paradoxical, ahistorical fashion. They claimed that revelation occurs in an individual encounter with God that takes place in a timeless present beyond everyday language and subsequently outside of history. In *I and Thou*, Buber described the paradox of revelation as a "metacosmic primal form of duality" demonstrated in the tension between turning away from the primal unity of the I-Thou relationship to an I-It objectification of the world, followed by the momentary return to this common center in relationship. Moreover, he asserted that the continuing dialectic between "dissolution and renewal" of the I-Thou relationship really constitutes "one way, *the* way."[41]

Rosenzweig's paradoxical portrayal of revelation is quite similar to that of Schoeps. Rosenzweig described this paradox in terms of the love one receives from God, which "can be stable only by living wholly in the Unstable, in the moment."[42] Because the experience of divine love is so spontaneous, the beloved must shamefully acknowledge her prior faithlessness up to that moment. For Rosenzweig, like Schoeps, this admission of faithlessness at the moment of revelation is an acknowledgment of sin, yet "not as transpired 'sin,' but as sinfulness yet present." Ultimately, the climax and achievement of revelation is the prayer for the possibility of redemption from sin.[43]

Yet while Schoeps's portrayal of revelation is similar to that of Rosenzweig, his understanding of Jewish identity is slightly different in the sense that he portrays a bipartite essence of Judaism consisting of both biological and dogmatic elements. Lease claims that Schoeps's portrayal of Jewish identity was based not on race but only on theological facts such as God, creation, and the revelational covenant of Sinai.[44] Yet Lease's critique does not take into account Schoeps's apparent ambivalence regarding the importance of race and dogma in the construction of Jewish identity. In his effort to establish a viable Prussian-

Jewish nationalism in the face of Nazi racism and antisemitism, Schoeps at times conflated the biologically rooted divine essence of the Jew with a dogmatic position of faith. This is evident in the fact that he selectively drew upon statements by Saadia Gaon and Steinheim that ground Jewish identity on religious teachings and faith.[45] Hence, by portraying Judaism more as a religion than an ethnicity, Schoeps wanted to show that Jews are members of the Prussian nation based on a religious decision to work with the German people in the universal process of redemption. Drawing upon a term used by Barth, Schoeps affirms that in "redemptive history," German and Jewish identities converge, and blood should not be taken into consideration. Redemptive history is constituted by the efforts of all people to perpetuate the order of creation "through human history."[46]

In *Jüdischer Glaube*, Schoeps illustrates this theological convergence of Jewish and German identities when a Jew is politically aligned with Germany:

> Being Jewish incorporates no worldly-historical, rather only a spiritual-salvation historical destiny. Only the one who as a German of Jewish faith (and origin), is prepared to live and die for Germany, has a historical destiny in the worldly sense. His private existence becomes historical only when he knows that his destiny is insolubly connected with the destiny of the nation, and he is no more able to escape the historical event that has become the order of the whole.[47]

Here, Schoeps is describing a Prussian-Jewish nationalism that leads to a unique existential intersection of Judaism and German culture occurring in the formation of the ideal Prussian state, an event in which spiritual and historical destinies converge. This theological-historical confluence is demonstrated in the fact that the state is responsible to both God and the people to maintain social order, which is a reflection of the divinely established order of creation. In this instance, the state sees itself as appointed by God to follow divine commandments and subsequently preserve the meaning and substance of its existence.[48] Ultimately, Schoeps believed that the Prussian state was the only authentic nation among the German cultural groups that represented and fulfilled not only German societal order but also "the order of the whole" of creation.

Schoeps argued that because the principles of statehood originate with a universal God, Jews as well as Christians must embrace Prussia in order to take responsibility for its past development and future destiny.[49] To this end, he organized the Deutscher Vortrupp, which would be the vanguard for a spiritual revolution among the Prussian youth and throughout the country. Through this collective self-renewal, the people of Germany would realize that a national identification with Germany stems from a common religious awareness of creatureliness.[50] In fact, he asserted that the "Germanness of Jews as well as the Germanness of Christians only ends when the peoples of the world cease to exist and from all ends of the world, the *shofar* is blown."[51]

In his debate with Blüher in 1932, Schoeps praised old conservative leaders of Prussia, Bismarck and Count York of Wartenburg, for recognizing the divine origin of the Prussian state. Schoeps distinguished them from the new leaders of Prussia, the Nazis, who rejected any belief in a transcendent order to the world.[52] Later, after being forced into exile in Sweden in 1938, Schoeps published an article anonymously, "Der Nationalsozialismus als verkappte Religion," in which he portrayed National Socialism as a "political religion" led by Hitler, who demanded the faith of an entire people in himself and his mission as if he were the "Messiah of all Germans" anointed by God. Schoeps argued that whereas "Hindenburg in the manner of Bismarck and the entire Prussian tradition could justify through his conscience all political action of his office into which God had placed him, the Christian thoughts of Adolf Hitler were completely foreign."[53] Finally, in contrast to Hitler's demand for a "political confession," Schoeps encouraged Jews to make a religious confession to the Prussian idea of societal order as reflecting the order of creation. Even after the war, Schoeps continued to promote Prussian nationalism by being one of the few Jews to return to Germany, calling for a return to the Prussian monarchy.[54]

Despite his protests against Hitler, however, Schoeps's theologically based Prussian-Jewish nationalism was misunderstood by his Jewish critics, especially Robert Weltsch, a leader of postwar German Jewry. Weltsch, not surprisingly, was led to the inaccurate conclusion that Schoeps was allied with Hitler because of his "unwanted professions of supra-nationalist German loyalty (even to the Nazi-Regime)." Schoeps was even called a Nazi and accused by Nicolas Becker of "having tempted the Jews to buy into antisemitism."[55] Ultimately, Schoeps's Prussian-Jewish nationalism and his own reputation became captive to the destruction of German Jewry in the Holocaust.

Nonetheless, Schoeps's existential theology of Judaism was inextricably connected to a Prussian identity. Ironically, Rosenzweig's existential theology led him to reject Prussian nationalism. Whereas Rosenzweig grew disillusioned with Prussian imperialism following World War I, Schoeps appeared to re-idealize the old Prussian state in the face of rising Nazi antisemitism and the onslaught of World War II. Subsequently, their once similar portrayals of Jewish identity diverged from one another: Schoeps's biologically rooted essence of Judaism assumed a religious, dogmatic form that became fused with political concreteness, while Rosenzweig's eternal people remained outside of history, "free of the parochial and invidious claims of geography and politics."[56]

Schoeps's Pluralistic Theology:
Transcending Jewish and Christian Borders

Both Rosenzweig and Schoeps constructed Jewish theologies in response to religious and cultural dilemmas shared by their Christian contemporaries, and they both drew upon a shared Jewish-Christian discourse to confront those challenges. Each first went through a religious identity crisis in which he turned to Christian mentors for support, ultimately constructing his Jewish identity as a result. After receiving guidance from their Christian counterparts, both Rosenzweig and Schoeps developed theologies in conversation with Christianity, subsequently discovering natural bridges between Jewish and Christian boundaries across which Jews and Christians might walk as they seek theological explanations for cultural phenomena. Like Rosenzweig, Schoeps constructed his Jewish identity by engaging his Christian milieu, yet Schoeps tended to blend Judaism and Christianity even while allowing each to retain a level of uniqueness. As a result, he himself became a uniquely heterogeneous amalgamation of Jew and Christian. This integration of Christian and Jewish motifs is clearly illustrated in his theology and his portrayal of the relationship between Judaism and Christianity. In addition, it appears to be the motivation behind some of his historiographical work.

Influenced by the largely Protestant and Lutheran culture of his youth, Schoeps was deeply disturbed by the modern Jewish participation in what he considered to be a general, "western history of fallenness" characterized by "the practical and theoretical elimination of God-consciousness." According to Schoeps, this was generated by the idealistic historicism of liberalism as well as the spiritless legalism of orthodoxy.[57] In his own childhood, Schoeps had been turned off by the self-righteous "moralistic babbling" of his Jewish religious school. He claimed that the only reason that he did not break away from Judaism entirely was the fact that he, like every other human being, was born into a "life inheritance," which one has to fill with one's existence whether or not he or she is sympathetic to it.[58]

Already at age seventeen, Schoeps was guilt ridden regarding the sin of estrangement from God committed by his generation, and he subsequently began a dialogue in 1926 with his Lutheran friend Eberhard Beyer, whom he had met in the German youth movement. He wanted to find out how he could come to experience a merciful God. Beyer told him that his life would be wasted unless he was able to believe in divine justification solely out of faith. Beyer argued that justification is exclusively God's work, and that even when one comes to a position of faith, it results not from human merit but from "God's freely chosen grace" (Eph. 1–2). At first, Schoeps strongly rejected this idea because he could not accept the prospect that good deeds did not count at all and that his striving for justice would not be recognized.[59] Yet many years later, Schoeps read Karl Holl's work on Luther, realizing that Holl had been Beyer's professor at the University of Berlin. Holl's Luther studies were first published in 1921 and initiated a renewal of Lutheranism characterized by newly available resources from the Weimar Edition of Luther's works and some earlier unpublished writings. The studies emphasized Luther's personal views rather than Lutheran confessional writings and concentrated on particular aspects of Luther's work.

Holl's portrayal of Luther was based on a philosophical approach that explores the "psychological preconditions" of religion.[60]

After reading Luther with Holl's lenses, Schoeps became attracted to the idea that in God's demand for judgment, we can experience divine grace.[61] Recalling Beyer's earlier words, Schoeps began to reexamine his position on the Lutheran concept of justification solely based on faith. He came to accept Luther's realization, described by Holl, that the sinner can never achieve personal union with and recognition by God as the reward for human struggle and sacrifice, but only if God freely gives it. Similarly, Schoeps claimed that while Israel must be obedient to God, it must also view salvation from sin as "the free merciful gift of God." In fact, Schoeps argued that even the ability to hear God's Word, that is the foundation for the decision of faith, is given by God through "the merciful choosing of the covenant of Israel."[62]

Schoeps observed that while Holl disagreed with the dialectical theology expressed by Barth in the 1920s, Holl appeared to be hypnotized by it, and similarly, Schoeps himself felt mesmerized.[63] Holl disagreed with the ahistorical eschatology of the dialectical theologians and contrasted it with that of Luther, who "clearly recognized the true characteristics of the Kingdom of God and correspondingly its relationship to the world and its communities and tasks."[64] Nevertheless, in his desire to experience a merciful God, Schoeps would also identify with the dialectical theology developed by Karl Barth and continued by his Protestant disciples. They recognized the urgent need to redevelop a "consciousness to the reality of the fact of revelation" and rethink fundamental issues based on it, such as the significance of faith, how it is viewed by humanity, and what is the nature of salvation that God has awarded humanity through revelation. Furthermore, Schoeps acknowledged Protestantism in general and Karl Barth's work in particular as the prototypical example of the "self-limitation of theological understanding and speech." This is illustrated in the restriction of theological words to "words only truly confessing God and his sanctifying will that stand in the power of no human, and can only be asked for through speech in prayer as a gift."[65]

However, like Rosenzweig, Schoeps attempted to maintain his connection to the Jewish community despite his Christian leanings. On the verge of despair, Schoeps turned to a rabbi to confirm whether or not good works counted toward salvation or whether everything depends on faith alone. The rabbi recounted familiar *midrashim* about humans having a good and evil urge and that, if they make an effort toward the good, the good urge will triumph, and they will ultimately be redeemed. Yet instead of being reassured about his traditional Jewish identity, Schoeps realized that he disagreed with these rabbinic teachings and branded the rabbi a humanist.[66]

In contrast to Rosenzweig, who had returned to Judaism wholeheartedly following his Day of Atonement experience, Schoeps had come to understand himself as a Jew with a "Protestant thought structure."[67] In fact, it could be argued that he identified his rejection of rabbinic legalism with Luther's opposition to the Catholic concept of salvation based on the merit of human action.[68] Another Christian colleague, Fritz Meier, had told him that Luther's formation of a separate church was unnecessary. Meier argued that Luther's theological endeavor would have been justifiable within the Catholic Church, had he not "made his own existential structure absolute." This conversation opened Schoeps's eyes to the fact that his "entire existential structure had always been a Protestant and Lutheran one."[69] Hence, Meier provided Schoeps a formula for his own bifurcated Jewish-Christian existence. This allowed him to accomplish what Luther could not, namely, maintain his Protestant and Lutheran existential structure *in potentia* without having to convert to Christianity.

Schoeps even claimed to have a "Critical-Protestant" approach to Jewish theology, in an attempt to return to an irrational biblical revelation. Schoeps argued that contemporary Jews could not avoid what he considered to be Protestant questions dealing with revelation that to some extent were already raised by the Karaites and later addressed by Steinheim. Specifically, these include questions regarding whether or not the tradition continues to have sacred content or whether the Oral Torah comprises revelation at all. Schoeps asked whether revelation should instead be identified with "the Divine Word in its absolute concreteness," which contemporary Jews have ceased to hear because of their alliance with the Enlightenment and liberalism. According to Schoeps, the ability to hear God's Word can be restored only through reverential piety.[70]

While his theology was clearly influenced by Barth, Schoeps identified more with Holl's portrayal of Luther's theology as a structural paradigm for his "critical Protestant Judaism," because of its greater affinity to his own Jewish belief. In fact, Schoeps himself asserted that it was through "Holl's Luther" that Beyer converted him to Judaism, and not through his Jewish religious education.[71] Yet he continued to assert his Jewishness because of the fact that he possessed the "inheritance of Israelite prophecy" in his blood, and that he could never accept the "divine sonship of Jesus."[72] He concluded that his encounter with Beyer led him to a point of "religious isolation," which I would characterize as an intermediate point between Jewish and Christian theologies that is neither fully Jewish nor Christian, illustrating a multiple subjectivity.[73] It becomes clear why Schoeps, as a Jew on the border between Judaism and Christianity, would write about the history of individuals and groups who also appeared to stand on the border between these two religions: Paul, the Jewish-Christian Ebionites, and philosemites in the Baroque period.[74]

In fact, one could argue that Schoeps identified with the Lutheran anti-Jewish understanding of Paul's distinction between faith and works. In his book on Paul, Schoeps wrote that Paul's criticism of the law as being unfulfillable is a problem intrinsic to Judaism. Schoeps agreed with Paul that there must be an attitude of faith prior to doing the law, yet faith not in Christ but in the God of Sinai. He stated that this doubt and radical questioning originally developed from a "border situation" in the first century, when Hellenism led to rampant assimilation, and has again occurred in the modern period. Schoeps argued that because the Rabbis presupposed an attitude of faith, they never considered it necessary to develop an independent doctrine on faith in addition to the doctrine of the law. Schoeps asserted that now in the face of renewed assimilation, instead of moving beyond the bounds of Judaism as did Paul, Jews must incorporate Paul's warnings into Jewish life, specifically regarding the avoidance of rabbinic legalism that makes the law into an "arid formality."[75]

Moreover, he claimed that the legacy of Paul's criticism against the law is an "eternal warning against the desire of Judaism to fulfill the will of God often too quickly and too rectilinearly. . . . It is not the law which makes man righteous, but God, the Lord of the covenant." Schoeps then made an antirabbinic critique based on Pauline dualism, claiming that because of rabbinic preference of orthopraxis over orthodoxy, it became impossible to distinguish between the literal and the deeper understanding of the law as an expression of God's will that must be fulfilled in faith. Hence, while Schoeps expressed the need to stay within the bounds of Judaism, he clearly demonstrated its fluid border with Christianity and appeared to occupy Paul's intermediate position on that border.[76] Ironically, Barth already made this identification of Schoeps with Paul in his February 1933 letter to Schoeps. In a passing reference, Barth asked Schoeps if he was aware that he held a Paulinian perspective regarding revelation, election, law, grace, forgiveness, and return. He asserted that these terms "shockingly indicate what Paul recognized as the law and justification of the law, and had referred to as the border between Christ and the Jews."[77]

Because of his seemingly contradictory Jewish-Christian theology, both Jews and Christians criticized Schoeps. While Schoeps's Jewish critics claimed that his theology was permeated with Barthian dialectical categories, Barth himself alluded to certain areas where it diverges from his position. Those areas in Schoeps's work that are considered neither Jewish nor Protestant illustrate a unique Jewish-Christian amalgamation that appears to be based on Holl's portrayal of Luther.

In his 1935 critique of Schoeps's theology, Alexander Altmann described Schoeps as a "Jewish Barthian student" and made the following argument regarding his theology:

> Of Schoeps it can only be said, that he, in a completely naïve manner, has taken over the conceptual framework of dialectical theology for Judaism. His "Prolegomenon to the Foundation of a Systematic Theology of Judaism" corresponds in its structure and even in its terminology and its pathos with Barth's "Prolegomenon to Christian Dogmatics." Also for him, the theological "decision" entails the complete removal of theology from intellectual history . . . the radical rejection of idealism.[78]

In his later appraisal of Schoeps's work, Altmann basically reiterated his original position, asserting that Schoeps "introduced a fully-fledged Barthianism, only slightly modified to suit the Jewish requirements." He concluded that German Jewry felt spiritually safer with Buber and Rosenzweig than with "Karl Barth and his Jewish disciple."[79] Altmann's critique of Schoeps was based on the claim that Schoeps drew upon five Barthian theological criteria: First, Altmann observed that, like Barth, Schoeps described the need for an existential "decision" by the modern individual to return to God and to recognize one's absolute reliance upon the master of the world, which involves a "total reversal of existence 180 degrees."[80]

Second, this relationship between God and humanity represents the ultimate paradox of existence, the fact that one can attain knowledge of God only through the hearing of the Divine Word and not through any humanly projected ideal, despite the fact that theological proclamation is a human undertaking. This paradox is predicated on the "'dialectic of the qualitative difference between time and eternity,' between humanity and God, reason and revelation."[81] Third, Altmann asserted that, like Barth, Schoeps portrays a devaluation of creation resulting from the fallenness of humanity.[82] Fourth, Altmann argued that Schoeps's idea of Israel's "sacrality in its blood inheritance" could be understood only in comparison with Barth's interpretation of Christian baptism. Just as Barth portrays baptism as a symbol that provides the individual the possibility of hearing God's word, "the election of the 'seed of Israel' means for Schoeps . . . indeed nothing more than the sacred institution of the synagogue in which the individual is presented with the possibility of receiving 'unmediated revelation.'"[83] Altmann claimed that Schoeps reduced the concrete existence of the people Israel to "the shadowy phenomenon of the synagogue," and thus failed to take into account Israel's historical consciousness. Moreover, he argued that, like Barth, Schoeps expected individuals to see their lives as being concurrent with an otherworldly *Urgeschichte*, or prehistory.[84]

In his response to Schoeps's *Jüdischer Glaube*, Gershom Scholem also criticized Schoeps for abandoning "tradition as an essential category of the religious way of life in Judaism" by attempting to return to an ahistorical biblical theology based on the "questionable terminology" of Karl Barth. Scholem described Schoeps's theology as leading to a "neutralization of Jewish historical consciousness." He asked, if Schoeps wanted to return to an ahistorical, irrational faith, why did he not reject biblical revelation along with the Oral Torah, when both would appear to the modern person as being obsolete? Scholem argued that because this question cannot be answered from a Jewish perspective, "it must obviously lead back to Schoeps's fixation on a Protestant discussion, an abyss into which Rosenzweig, although obviously coming from a Christian discussion as well, did not fall." Subsequently, Scholem concluded that Schoeps's existentialist position was "in danger of slipping into subjectivism."[85]

We have seen however, that while Schoeps clearly placed Jews in an ahistorical *Heilsgeschichte*, he also promoted their entrance into history as participants in the formation of the Prussian state. Because the Prussian leaders are representatives of God in history, Jews must serve them in their efforts to bring divine order to the world. Thus, Schoeps claimed that Jews have a responsibility to promote Prussian nationalism because of its spiritual as well as historical importance. This support for worldly historical institutions goes directly against the dehistoricized eschatology of Barth. As we saw in the last chapter, Barth viewed Christian historical existence as absurd because of its original eschatological roots and consequently rejected Protestant attempts to equate Christianity with cultural progress. Moreover, while Rosenzweig did not reject the historically based oral tradition of Judaism, his ahistorical portrayal of Israel corresponds more with Barth's eschatology than does that of Schoeps, because of Rosenzweig's consistent claim that the Jews are independent from history and subsequently must deny themselves any participation in any nation-state.[86]

Finally, Altmann maintained that "Schoeps shows his dependence on Barth most clearly in his taking over of the Protestant "principle of Scripture." This was demonstrated by the fact that Schoeps refused to equate the Scripture with revelation, insisting that faith dialectically "confesses the hidden in the visible, hears God's Word within the shell of the human word, hears the Word through the words of Scripture."[87] Like Barth, Schoeps argued that God's Word must not be understood as an eternal truth to be found in the Scripture but as an event that has occurred. Ultimately, Schoeps agreed with Barth that "the Word of God is never at the disposal of any human, even the best theologian."[88]

However, Barth's own critique of Schoeps's work calls into question Altmann's claim that Schoeps's theology demonstrated "a fully fledged Barthianism." Schoeps's theology may be more appropriately placed at the border between Judaism and Christianity. In his February 1933 letter to Schoeps, Barth described his Jewish theology as "fundamentally strange because it is indeed an epistemology which corresponds to a Jewish teaching of the 'Fall,' original sin, divine likeness after the Fall, and justification; however, in addition, perhaps above all, the Jewish omission of the trinity."[89] Moreover, Barth asserted that any contemporary Jewish theology "must culminate in the proof that Christ had to be crucified."[90] Along with his Christocentric approach, Barth's positions on the other issues clearly differed from those of Schoeps.

Schoeps presented his own version of the Fall and original sin that is different from Barth's. Schoeps claimed that because Adam set the historical precedent, each human has the tendency to sin but is not a sinner. As we saw earlier, Schoeps argued that each individual is personally responsible for the sin that he or she chooses. When discovering sin as one's separation from God, the individual realizes that it has already occurred as his or her own sin.[91] Despite his rejection of what he considered to be rabbinic humanism, Schoeps's formulation of sin actually corresponded in part to the rabbinic idea of the *Yetzer Ha-ra*, or "evil urge," which provides humanity with the potential to sin but can be counteracted by the *Yetzer Ha-tov*, or "good urge."[92] Conversely, Barth argued that sin is not an event that occurred only to Adam but rather is a "presupposition that underlies every human event and conditions every human status. Sin is the characteristic mark of human nature as such . . . it is the Fall which occurred with the emergence of human life."[93]

In contrast to Barth, Schoeps argued, "The human is not born in sin, but rather in purity, because in the birth of each person, the creation of the beginning repeats itself." In fact, Schoeps asserted that because human beings are "created in the Spirit," they retain that status after the Fall.[94] Hence, contrary to Altmann's claim, Schoeps's theology does not devalue creation entirely but expresses a tension between this-worldly optimism and apocalyptic pessimism.

Barth's position regarding the issue of divine likeness appeared to change during the course of his career, yet he always maintained that there was no divine likeness after the Fall. In his *Epistle to the Romans*, Barth claimed that all humanity have fallen from "their union with God." Yet he viewed the revelation in Christ as a miraculous restoration of the human immediacy to God. While Christ had experienced the death of Adam, he was no longer under the power of sin.[95] Later, in his *Church Dogmatics*, Barth would offer a more positive treatment of the divine likeness in creation, acknowledging in Gen. 1:26–27 that God created male and female in the divine image. Based on the plural subject in verse 26, Barth perceived an analogy between the I and Thou within God in the Trinity and the I-Thou relationship between male and female. Yet he maintained that an analogy does not entail divine likeness but rather "a correspondence of the unlike." In fact, he argued against the Reformation thesis regarding the loss of the divine likeness after the Fall, asserting, "What man does not possess, he can neither bequeath nor forfeit."[96]

While both Schoeps and Barth used the Christian term "justification" to refer to the divine forgiveness of sins, they each described the process differently. Barth portrayed a Christological event in which the individual is transformed externally through the divine mediation of Christ from a sinful creature into a person who is righteous and holy before God. Barth explicitly wanted to deny the existence of any capacity within humans to experience or attain knowledge of God associated with the Spirit. In fact, he argued that the Spirit implanted in humanity is not a secure possession over which humans have control. Individuals cannot say, "We have the Spirit" because they are possessed *by* it. Consequently, one can never really have faith but can only receive it miraculously from moment to moment.[97]

In comparison to the objective Christocentric transformation portrayed by Barth, Schoeps described a more theocentric process of justification that appears to combine both objective and subjective elements. Schoeps's portrayal of justification appears to be an objective, externally based experience in which "the person can be addressed by God, thereby the person herself is not addressing or even being spoken to through reason." However, he claimed that the person is actually addressed by the "Holy Spirit that sanctifies the individual and enables the person to become just, through repentance, charity and prayer."[98] This now appears to shift from an objective experience originating from outside of the person to an inner subjective experience in which the person decides to complete the process of justification by acting on it. In contrast to Barth's doctrine of justification, Schoeps claimed that the individual "has the ability to decide to hear" God's Word, which Schoeps associated with the Spirit.[99] Moreover, by using the term "Holy Spirit" here instead of "God," Schoeps may have been portraying an inner divine presence that is not fully theonomous but is a divine filament that can be ignited by humanity for its own action.

While it appears that Schoeps could envision an intermediate level of divinity at work in the process of justification, he could never accept Barth's perception of Christ as the second person of the Trinity or as the mediator of divine revelation. Whereas Barth argued that Christ is the creaturely medium of divine self-revelation, Schoeps consistently argued that Israel received an unmediated revelation of God's Word in its "absolute concreteness" at Sinai. Moreover, contemporary Jews must strive to return to this "unmediated hearing of the Word of God."[100] Whereas Scholem asserted the necessity in Judaism of mediating revelation with oral tradition, Schoeps claimed that since the era of emancipation, Jewish tradition has fallen apart because of Western secularization.[101] He argued that "the traditional access to faith is then of no use at all if the reality has become godless, the claim of the law is empty and it is our task . . . to again become aware of the Word of revelation."[102] Schoeps believed that if Jews could confess how historicized their consciousness had become, they would hopefully be able to realize the concreteness of revelation again in their time. In constructing his theology, Schoeps affirmed that he ultimately relied on Steinheim's position that biblical revelation is "an essential and cognitive priority over tradition."[103]

However, while Schoeps found a Jewish model in Steinheim, one can also look to Holl's Luther as a possible Christian paradigm for his work in order to understand the elements of his theology that are neither Barthian nor particularly consistent with Judaism. Specifically, Schoeps's rejection of inherited sin corresponds directly with that of Luther as conveyed by Holl. Both Holl's Luther and Schoeps recognized the importance of personal responsibility in committing sin, despite the fact that human beings descend from Adam, who committed the first sin.[104]

In regard to divine likeness after the Fall, Luther claimed that every Christian has a dual self-awareness as sinner and saint. While the individual is a "self-seeking ego," at the same time, "every Christian ought to acknowledge himself to be great, because on account of the faith of Christ dwelling in him, he is God, son of God, and infinite, because God is now in him." This characteristic of greatness is demonstrated by exhibiting patience and forgiveness, qualities that God has provided. Here, Luther confirms the existence of divine likeness after the Fall in the form of love for one's neighbor, "for the divine nature is nothing other than pure beneficence."[105]

Moreover, Holl maintained that for Luther this ethical behavior was one's God-given duty to be performed in this world, and that it should be mediated by the political and social order. In fact, the state becomes God's instrument for preserving the gospel through its attempts to ensure peace and order in the world. Here it could be argued that Schoeps found a paradigm for his theological-political approach to Prussian nationalism.[106] Hence, Schoeps's tension between this-worldly optimism and apocalyptic pessimism is clearly more consistent with Luther's bipartite description of human behavior than with Barth's portrayal of human fallenness.

When examining Luther's understanding of justification as described by Holl, one can see a clear parallel with that of Schoeps in the fact that both describe a theocentric process that is characterized by objective and subjective elements. According to Holl, the process of justification began objectively for Luther in *Anfechtungen*: spontaneous, unexpected experiences in which God confronted him directly in judgment, resulting in intense feelings of guilt and self-condemnation. At times, the assault appeared to be a temptation by Satan, whom he thought was trying to separate him from God. At other times, Christ would intervene on his behalf, and at still other times, Satan would come in the guise of Christ. Ultimately, when Christ would recede from view, God would save Luther directly through the reissuing of the First Commandment, impressing upon him the feeling of obligation to God even when it seemed most difficult to obey.[107]

The subjective phase of the process began when Luther realized that although God could crush the sinner with judgment, God chooses to save the individual, which implies the hope of forgiveness. Here, according to Holl, Luther realized that the individual must intuit the true will of God beneath divine anger. Out of a sense of obligation, one must now take the leap of faith and decide to believe in God's love despite the fact that his conscience indicates that he is under God's wrath. In terms similar to those later used by Schoeps, Luther attributed this inner realization of divine love with the working of the Holy Spirit and claimed that it should be followed with prayers of thanksgiving, acts of love, and forgiveness.[108]

Holl's reading of Luther differed from that of the "theology of crisis school," a group of Protestant theologians, among them Paul Tillich, Karl Barth, Rudolf Bultmann, and its spokesman, Friedrich Gogarten, who in the early 1920s responded to World War I by rejecting the anthropocentric optimism of nineteenth-century liberal theology.[109] Specifically, Gogarten raised three criticisms of Holl's portrayal of Luther that allude to the same distinctions that exist between the theologies of Barth and Schoeps. First, he objected to Holl's inadequate Christology in which Christ is given only secondary importance. Second, he disagreed with Holl's portrayal of justification, arguing that in it, he viewed forgiveness merely as a "rational inference from the fact of the moral consciousness." Third, he accused Holl of ethicizing Luther by viewing ethical behavior in this relative world as a means to "the absolute world of the gospel of eternal salvation."[110]

After examining the direct parallels between Holl's depiction of Luther and Schoeps's theology along with the distinctions observed between Holl and Gogarten, it becomes apparent why Holl's portrayal of Luther inspired Schoeps to such an extent that he constructed a "Critical-Protestant" Judaism. In Holl's work, Schoeps found a Luther who advocated the theological positions on human sin, divine judgment, and forgiveness with which he identified. At the same time, Holl's Luther lacked Barth's Christocentrism, his purely objective portrayal of justification, and his dehistoricized eschatology with which Schoeps disagreed. Moreover, by using Holl's Luther as a model for his own theology, it appears as if Schoeps benefited from a shared discourse with Christianity in order to adequately respond to what he considered to be an existential crisis, without losing his Jewish identity.

A Dialogical Portrayal of the Jewish-Christian Relationship

In his description of the Jewish-Christian relationship, Schoeps acknowledged the ongoing reconfiguration of boundaries between the two religions, going further than Rosenzweig in truly recognizing Christian otherness, while at the same time acknowledging its indissoluble connection to Judaism. In his debate with Hans Blüher in 1932, Schoeps repeated some of the overtures that Rosenzweig had made toward Christianity, yet unlike Rosenzweig, he did not appear to circumscribe Christianity in his own Jewish framework. Like Rosenzweig, Schoeps portrayed Christianity as having the task of revealing God's presence to the rest of the world through Christ. Consequently, Schoeps described Christianity as having a distinct role in redeeming the world, yet unlike Rosenzweig, this participation in redemption did not amount to Judaicizing a world in which Judaism was already redeemed.[111]

Instead, Schoeps referred to a "Jewish-Christian concept of redemptive history" upon which the endurance of creation in human history is based.[112] Here, both Jews and Christians equally participate in the work of world redemption. In his debate with Blüher, Schoeps at times portrayed Israel with a biological predisposition toward salvation; at other times, he claimed that its election signified "the continuing possibility of a correct relationship to God." Nonetheless, he asserted that Jews have no advantage over Christians, maintaining that in and of themselves, they are not saints, and in fact are equally sinning people.[113] When examining Schoeps's other writings, it is clear that this statement was not merely an apologetic; it corresponds to his statements regarding the Jewish involvement in the "western history of fallenness" and the fact that Jews have forgotten their "blood inheritance of chosenness."[114]

Moreover, in his letter to Karl Barth in October 1929, Schoeps had acknowledged that Jews and Christians stand together in sin before God and must attempt to recover their sense of "creature feeling" in the face of God as "Wholly other." Subsequently, in *Jüdischer Glaube*, Schoeps linked the Synagogue to the Church in terms of their mutual responsibility of proclaiming God's Word to a fallen world. In addition, just as Rosenzweig had compared the eternal way of Christianity based on dogma with the eternal life of the Jews based on blood, Schoeps compared Israel's "sacrality of the blood inheritance" to "the Church as the sacred institution of Christianity."[115]

However, in his book *The Jewish-Christian Argument* (1937), Schoeps maintained, as did Rosenzweig, that Christian baptism is essentially different from Jewish lineage in the sense that Jews can return to the original birth of their people in Abraham's bosom by virtue of their own eternal biological connection, in contrast to Christians who must be cleansed in faith "for a second birth, the rebirth in the Holy Spirit."[116] This appears to go against Altmann's comparison between Schoeps's idea of "sacrality of the blood inheritance" and Barth's idea of baptism. Although Schoeps appeared to go further than Rosenzweig in breaking down the boundaries between Judaism and Christianity, he was still engaged in a similar dialectic between fascination and aversion for Christian categories.

This interdependence between polemics and reception of Christian influence was evident in Schoeps's contrast of the Christian claim of Jesus as the Son of God with what he claimed to be the true biblical portrayal of all Israelites as the sons of God. In his debate with Blüher, Schoeps asked him to take literally various direct and indirect biblical references to Israel as the sons of God.[117] In his February 1933 letter to Schoeps, Karl Barth claimed that in this instance, Schoeps was unconsciously exhibiting "anti-Christian elaborations."[118] In fact, this apparently polemical contrast was similar to that of Yehuda Halevi, who argued in *The Kuzari* that because of their possession of the *amr ilahi* (divine Logos), all the children of Israel are "sons of God," in contrast to the Christian claim that only Christ is the Son of God and incarnate Logos.[119]

However, while coming to the same conclusion as Halevi, Schoeps took an opposite approach. Whereas Halevi based Israel's status as "sons of God" on a spiritual foundation, Schoeps claimed that it was based on the biblical description of Israel as a "holy body." His argument was based on an interpretation of *goy kadosh* in Exod. 19:6 that was brought to his attention in a letter by Martin Buber. Instead of translating it as "holy nation," Buber defined *goy* based on its connection to the Hebrew word *geviyah*, meaning "body," which shares the same root, *gvh*.[120]

Moreover, in an apparent reference to Christ, Schoeps argued, "every part of this body which spreads out through time is now indeed sanctified not through its mere existence, but rather because of the influence of holiness." Here he compared the portrayal of the Church as forming the body of Christ to the Synagogue as constituting the body of Israel. Yet, in a more dialogical tone, Schoeps concluded that Israel "has the fleshly predisposition to the supernatural within itself, just as for the Christians, their savior is the supernatural in and of himself."[121] In this instance, he seemed to cross over the essential boundaries constructed between Judaism and Christianity by his Jewish and Christian contemporaries, by making a direct comparison between the divinity of Christ and Israel. In fact, Schoeps was accused by Blüher of taking "one step over the Rubicon" because of his reference to Christ as one of the "blessed miracles" that have occurred outside Israel. In Blüher's eyes, Schoeps was using terms to refer to Christ that a Jew was not supposed to use. Blüher observed that Schoeps had appropriated much from his Christian colleagues. He even commented, "I almost believe that Karl Barth's school will lead more Jews back to Judaism than it will Christians back to the Church."[122]

While Schoeps maintained his Jewish identity in some measure, he went further than Rosenzweig in recognizing Christian difference by using the term "new covenant" to refer to God's relationship with Christians articulated in the New Testament, maintaining that for Jews this was an "inscrutable fact."[123] He concluded that in his opinion, "a modern Jew should have no fundamental difficulties acknowledging such a covenant between God and humanity which indeed does not affect himself and his certainty of salvation."[124] Here he attempted to provide a truly dialogical model of Jewish-Christian reality in which Jews could recognize Christianity on its own terms without compromising their identities. Ultimately, Schoeps expressed the interdependence of Jewish and Christian identity construction when he asserted that Israel could be comprehended only in analogy to the Christian Church, because they are both the children of God.[125]

Unlike Rosenzweig, who portrayed a Jewish eternality in contrast to the Christian historical confrontation with paganism, Schoeps placed the two religions in the same predicament of secularization during the modern period, perceiving a parallel between "the modern post-Jewish existence and that of the post-Christian." In his book *Die letzen dreissig Jahre* (1956), Schoeps claimed that the traumatic events of the past twenty years had provided him with the religious insight that "the fight against Judaism also leads in its consequences to a fight against the Christian Church, because the Jewish element in Christianity is affected by the fight against the synagogue."[126] The fact that the attack was targeted against the Hebrew Bible as a "special element of the Christian proclamation" confirmed for Schoeps how closely related Judaism and Christianity are. Schoeps concluded that the two religions "have a common enemy: the universal godlessness which denies the otherworldly powers and connections."[127]

From his initial confrontation with universal faithlessness in the early days of Nazi Germany to his post-Holocaust stand against it, Schoeps consistently advocated a Jewish-Christian solution composed of the elements of Lutheranism, Protestantism, and Judaism that he believed most effectively combated this common enemy. Thus, in his "Critical-Protestant" theology of Judaism and his portrayal of the Jewish-Christian relationship, Schoeps demonstrated a more porous boundary between Judaism and Christianity in an era in which this boundary was firmly essentialized in German consciousness. As a result, his work was marginalized by both Jews and Christians who viewed it as inauthentic in either category. His critics on the Jewish side, Altmann and Scholem, claimed that he had moved too far toward Protestantism and specifically Karl Barth. Moreover, his effort to ground a Prussian-Jewish nationalism in an existential, "Critical-Protestant" Judaism was met by fierce opposition from Jews who actually saw him as an antisemite who was pro-Hitler. Alternatively, on the Christian side, Barth criticized Schoeps for trying to Judaize certain Protestant categories and failing to recognize Jewish complicity in the crucifixion of Christ.

Rosenzweig also constructed a Jewish theology in conversation with Christianity that was quite similar to Schoeps in its distinction from Liberal and Orthodox Judaism. However, the Jewish intellectual establishment did not marginalize him. In fact, both Jewish and Christian scholars following the Holocaust have seen his work as a model for Jewish-Christian dialogue. Yet Rosenzweig actually perpetuated a Jewish-Christian dialectic through his approximation of Augustinian categories and use of Christian anti-Jewish motifs against their grain, as well as his tendency to subordinate Christianity to Judaism. Consequently, it could be argued that his attempt to reify essential Jewish and Christian boundaries explains, at least in part, the continued inclusion of his work in the Jewish intellectual canon.[128]

Although Schoeps retained a dialectical approach to some extent, he seemed to transcend Jewish and Christian borders in his own theology and in his portrayal of the Jewish-Christian relationship. In Holl's portrayal of Luther, Schoeps found a model for his own amalgamation of Judaism and Christianity, enabling him to realize his attraction to Lutheran and Protestant theological motifs while at the same time remembering his Jewish blood inheritance. Consistent with his own integrated identity, Schoeps tried to allow for Christian difference without fear of Jewish negation in his portrayal of the Jewish-Christian relationship.

Yet in his critique of rabbinic legalism, Schoeps was clearly examining rabbinic literature from a Lutheran, anti-Jewish understanding of Paul, and at times Schoeps seemed to negate the very Jewish identity that he intended to uphold. Ironically, in his attempt to preserve Christian difference, he tended to dilute Jewish identity to an extent. His reading of rabbinic literature with Lutheran/Pauline lenses foreshadows the post-Holocaust work of Richard Rubenstein, who would later make a similar critique, yet for the opposite reason. Whereas Schoeps criticized the Rabbis for paying more attention to law than to faith in a transcendent God, Rubenstein criticized them for paying too much attention to law because of their belief in a transcendent God. While Schoeps still had confidence in the biblical God of Sinai to bring Jews and Christians together toward redemption in the early stages of World War II, Rubenstein would no longer accept the image of an omnipotent God who could conceivably punish six million Jews for their sins in the Holocaust. Both leading up to and following the Holocaust, these two Jewish thinkers would stand outside of the Jewish establishment and critique it from a Christian vantage point, thus illustrating the already blurred boundaries with Christianity within which they claimed to remain.

3

Beyond Borders

Richard Rubenstein's Critique of Judaism in
Relation to Christianity after the Holocaust

Following the Holocaust, Richard Rubenstein did not share
Schoeps's optimism in a shared redemptive history for Jews and
Christians because he was unable to reconcile the image of God as
"the ultimate, omnipotent actor in the historical drama" with the
historical reality of the death camps.[1] For Rubenstein, this portrayal
of the biblical God of history must ultimately lead to the interpretation of the Holocaust as part of "God's providential way of leading
humanity to its final redemption."[2] As a result, Rubenstein came to
the agonizing conclusion that after the Holocaust we are now in the
age of the death of the historical God. Moreover, he rejected the
Jewish mythical claim of chosenness associated with this transcendent God that has ignited a "two thousand year old sibling rivalry of
Jew and Christian over who is the Father's beloved child."[3] In his
landmark book *After Auschwitz* (1966), Rubenstein criticizes the use
of both Jewish and Christian religious myths because they created
the historical climate for the Holocaust. He maintains that they
should be abandoned to provide an opportunity for genuine dialogue
between the two religious communities.

In the tradition of Jules Isaac and James Parkes, Rubenstein
perceives a direct link between Christian anti-Judaism in antiquity
and the Holocaust. While acknowledging that Nazism was an anti-
Christian movement, Rubenstein argues that it was dialectically
related to Christianity in the sense that the Nazis were able to negate
Christianity by using its anti-Jewish myths for their own purposes.
Consequently, they transformed a theological conflict "into a biological struggle in which only one conclusion was thinkable—the total

extermination of every living Jew."[4] He asserts that Nazi ideology grew out of the nineteenth-century German condemnation of Christianity, articulated by Hegel, for displacing its Teutonic Gods with Jewish gods and myths in place of their own. Because the Nazis could not eliminate the powerful Christian Church, they vented their frustration on the weaker Jewish community.[5] Rubenstein then links the Nazi agenda with the Jewish-Christian conflict over the myth of chosenness, arguing the following: "The ancient Jewish-Christian quarrel over the true Israel led to the utilization of the original Israel as a surrogate victim for the presumed sins of the New Israel in effecting the alienation of the German people from their native traditions."[6]

Moreover, Rubenstein sees the Holocaust as the culmination of a mythical drama in which the Jews are the central actors. In this drama, the Jew has been historically identified as the incarnate God, his betrayer Judas, or those who reject and crucify him. Subsequently in the Holocaust, the Jewish people must ultimately be forced to play its "final role in the domain of the sacred, that of sacrificial victim." Rubenstein describes the death camps as "one huge act of ritual murder in which the perpetrators were convinced that only through the elimination of the Jews could Germany's safety be vouchsafed."[7]

Alternatively, in the eyes of certain types of evangelical philosemites and some ultra-Orthodox Jewish leaders like Rabbi Yoel Taitelbaum, the Holocaust is understood as part of a *Heilsgeschichte* in which it was God's will that Hitler would exterminate the Jews to punish the chosen people for their sins.[8] These sentiments were also expressed by a renowned Lutheran clergyman, Heinrich Gruber, dean of the Evangelical Church of East and West Berlin. Gruber had a long-established friendship with the Jews, and his opposition to the Nazis led to his imprisonment and near death at Dachau. Yet, in a meeting with Rubenstein in 1961, Gruber stated that it was God's plan that the Jews die in the Holocaust for their sins and that, like the biblical figure Nebuchadnezzar, Hitler was one of the "rods of God's anger."[9] Although Gruber was clearly not an antisemite, Rubenstein concluded that his mind-set thoroughly reflected the New Testament perspective that God was the omnipotent master of the world and that the Jews were being punished for their crime of deicide. Despite the fact that he had risked his life to save Jews, Gruber was incapable of seeing them as "normal human beings with the same range of failings and virtues as any other people."[10] Because they are considered God's chosen people, Gruber expected the Jews to act in superlative ways that are appropriate with divine commandments.[11]

Following his meeting with Gruber, Rubenstein realized that at the root of the antisemitism leading to the Holocaust lay a fundamental problem, "that it may be impossible for Christians to remain Christians without regarding Jews in mythic, magic and theological categories."[12] Moreover, the cause of this problem actually rests with an exclusive Jewish theology that leaves Jews open to the theological conclusions of Dean Gruber, as well as Orthodox Jewish thinkers regarding the Holocaust.[13] Rubenstein argued that both Jews and Christians have been involved in an inherited dialectic in which each is the "disconfirming other par excellence." He disagreed with those psychohistorians who offer pathological and projective interpretations of antisemitism that make Jews look like "neutral objects of the assaults of others rather than participants in a two-way conflict."[14] When viewing a Christian *Heilsgeschichte* potentially leading to murder, he could not forget its Jewish origin. Rubenstein stated that despite not having chosen it, as a Jew, he possesses "an unwanted superordinate significance for others" because non-Jews took his "ancestors seriously when they claimed for themselves a special religious destiny." Following the Holocaust, he neither desired nor expected any "special religious destiny" for himself or his community. For him, the religiohistoric myths of Judaism and Christianity not only "impede meaningful community; they absolutely preclude it."[15] Consequently, Rubenstein challenged Jews and Christians to demythologize their sacred traditions in order to have "true dialogue, the genuine meeting of persons."[16]

Just as Schoeps had tried to bridge the gap between Jews and Christians in the early years of World War II, Rubenstein tried to achieve reconciliation between the two communities after the horror of the Holocaust that had grown out of their opposition. Yet, while Schoeps tried to link German Jews and Christians together as sinful creatures who must return to a revelatory God, Rubenstein wanted to unify Jews and Christians in general after the Holocaust as guilt-ridden human beings, heirs to a religious conflict that they did not create based on their shared detrimental theology of a historical God. He first stated this position in German at the Fifteenth Annual Conference on Church and Judaism in Recklinghausen, Germany, in 1963. Ironically, in that lecture, he reached out to the same German Christians to whom Schoeps had appealed, but with a different message: "If we concentrate less on what our religious inheritances promise and threaten and more on the human existence that we share through these traditions, we will achieve the superlative yet simple knowledge of who we truly are."[17]

Yet, while he condemned Jewish-Christian antagonism stemming from their "religiohistoric myths," Rubenstein appeared to internalize Christian anti-Jewish mythical perceptions in his profoundly ambivalent portrayal of rabbinic Judaism and Jewish obedience to an omnipotent, punitive Father God. On the one hand, Rubenstein praised the Rabbis for requiring observance of Jewish law because it was given by God as a realistic measure of freedom in a limited universe.[18] Rubenstein defended obedience to an omnipotent God throughout history as a way of giving Jews hope to escape their powerless existence, yet he criticized rabbinic legalism because it led to "self-blame, self-punishment," and increased guilt.[19] This analysis concentrates on six constitutive components of that critique that arise largely out of his encounter with Christian theology and culture: First, when examining Rubenstein's intellectual development in the context of his biography, one can detect his early tension between attraction to and repulsion by Christianity that contributed to his personal sense of Jewish powerlessness and quest for power. As Jocelyn Hellig has pointed out, while it is rare for a theologian's life and work to be so closely interconnected, Rubenstein's theology is so personal and subjective that "an exposition of it in isolation from his life circumstances would tend to falsify his statements." In fact, Rubenstein himself has said that there is no substitute for life experiences as the foundation for a meaningful theology.[20] This is demonstrated in the fact that he developed a sense of impotence in the presence of a transcendent God based on personal experiences in his childhood and later adult life that were significant factors in the construction of his death of God theology after the Holocaust.

Second, in an attempt to understand his own inability to fulfill the commandments, Rubenstein constructed a critique of rabbinic legalism in his books *The Religious Imagination* (1968) and *My Brother Paul* (1972) similar to that of German Lutheran and Protestant interpreters of Paul. In general, these New Testament scholars claimed that Paul rejected the Law as a result of a sense of inadequacy because of the rabbinic expectation that Jews strive to observe all of the commandments in order to obtain salvation.[21] Rubenstein did not reject Jewish rituals and in fact viewed those with a sacrificial and priestly aspect, as having an important psychological function of addressing the deepest fears, aspirations, and yearnings of the individual and community in crucial life circumstances such as birth, puberty, marriage, sickness, and death.[22] However, he did reject the heteronomous authority of *Halakhah* in contemporary society and what he perceived to be excessively rigid rabbinic expectations regarding fulfillment of the commandments.

Third, Rubenstein related his own feeling of powerlessness to what he perceived to be a history of Jewish powerlessness in the face of Christian hegemony. In addition, he portrayed the development of a servile Jewish consciousness due to behavioral restraints imposed by the Rabbis who, he argued, interpreted every misfortune as a deserved punishment by an angry Father God. Fourth, following the Holocaust, Rubenstein appeared to assimilate the theistic God of Judaism and Christianity to the negative image of the Jewish God portrayed in the Marcionite dichotomy between a wrathful creator God and the loving savior God manifest in Christ.[23] In contrast to this transcendent and controlling "Lord of Nature," he conceived of a post-Holocaust, immanent God as the maternal "Ground of Being."[24] While this "cannibal Earth Mother" is no less threatening than the biblical God, this divinity of the earth is not intentionally punitive like the omnipotent God of the Hebrew Bible.[25] Fifth, Rubenstein contrasted rabbinic misogynist symbols of God with a return to feminine divine imagery after the Holocaust. Here Rubenstein exhibited elements of the anti-Jewish critique later illustrated in the work of Christian feminists, who blame Judaism for patriarchy and present it as the antithesis of feminist reconstructions of early Christianity. By distinguishing feminine, immanent images of a post-Holocaust

God from the transcendent Lord of history, Rubenstein anticipates those post-Christian feminists who present Judaism as the inferior antithesis of Goddess-centered religion.[26]

Finally, in his psychoanalysis of Judaism in relation to Christianity, Rubenstein appeared to perpetuate the Christian supersessionist claim by concluding that Pauline Christianity demonstrated a psychological advance beyond rabbinic Judaism through rituals such as baptism and the Eucharist that recover an archaic pagan identification with God as a "Ground of Being" that had been repressed by the Rabbis through halakhic stipulations.[27] In another indication of his ambivalence toward rabbinic Judaism, Rubenstein praised the Rabbis for acknowledging the potency of pagan rituals like human sacrifice that demonstrate the insight of overcoming intergenerational hostility. By constructing the symbolic, monetary transaction of redeeming the firstborn Jewish male with a coin, the Rabbis recognized the insight of the pagan ritual while channeling its murderous expression in order to eliminate its danger. However, he also criticized the same rabbinic sublimation of archaic strivings as an attempt to reduce anxiety about the distance between God and humanity. Ultimately, he argues that Pauline Christianity went further than the Rabbis in allowing for a greater recognition of the deepest human yearnings to become closer to God that the Rabbis had merely sublimated.

Rubenstein's complex path toward identity illustrates the contradictory and multiple nature of Jewish subjectivity. He should be neither marginalized nor seen as a "loyal son of Israel" who only seeks to defend the Jewish community, as Zachary Braiterman argues.[28] Throughout much of his career, Rubenstein has been a modern-day Paul who stands on the border between Judaism and Christianity, offering an intra-Jewish critique constructed out of his encounter with Christian religion and culture. While appearing to move beyond the Jewish-Christian dialectic, Rubenstein has perpetuated it by preserving Jewish and Christian myths.

Moving In and Out of the Shadow of Christianity:
A Biographical Sketch

Ironically, in his attempt to demythologize Judaism, Rubenstein perpetuated the mythical perception of Judaism by Christianity that he decried, by often viewing his life and that of his community through Christian mythical lenses. In his effort to achieve self-mastery with psychoanalysis, Rubenstein clearly illustrated a dialectic between fascination for and aversion to Christianity. Throughout his life, Christian antisemitism and even philosemitic Christian perceptions of Jews fueled his impression of Jewish powerlessness that was already developing as a result of his own sense of impotence in the face of a commanding God.[29] He was born in 1924 in New York to a poverty-stricken family. Rubenstein's psychological predicament stems in great respect from his own sense of personal weakness and isolation that developed during his childhood and resurfaced throughout his life. This dual sense of insecurity originated from the shame he felt at being too poor for the neighborhood in which his family lived, and his fear that he would end up a "beaten man" like his father, whose business had failed during the Great Depression. At the same time, his overbearing mother made him feel superior to other children because she claimed to be intellectually superior to their mothers, due to her college education. As a result, Rubenstein attempted to defend himself from the children of wealthier families by proving he was smarter than them, yet because of this, he was isolated even more as an outsider.[30]

By searching for knowledge, Rubenstein was able to deflect criticism from what he perceived to be a disgraceful physical experience demonstrated by his cheap, shabby clothing. His anxiety regarding his body image was also reflected in his strong doubts that he was sexually attractive to women and his later perception that he was not a "fully competent adult male" even as a husband and father. In therapy, he discovered that the root of this ongoing neurosis lay in the fact that he was not allowed to have a Bar Mitzvah, partly for financial reasons and partly because of his parents' rejection of traditional Judaism. In his eyes, this rite of passage would have enabled him to officially become a man sexually as well as religiously. He also realized that not having a Bar Mitzvah intensified his feeling of being an outsider to his fellow Jews, which he never relinquished.[31]

As a teenager in 1938, Rubenstein encountered three drunken Irish men yelling, "God damned dirty Jews." Refusing to be passive, he confronted the men and was seriously beaten. Later, instead of being helped by the police, he was insultingly accused in front of his father of being a delinquent. When his father failed to support him in front of the police, Rubenstein saw his passivity as a form of Jewish powerlessness in the face of antisemitism. He now concluded that the Nazis chose to exterminate the Jews because they were powerless to stop them.[32] Through psychoanalysis beginning in 1953, Rubenstein realized that in his earlier desire to escape the impotence he felt from his antisemitic encounter, he wanted to acquire the psychological, sacramental power of the priest. He realized that his decision to be a preacher was partly rooted in his desire to control the way people would look at him by wearing a special robe and dominating them with hypnotic sermons. He even surmised that the confessional elements of his theological writings arose out of the same motives.[33] In a personal interview in 1997, he stated that psychoanalysis enabled him to realize how much he appreciated Christianity, which helped him to ultimately strengthen his Jewish identity.[34] The anti-Trinitarian Christian sect of Unitarianism offered Rubenstein the sacramental power of Christianity without a belief in the divinity of Christ.[35]

For Rubenstein and other American Jews in the late 1930s, Unitarianism represented an attractive intermediate zone between Judaism and Christianity.

Facing the growing threat of Hitler overseas and an emerging isolationism at home, there was a general sense of impotence by American Jews corresponding to that expressed by Rubenstein. Having achieved some socioeconomic advancement, this second generation of American Jews tried to integrate into the larger Gentile world through organizations outside the Jewish community, yet because of their rapid mobility, they paradoxically encountered increased antisemitism.[36] As a result, American rabbis resorted to apologetics, attempting to secure an unbreakable bond between Judaism and America by promoting a common "Judeo-Christian heritage." While not completely assimilating the two faiths, both Conservative and Reform rabbis claimed that Judaism and Christianity were "fundamentally" alike. In *The Chosen People in America*, Arnold Eisen observes that identifying Judaism with America paradoxically "rendered the abandonment of Judaism . . . unnecessary, even if it also made 'apostasy' more reasonable."[37] It appears that this dilemma was most prevalent within the Reform movement. In 1923, one of its own rabbis had already accused the movement of preaching a "colorless universalistic liberalism" and "Christless Christianity" that led congregants to leave the synagogue. In his essay "The Uniqueness of Israel" (1923), Felix Levy argued that promotion of a belief in God "as one and not triune" was not enough to distinguish Jews from Christianity.[38]

It was this belief in religious universalism, the concept of the unity of God, and the preaching of an eschatological "Religion of Humanity" that Reform Judaism shared with Unitarianism. Following the Pittsburgh Platform in 1885 laying out the fundamental ideas of Reform Judaism, there were calls by both Jews and non-Jews in the last third of the nineteenth-century for a merger between Reform Judaism and Unitarianism because of their perceived identical beliefs and the Jewish fear of becoming a weaker minority. However, these calls were at times motivated by polemics initiated by conservatives in both camps who derided their liberal counterparts for abandoning the central tenets of their faiths. Even among Reform rabbis, there was still an ambivalent attitude toward Unitarianism reflected in their simultaneous acknowledgment of surface similarities and their attempt to articulate fundamental distinctions between the two religious movements.[39] In fact, when Rubenstein discussed his interest in the clergy with a Unitarian minister, he was actually encouraged to become a Reform rabbi because of the common beliefs that Unitarians and liberal Jews share. Yet he decided to become a Unitarian minister because he "saw the clerical office as a magic vocation and as a further defense against the curse of Jewishness and its impotence."[40] Although he realized that Unitarian ministers were probably the least priestly in their duties out of all Christian clergy, Rubenstein still wanted to obtain their magic not only to ward off his self-perceived powerlessness but also to "neutralize" antisemitic hatred.[41]

However, Rubenstein's confusion over his identity intensified when he realized that Unitarianism was more Christocentric than he had thought. Initially repulsed by the Eucharist, he would later become attracted to its symbolism. Rubenstein later claimed that by converting to Unitarianism, he had acted out his mother's rejection of Judaism and then rebelled against her wishes that he not become a priest. His anxiety and confusion reached a climax when he was asked to change his name for fear of antisemitism. He reacted to this by abandoning Unitarianism and returning to Judaism. At that point, he realized that by trying to flee Jewish impotence, he would become even more powerless by resorting to self-falsification and self-rejection. He decided to be true to himself and not try to hide his real identity, even though it was elusive.[42] In his essay "The Making of a Rabbi" (1966), Rubenstein claims that he decided to remain a Jew not because Judaism possesses any positive significance but because he refused to let anyone else determine how he should think of himself or the religious community that he inherited. He offers the following rationale for preserving his Jewish identity:

> Self-acceptance as a Jew has made it possible for me to accept myself as a man and to learn how to live . . . in terms of my own needs and my own perspectives. Had I rejected myself as a Jew, I would have had to enthrone the opinions of others as ultimately decisive for my inner life. I could not grant the world that tyranny over me. . . . By accepting myself as a Jew, I have liberated myself from the most futile and degrading of servilities, that of forever attempting to appease the irrational mythology that the Christian world has constructed of the Jew.[43]

Yet Rubenstein later realized that by remaining true to himself and his beliefs, he would ultimately be unable to remain an active participant in the very Jewish community to which he had returned. Ironically, by returning to the Jewish community, he would often define Jewish identity based on the mythical construction of the Jew by the Christian world. He would forever be standing beyond the established borders of Judaism viewing his community from the outside, first from the Christian perspective and later from that of the Buddhist.

To some extent, Rubenstein's identity crisis reflects a general sense of Jewish positionlessness during this time. Jews truly lived on the boundary between a Jewish world that they wanted to escape and a Gentile world that would not allow them to fully enter. In 1941, the social psychologist Kurt Lewin warned of "self-hatred" among Jews stemming from their precarious position at the barrier between the Jewish and Gentile worlds.[44] Moreover, Eisen points out that during this time, portrayals "of the Jews' 'sickness' or 'abnormality' or even 'pathology' are quite common in the writings of lay and rabbinic observers alike."[45] Ultimately, it appears that Rubenstein's conflict regarding Jewish identity was initially caused more by psychological than by social reasons, yet it was perpetuated by his dialectic of attraction and repulsion for Christian theology and culture. One could argue that his perception of historical Jewish powerlessness was an extension of his own personal and family difficulties growing up in the depression on the eve of World War II, and this perception developed further as a result of his encounter with Christianity.[46]

Upon his return to Judaism, Rubenstein became attracted to Reform Judaism, which he perceived to be a Jewish form of Unitarianism. He then enrolled at the Hebrew Union College in 1942 with the intention of becoming a Reform rabbi, but he could not accept the classical Reform positions of anti-Zionism and emphasis on ethical monotheism in light of the disclosure of the Nazi death camps. Responding to the Nazi extermination of the Jews, Rubenstein became angry and fearful at the same time. His greatest fear was that his anger toward the Nazis would be equal to their hatred against Jews. To stem his own rage and provide discipline in his life, he submitted himself to the dictates of *Halakhah*. He began to receive private instruction in Talmud at an Orthodox yeshiva, Mesivta Chaim Berlin, in 1947, yet because of a lack of traditional Jewish education and an insufficient amount of time, he decided to acquire the discipline he was seeking by enrolling in the Conservative rabbinical school, the Jewish Theological Seminary, in 1948.[47]

However, as Rubenstein became obsessed with observing all the commandments, he grew more anxious and guilt ridden about disobeying them. He agreed with the apostle Paul's description of the law making one aware of sin by its very prohibition against it. He observed that by imposing limits on human autonomy, "the Law incites men to rebel against its Author." Consequently, Rubenstein himself developed hatred toward God that paradoxically incited him to rebel at the same time he submitted to each commandment. Furthermore, he observed that as long as "the inclination to rebel continues, feelings of guilt and self-reproach are inevitable. . . . Such irrational anxiety and guilt encourage further attempts to obey wholeheartedly."[48] Through psychoanalytic reconstruction, he later realized that his desire to observe all the commandments reflected a subconscious desire to attain immortality and omnipotence. In his unconscious fantasy, he thought that if he were a completely obedient son to the omnipotent Father, then God would make him divine. As a result of his infant son's death in 1950, Rubenstein slowly came to realize that no matter how well he observed the commandments, he was destined to die like his son, who was too young to have even sinned.[49]

Yet despite the tragedy of his son's death and his own anxiety regarding *Halakhah*, Rubenstein continued his rabbinic education and was ordained as a Conservative rabbi in 1952 at the Jewish Theological Seminary in New York. Eight years later, Rubenstein obtained his doctorate from Harvard University. His thesis, "Psychoanalysis and the Image of the Wicked in Rabbinic Judaism," was later revised and published as *The Religious Imagination* in 1968. In it, he attempted to explain the psychological neuroses that he encountered when attempting to fulfill the commandments by undertaking a Freudian analysis of rabbinic *Aggadah*. He also attempted to understand his own sense of powerlessness by explaining how the Rabbis coped psychologically with the destruction of the Second Temple and their historical powerlessness that ensued.[50]

Rubenstein's personal struggles between obedience to and rebelliousness against God culminated in the writing of his book *After Auschwitz* (1966), in which he rejected the omnipotent historical God who had the power to enlist Hitler as a divine agent to exterminate six million Jews for their failure to uphold the covenant. In response to his "death of God theology," in *After Auschwitz*, Rubenstein was "bureaucratically excommunicated" from the American Jewish community and found it nearly impossible to find a job in any institution funded by Jews, as he discovered when forced to leave his position as a campus rabbi at the University of Pittsburgh. As a result, in 1970 he was offered an academic position at Florida State University, where he later became the Robert O. Lawton Distinguished Professor of Religion in 1977. Ironically, Rubenstein taught about the Jews while in exile from them until 1987, when he was finally acknowledged for his work by the same institution from which he had been ordained as a rabbi, the Jewish Theological Seminary, which awarded him the degree of doctor of Hebrew letters, *honoris causa*.[51]

However, Rubenstein continued to work in non-Jewish academic institutions, in 1995 becoming the president of the University of Bridgeport, an institution associated with Reverend Moon's Unification Church, where he is now president emeritus. In the latter stages of his career, Rubenstein focused more on the implications of general secularization and rationality that led to the Holocaust while also pursuing Asian thought, entering into dialogue with the Buddhist thinker Masao Abe. Most recently he has examined the religious motivations of communal conflict, population elimination, and genocide in the modern period in a book entitled *Holy War and Ethnic Cleansing*.[52] Spending much of his career in the shadow of Christianity, Rubenstein illustrates the dynamic of the modern Jewish thinker formulating identity in dialogue with his Christian Other.

Echoing Christian Anti-Jewish Myths: Rubenstein's Critique of Rabbinic Legalism

In his book *The Religious Imagination* (1968), Rubenstein relates his own anxiety regarding rabbinic legalism to the anxiety that he argues is expressed in rabbinic *Aggadah*. He claims that the rabbinic legends about Korah's rebellion against Moses reflect a subterranean rabbinic attack on "the Law" as both arbitrary and unethical. The arbitrary and irrational character of the Torah is reflected in a few *midrashim* where Korah is depicted as asking Moses questions regarding commandments that appear to make no sense. In one instance, Korah wonders why one must still add a purple fringe to an entirely purple garment in order to fulfill the commandment in Num. 15:38.[53] In another *midrash*, Korah rallies the entire congregation of Israel against Moses and Aaron because they have imposed a cruel law upon a poor widow that leads to her "progressive impoverishment." At every turn, the woman submits to a different commandment regarding the harvest that eventually leads to the confiscation of her only remaining possession, her sheep. Rubenstein compares this *midrash* to Kierkegaard's interpretation of Abraham's binding of Isaac because both present a conflict between the ethical and the religious. Yet, whereas Kierkegaard could devalue religious authority, the Rabbis represented the religious establishment and therefore could only express the tension through a "discredited rebel" who was destroyed by an overwhelmingly powerful God.[54]

According to Rubenstein, the Rabbis used the Korah *midrashim* to sublimate the anarchic and rebellious tendencies of their community in fantasy and to reaffirm obedience to an omnipotent God. He agrees with Paul that rabbinic sublimation was "a never ending treadmill," concluding that the harder one tried to improve one's relationship with God, the more one realized how much distance remained between God and humanity. Rubenstein claims that by "settling the question of religious authority in favor of God's power, Jews enormously enhanced their feelings of anxiety, guilt, and self-accusation." He finds that these feelings are constantly reinforced by the Jewish liturgy with the *mipnei ha-ta-enu* concept, which asserts that Jews were exiled from their land because of their sins.[55]

However, in "Because of Our Sins," Elliot Gertel argues that for "all the 'guilt complexes' supposedly fostered by the Liturgy, there is no advocacy of self-destruction." Instead of invoking a sense of destructive guilt, or original sin, the Rabbis sought out "the *human* source of guilt" which is the result of human existence and action, rather than being equated with it or seen as a source for it. Consequently, Gertel denies the association of Jewish guilt with the destructive guilt of the "super-ego."[56] Rubenstein acknowledged that the Rabbis did not explicitly see their relationship with God in this way, but he claimed that they did express these sentiments unconsciously through *Aggadah*. Moreover, he claimed that subsequent generations of Jews have illustrated this sense of self-destructive guilt throughout history.

For Rubenstein, this sense of powerlessness before God and the resulting self-hate were reinforced by Christian antisemitism. Rubenstein argued that the "biblical-rabbinic theology of history, of which the Korah stories are an important example, was devastatingly employed against the Jewish community throughout the history of the Christian Church." Specifically, in the *Dialogue with Trypho*, Justin Martyr interpreted the Jewish defeat in the Hadrianic War (132–35) as a divine rejection of the Jews in favor of Christianity, just as the Rabbis interpreted Korah's destruction by God as proof that his protest was rejected in favor of Moses. Rubenstein went on to argue that the Rabbis actually agreed with Justin's contention that God punished the Jews for their sins, but they disagreed with what those sins were. Yet later he stated that even the Christian claim that Jews were punished for rejecting Jesus had a strong impact on their negative self-image, and the deicide accusation ultimately reinforced Jewish self-accusation.[57]

Ironically, it was Rubenstein himself who seemed to internalize Christian anti-Jewish claims when examining rabbinic Judaism. Specifically, his portrayal of Paul approximated much of what is considered to be the pre-Holocaust, German Lutheran and Protestant reading of Paul's disillusionment with Judaism because of its commitment to a "legalistic works-righteousness."[58] Rubenstein accepted the accounts of Paul and rabbinic Judaism that portrayed the law as leading to a sense of inadequacy because of the requirement that one must intend to fulfill it completely in order to attain salvation.[59] However, he rejected the idea that the Pharisees and later Rabbis were self-righteous and hypocritical in their observance of the commandments. In fact, he emphasized their "moral and psychological honesty," which is illustrated in their "disguised admiration for the worst sinners" and their expression of ambivalence toward Halakhah reflected in the Aggadah.[60] Moreover, Rubenstein pointed out the rabbinic perception of Halakhah as a gift by a caring Father God "to allow as much freedom as is consistent with the inherent limitations and structure of the created order."[61] Hence the Torah was considered a tool with which one can realistically accept the limits of existence imposed by suffering and death and live a free and fulfilled life. He argued that on the surface at least, the Rabbis never believed "that the biblical commandments they obeyed were the arbitrary and irrational fiat of an Omnipotent Autocrat." However, he also observed that they "did not have any sense that their religious careers were fundamentally enslaved. . . . It is possible that the Rabbinic 'slave' did not know his own chains."[62]

Furthermore, by highlighting the unconscious rabbinic perception of Halakhah as arbitrary, irrational, and unethical, Rubenstein was articulating at the very least a classical Reform position regarding Halakhah, or more possibly expressing the anti-Jewish viewpoint of Protestant New Testament scholars like Bultmann who claimed that in the Talmud, ritual commandments became more important than ethical ones, and as a result, Jews lost sight of their social and cultural responsibilities. Bultmann argued that prior to the destruction of the Second Temple, Jews were able to observe the Sabbath and basic laws of purity without a problem. Yet, after the elaboration of such a vast number of regulations in the Mishna and Talmud, to "take them seriously meant making life an intolerable burden."[63]

Moreover, Bultmann observed that because of the legalistic, rabbinic conception of obedience, Jew were never sure if they had done enough good works in order to be saved. "The prospect of meeting God as their Judge awakened in the conscientious a scrupulous anxiety and a morbid sense of guilt." He admitted that Jews could repent for their sins but argued that eventually repentance itself became a good work that insured merit and grace, making the entire relationship with God into one predicated on merit.[64] Like Bultmann, Rubenstein viewed repentance as a task that must be legalistically performed in order to earn God's mercy. Yet he saw that even this exercise was futile because it would only lead to more anxiety and estrangement from God, resulting from the inability to be fully obedient to God's commandments. In his book, *My Brother Paul* (1972), Rubenstein agreed with the German Protestant and Lutheran perception that within rabbinic culture, individuals never make themselves right before God. He argued that repentance is never complete because there is always some remnant of satisfaction for making the offense. He claimed that while it "is impossible to obey all the Law; it is probably impossible fully to repent for one's inability to achieve perfect obedience."[65] For Rubenstein, Paul and the sacramental Christian religious motifs and rituals associated with him provided a penultimate example of a rabbinic Jew who "understood the inability of the Jewish religious system to overcome the anxiety and guilt it engendered." This anxiety reflected the sense of Jewish impotence before an omnipotent God and the fear of punishment for not observing all of God's commandments. Through psychoanalysis and his exploration of Paul, Rubenstein rejected what he considered to be a rabbinic sublimation of guilt, and he attempted to uncover and give expression to the repressed elements in Jewish consciousness.[66]

In *The Religious Imagination*, Rubenstein argued that the rabbinic conception of God and religious belief in general are projections of an inner psychic conflict into the cosmic sphere, "an act of self-therapy and self-cure." He compared this concept of God with that of the superego, which is not only a hostile and censoring faculty but also an "ego ideal" that possesses a loving and rewarding element. The rabbinic construction of divine imagery corresponds to children who introject parental standards into their behavior but often perpetuate their dependence on their parents beyond the period of its relevance. Similarly, few "contemporary Jews are willing to restrict their personal behavior to the very stringent limits which the rabbis, against enormously potent inner promptings, imposed upon themselves."[67]

Through psychoanalysis and the teachings of the Protestant thinker Paul Tillich, Rubenstein came to realize that his own quest for heteronomy was a form of false consciousness, and the whole concept of divine mercy and love of God is therefore fallacious. For Rubenstein, this indicates the psychological construction of a heteronomous authority to ensure stability and security in a precarious world.[68] While he did not deny the majority of others the need for heteronomous authority, his "psychoanalytic identity" gave him the ability to make completely autonomous decisions without any political, moral, social, or religious authority. Theologically speaking, he could no longer accept the rabbinic idea of God either loving or even hating Israel, because of his rejection of an omnipotent theistic God who is responsible for the "gratuitous human evil" of the Holocaust.[69]

Projecting Passivity onto the Rabbis: Reading Half of a Tradition

Although Rubenstein admitted that it is problematic to reduce the cause of the Holocaust to the psychological factor of Jewish self-blame, he clearly observed a historical pattern of self-hatred and submissive obedience to an omnipotent God that culminated in the Holocaust.[70] In his autobiography, *Power Struggle* (1974), Rubenstein acknowledged that this historical pattern that he had observed was an outgrowth and completion of his own personal psychoanalysis.[71] He traced this pattern back to the Rabbis, and especially Rabban Yochanan ben Zakkai, whose theodicy in the wake of the destruction of the Temple contributed to the development of what he considered to be a "servile consciousness" that became normative for Jews up through the twentieth century, resulting in their ultimate undoing in the Holocaust. Rubenstein argued that this theodicy was based on the attempt in "normative Jewish theology" to impose meaning on human experience by interpreting it as a drama with God as the "First Actor," the various nations of the earth as subordinate actors, and the Jewish people with the starring role. He observed that a distinctive characteristic of this drama is that the First Actor inflicts misfortune and death upon the subordinate actors for failing to comply with divine will.[72]

> Yohanan's contribution was to interpret the fall of Jerusalem as the First Actor's punitive response to the failure of the Jewish people to maintain fidelity to his law. The military defeat only seemed to be the victory of Roman imperial power. In reality, the Romans were the First Actor's instruments of his punitive design. Yohanan's view implied a practical program: if the people took heed to what had befallen them and applied themselves diligently to the study and practice of God's law, they might yet incline the First Actor to undo his punitive action.[73]

Rubenstein argued that this theodicy reflects what Jacob Neusner describes as a political deal with the Romans.[74] In "Yohanan's bargain," the Pharisees, under his leadership, would give the Romans "the tokens of submission they demanded, foreswearing all resort to power in their dealings with their overlords," in exchange for an internal autonomy centered around spirituality.[75] Rubenstein viewed "Yohanan's bargain" as politically expedient and essential for Jewish survival throughout history. However, he argued that there are social and psychological reasons why there is no longer any justification after the Holocaust for maintaining the bargain "or the religio-cultural institutions which affirm it as the normative expression of Jewish life." First, Rubenstein observed that because the bargain was so mystified by later generations, Jews confused disobedience to rabbinic authority with a rebellion against God, and the social cost was an "alienation of consciousness." In addition, the submissive rabbinic culture growing out of Yohanan's bargain incurred psychological costs on the Jewish people, specifically "the repression of the aesthetic and sensual side of existence and the overemphasis on the abstract" which were barely understood.[76]

The most fundamental reason for rejecting the rabbinic culture that evolved out of Yohanan's bargain is that in the twentieth century it has been broken by the Nazis. Rubenstein argued that "Rabban Yohanan's culture made sense in coming to terms with an overlord who sought Jewish submission; it became suicidal when the Jews were confronted with an adversary whose goal was extermination."[77] Moreover, Rubenstein observed that it is hideously ironic that "the instinctively law-abiding character of the Jewish community greatly contributed to its total destruction." He argued that because Jews have always been disciplined to observe the commandments without question, they had an automatic tendency to obey the secular and religious rules of the societies in which they lived. Hence, when the Nazis took over the European nations in which Jews lived, they were instinctively obeyed. Just as Moses never replies to Korah's complaints about the law being cruel and arbitrary in the *Aggadah*, Jews were supposed to obey the law of God or any other powerful authority, no matter how vicious and despicable the decrees were.[78]

Furthermore, Dean Gruber unconsciously echoed Yohanan's theology of history. According to Rubenstein, Gruber's theological analysis of the Holocaust confirmed the historical phenomenon of Jewish self-reproach and the Jews' passive acceptance of their fate in the Holocaust. Moreover, Gruber's insistence that even in the Holocaust, God was responsible for the fate of Israel as the chosen people "was fully consistent with normative Jewish faith."[79] Rubenstein ultimately observed that just as in the situation of the Rabbis and Justin Martyr following the destruction of the Temple, "Europe's Jews and Christians were able to agree that Jewish degradation was the result of God's punishment, even when they could not agree upon the nature of the Jewish offense."[80] The interview with Gruber thus represented the culmination of Rubenstein's personal struggle between obedience and rebelliousness to the all-powerful, tyrannical God of Sinai that he perceived to be occurring in history on a collective level with the Jewish people. Following his encounter with Gruber, Rubenstein came to the conclusion that if "indeed such a God holds the destiny of mankind in his power, his resort to death camps to bring about his ends is so obscene that I would rather spend my life in perpetual revolt than render him even the slightest homage." For Rubenstein, this "perpetual revolt" manifested itself in his perception that "the transcendent Father-God of Jewish patriarchal monotheism is dead."[81]

In *After Auschwitz*, Rubenstein appears to waver regarding the preceding statement by saying that it is impossible for Jews to use the words "God is dead" because of their association with the Christian symbol of the cross. Yet he insists that Jews "must use these words of alien origin and connotation" because they "share the same cultural universe as the contemporary Christian thinker."

However, he later criticizes radical theologians who make the statement because it reveals nothing about God and only what the observer thinks. He argues that it "is more precise to assert that *we live in the time of the death of God* than to declare 'God is dead.'" Ultimately for Rubenstein, the relevance of theology is anthropological because its importance is based on what it reveals about the theologian and his or her culture.[82]

In his analysis of Rubenstein's reaction to Gruber, Braiterman claims that Rubenstein was rebelling not against Judaism but against a German pastor because he manipulated traditional assertions about God, covenant, and suffering in order to fault the Jewish people.[83] Yet I would argue that Rubenstein's response to Gruber clearly reflects his own revolt against a self-perceived acquiescent and repressive rabbinic culture that grew out of Yohanan's bargain and was now permanently dysfunctional after the Holocaust. When criticizing rabbinic Judaism, Rubenstein presents an overly reductionist account of Jewish history that only emphasizes the passive characteristic of diaspora Judaism without accounting for its political activism. It is problematic to argue that Jewish passivity in the diaspora was a precursor to a lack of resistance in the Holocaust because such an argument makes a false distinction between a passive diaspora mentality and an active, healthy mentality of the post-Holocaust Jew. In his analysis of this perceived passivity of diaspora Jewry, the historian Amos Funkenstein asserted that while Jews from antiquity to the medieval period expected persecution and always defended themselves with whatever means available, their relative passivity in the Holocaust stems from their general quality of disbelief that it was possible for people to engage in such horrific acts. In fact, as some scholars suggest, the rabbinic legal principle, "the law of the kingdom is the law" that was referred to by eighteenth century *maskilim*, or Jewish enlighteners, as a justification for the Jewish observance of state law, originally meant the opposite. The Rabbis argued that the law pertained only to matters of property rights and taxation, and they stipulated that only when a ruler acts according to the law of the land is one required to obey him.[84]

Nevertheless, it is clear that there was a rabbinic ideology of passive messianism reflecting God's omnipotence and Israel's promised political inaction in bringing about the messianic age. Funkenstein observed that following the destruction of the Second Temple, the Rabbis promoted what he called a cathartic theodicy inherited from the latter prophets, claiming that Jews were exiled from the land of Israel because of various sins of disobedience to God, neglect of scholars, internal hatred, social injustice, and a lack of leadership. According to this approach, the Rabbis believed that through exile they would be expiated and purified of their moral blemish by God, and that only God could call an end to the punishment.[85] This carthartic theodicy was further supported by a *midrash* in Babylonian Talmud *Ketubot* 3a that seeks to explain the three references to a divine oath made in the biblical narrative of the Song of Songs, in which God urges the daughters of Jerusalem to not precipitate love until it is ready. Funkenstein further pointed out that some rabbis interpreted these three oaths to refer to three oaths imposed on Israel and the nations after the destruction of the Second Temple that illustrated a type of passive messianism: First, Israel was required not to rebel against the nations that ruled over them. Second, Jews were not to try to hasten the coming of the messianic age. Third, the nations were not to oppress Israel too much. Hence, Jews who tried to "precipitate the end" and force God to bring about the messianic age through human initiative were considered rebels and would be punished further as a result. This was the position later taken by Rabbi Yoel Taitelbaum, who saw the Holocaust as the punishment for Zionist efforts to obtain sovereignty by attempting to form a Jewish state in Palestine.[86]

However, this theology reinforcing divine power was accompanied by an entirely new theology that reflected divine impotence through the exile of the *Shekhinah*, Divine presence, along with the Jews. In this case, God was seen as no longer intervening in history, and the possibility arose "for the Jews to take political action without direct divine dispensation." Amos Funkenstein called this theory "active-realistic messianism" because it illustrated the rabbinic desire for the restoration of Jewish sovereignty through political action. This theology was neither passive nor apocalyptic but instead "'neutralized' messianism by channeling it into a nonrevolutionary doctrine related to this world."[87] This ideology of "active-realistic messianism" supports the view that rather than being passive and apolitical leaders, the Rabbis led by Yohanan ben Zakkai were "pragmatic political realists who were determined to preserve their authority." According to this view, ben Zakkai supported the war against the Romans until it was too late, and instead of requesting Yavneh as a spiritual retreat, he was imprisoned there by the Romans.[88] Hence, while passivity and self-blame may have been predominant in Jewish history, it is clear that there was another tradition of rabbinic autonomy in which the Rabbis assert themselves in relation to God and "frequently depict human authorities whose status and power often equal and sometimes outweigh God's own."[89]

In (God) After Auschwitz, Braiterman recognizes that "Rubenstein as it were, reads only 'half' of any given traditional text" by underestimating the significance of classical Jewish protest literature. While acknowledging protests in rabbinic *Aggadah*, Rubenstein dismisses them as "muted and inferential," originating only from the mouths of discredited heretics. Braiterman concludes, "He has thus effectively marginalized any antitheodic counter-tradition . . . in order to represent 'The Tradition' as the theodic monolith that he must reject after the Holocaust."[90] Yet Braiterman portrays Rubenstein as a post-Holocaust thinker ultimately ambivalent toward Jewish tradition, whose "thought has swung between the rejection and revision of Jewish literary sources."[91] As a result, Braiterman describes Rubenstein as a revisionist, rather than a revolutionary, who attempts to construct a "counter-tradition" out of isolated Lurianic and Levitical texts. However, in the end, his post-Holocaust countertradition is

weakened by his failure to translate his theology into traditional Jewish categories and his inability to account for the antitheodic elements of biblical and rabbinic sources.[92]

While I agree with Braiterman that Rubenstein was ambivalent toward Jewish tradition, Braiterman does not go far enough in explaining the reasons for
Rubenstein's rejection of rabbinc theodicy and halakhic repression. Braiterman
recognizes that Rubenstein initiates his reorientation of Jewish thought through
the use of Greek, pagan categories. However, Braiterman's analysis of Rubenstein
is incomplete in the sense that it fails to account for the impact of personal, psychological neuroses and Christian anti-Jewish myths on the construction of his
antirabbinic polemic. By rejecting what he considered to be the omnipotent and
punitive God of rabbinic Judaism, Rubenstein's critique resembled a Christian
polemic against rabbinic Judaism. Using psychoanalysis, Rubenstein projected
his own anxiety and guilt regarding the fulfillment of commandments on to the
Rabbis and, in the process, confirmed the pre-Holocaust, German Lutheran and
Protestant portrayal of rabbinic Judaism as a legalistic, self-punitive culture. In
addition, based on his own experience with antisemitism and the writings of
Christian thinkers throughout history, Rubenstein unconsciously internalized
the powerless, pariah status of the Jew. As we have seen with Rosenzweig,
Rubenstein illustrates the postmodern concept of culture, as "the ensemble of
stigmata one group bears in the eyes of another group."[93] Yet instead of recu-
perating the view of the Christian and inverting it, Rubenstein condemned it
and blamed the Rabbis for creating it.

Rubenstein's Immanent Post-Holocaust God: A Mixture
of Philosophical and Religious Motifs with a Marcionite Trope

In *After Auschwitz*, Rubenstein replaced the biblical, theistic portrayal of God
and the divine-human relationship with a post-Holocaust, panentheistic image
of a God who unfolds in nature yet is ontologically distinct from it. In this scenario, "the cosmos in all of its temporal and spatial multiplicity is understood
as the manifestation of the single unified and unifying, self-unfolding, self-
realizing Divine Source, Ground, Spirit, or Absolute."[94] He later stated in *Power
Struggle* that his initial reconstruction of the divine image was influenced most
by the pagan leanings of the Protestant thinker Paul Tillich.[95] Nevertheless,
Rubenstein's post-Holocaust theology also reflects the Marcionite thrust in
Tillich's critique of "theological theism." In the 1992 edition of *After Auschwitz*,
Rubenstein refered to Tillich's depiction of "the Old Testament God as the harsh,
merciless, unforgiving Lawgiver in contrast to the gracious, self-sacrificing
Christ."[96] Rubenstein himself called this a false dichotomy because the loving
God of the New Testament requires the atoning sacrifice of the Son. In addi-
tion, he pointed out that Christianity maintains judicial constraints and the

punitive concept of hell.[97] However, in his post-Holocaust portrayal of God, Rubenstein approximated the tyrannical image of God in that dichotomy that was also present at times in rabbinic protest literature and applied it to the theodic God of both Judaism and Christianity.[98] He presented this image of an unrelenting biblical God as a foil to a nonpunitive, immanent "Source and Ground of Being" after the Holocaust.[99] Yet Rubenstein's post-Holocaust God of Nature is neither angry nor kind, but rather amoral, transcending the categories of good and evil. In fact, as Braiterman notes, Rubenstein's theology is "profoundly tragic" because it abandons any notion of purposeful divine redemption in the face of tragedy, leaving death as "the only ultimate redemption from uncertainty and trial." Nonetheless, Rubenstein would rather interpret historical Jewish suffering culminating in the Holocaust as tragic misfortune rather than a deserved punishment from an autocratic God.[100]

Drawing upon Tillich's portrayals of God as "'Being Itself,' 'Ground of Being,' and 'Source of Being,'" Rubenstein conceived of an intimate, maternal image of God that "creates as does a mother, in and through her very substance." Tillich wanted to show that humans possess self-consciousness apart from their Ground of Being yet at the same time remain immersed in it at all times and become reunified with it at death. For Rubenstein, the amoral God as the Ground of Being "participates in all the joys and sorrows of the drama of creation, which is at the same time, the deepest expression of the divine life."[101] In contrast, the "masculine sky God of biblical and rabbinic Judaism" is referred to as King, father, creator, and judge who, like a male, produces something external to himself when creating. "He remains essentially outside of and judges the creative processes He has initiated."[102] Rubenstein pointed out that the Rabbis did not see God as an inherently "arbitrary, capricious tyrant," yet he argues that by attacking God's commandments as cruel and arbitrary in the *Aggadah*, the Rabbis implicitly attack their author as well.[103] In his analysis of Rubenstein's philosophy, William Kaufman observed that "Rubenstein paints an especially repugnant, one-sided, and Christian picture of the God of the Old Testament as "an angry sky-god."[104] In addition, Rubenstein claimed that the Jews' only explanation for their two-thousand-year exile was that they were punished by a wrathful God and, as a result, experienced a pervasive sense of guilt and self-blame.

Braiterman has observed that Rubenstein ironically ignored or misread classical rabbinic protest literature and even the Book of Job that could have aided his own antitheodic reading of the Hebrew Bible. Specifically, while observing the theodic elements of *Lamentations Rabbah* in which the Rabbis attribute their national misfortune to sin, Rubenstein failed to mention the scene in which the Rabbis put God on trial for breaking the covenant by being silent in the face of Israel's suffering. This counterlawsuit genre was already reflected in the story of Job, whose author for most of the text constructs a courtroom drama in which Job is the plaintiff and prosecutor and his friends the witnesses, calling the defendant God to prove his innocence in the face of unjustified evil. However,

Rubenstein argued that while the story of Job once represented a powerful response to suffering, his refusal to reject God has no contemporary relevance in light of the Holocaust.[105] These instances where Rubenstein refused or was unable to account for antitheodic protests within biblical and rabbinic Judaism actually seem to lend more credibility to the argument that Rubenstein was stepping outside of his tradition and critiquing it from a Christian perspective.

In his earlier neopagan period, Rubenstein described the return of the Jews to the land of Israel as an expression of the return of humanity to its primal origins and a revitalization of nature in the twentieth century. This reunification with nature ends the dehumanization of history culminating in the Holocaust and enables humanity to reexperience a sense of eros. In returning to "*eros and the ethos of eros*," Rubenstein argued that individuals were no longer being punished by the omnipotent Lord of history for attempting to be what humans were created to be.[106]

In the 1992 edition of *After Auschwitz*, Rubenstein describes the divine-human relationship by drawing upon models of dialectical pantheism, *Kabbalah* (Jewish mysticism), and Buddhism. Using Hegelian terms, he observes an ongoing dialectic occurring between the essential unity of the Spirit and "the natural and historical world as epiphenomenal manifestation of the divine Reality." He points out that according to Hegel, there is a unified totality that is beyond "the empirical world of dichotomous oppositions and discrete, isolated entities."[107] Rubenstein links this self-unfolding of a unified totality with the quest for Buddhist enlightenment and contrasts it with the "dichotomizing *system of gaps*, such as faith in the radically transcendent Creator God of biblical religion, who bestows a covenant upon Israel for His own utterly inscrutable reasons." In Buddhism, nirvana or enlightenment cannot be provided by a transcendent deity over against oneself but can be achieved only through dissolution of the self or the realization of the illusion of the self.[108]

Earlier in his book *Morality and Eros* (1970), Rubenstein distinguished his post-Holocaust image of God as the "Holy Nothingness" from the Hegelian Spirit because he believed the process of divine self-unfolding has neither goal nor meaning, but rather "*the process itself may ultimately be a vast cosmic detour originating in God's Nothingness and finally terminating in God's Nothingness.*"[109] In the 1992 edition of *After Auschwitz*, Rubenstein related this cosmic process to Lurianic mysticism that describes God as the *Ein Sof* (Endless). Like the Holy Nothingness, the image of the *Ein Sof* represents the source of all being which cannot be defined. The *Shekhinah* (Divine Presence) is perceived to be exiled from the *Ein Sof*, and the goal of existence is to overcome the cosmic exile and restore the cosmos to unity with its primordial ground.[110] Braiterman observes that by drawing upon Lurianic *Kabbalah*, Rubenstein, like Gershom Scholem and Martin Buber with Hasidism, was bringing traditional Jewish motifs to the surface that had been marginalized by modern Jewish liberalism. He claims that Rubenstein was the first modern Jewish theologian to openly and self-consciously integrate Lurianic metaphor into his thought.[111] Braiterman argues that Rubenstein uses Lurianic motifs to reinvent the tradition he rejects, based on his "uneven attempt to construct a post-Holocaust Judaism predicated upon the radical rejection of theodicy and its texts."[112]

I agree with this critique but would argue further that Rubenstein is using Lurianic categories against their grain to highlight the immanent aspect of Jewish theism in contrast to a transcendent image of God fostered in a Christian anti-Jewish myth. Specifically, Rubenstein fails to take into account the interdependence between *Kabbalah* and *Halakhah* in the Lurianic system that reinforces the paradoxical notion of a transcendent, commanding God who at the same time demonstrates the ultimate in divine immanence. Scholem explains that according to Lurianic *Kabbalah*, the process of *tikkun*, or restitution, of the scattered and exiled divine sparks does not reach its final conclusion in God but depends on humanity to effect the final restoration. "The Jew who is in close contact with the divine life through the Torah, the fulfillment of the commandments, and through prayer, has it in his power to accelerate or hinder this process." Paradoxically, the Jew is required by a transcendent God to complete the divine enthronement and restore God to the "Kingdom of Heaven" to bring about the immanent return of all things to their source.[113] Thus, Lurianism brings the tension between divine transcendence and immanence to its height but maintains it, while Rubenstein clearly separates one from the other in his Marcionite type of dichotomy between the biblical God and the post-Holocaust Holy Nothingness. Moreover, Rubenstein uses Lurianic divine imagery to portray a God who is no longer an omnipotent King issuing commands but an immanent Ground of Being who participates in the joys and sorrows of creation without viewing them as rewards or punishments.

In addition to perpetuating a negative image of the biblical God shared by many Christian thinkers throughout history, Rubenstein finds a Christian theological model for his post-Holocaust God in the apocalyptic vision of the apostle Paul. According to Paul, Christ as the "Last Adam" destroys all vestiges of authority and power and ultimately submits himself to God "so that God may be all in all." Rubenstein interprets this vision as an indication that at the end of time, the distinction between God as transcendent subject and the cosmos as object will disappear, thus making Christ "the cosmic agent through whom the eschatological return of the cosmos to its originating Sacred Womb is finally attained."[114] He concludes that just as in the Lurianic myth, the *Shekhinah*'s exile from God ends when God is "all in all"; in Paul's vision, human exile from Eden as well as the exile of the cosmos from its Source is "terminated in the final restoration of all things to their Originating Ground."[115] With this interspersing of kabbalistic, Pauline, and pagan motifs, Rubenstein attempts to bridge the gap between God and nature, Judaism and paganism.

Rubenstein's dialectical-mystical paradigm accounts for the creativeness and destructiveness of his post-Holocaust God. Just as we are created and nurtured out of our maternal ground of being, we must also return to it in death. He describes the totality of the creative process in this way: "It is impossible to affirm the loving and the creative aspects of God's activity without also affirming that creation and destruction are part of an indivisible process. Each wave in the ocean of God's Nothingness has its moment, but it must inevitably give way to other waves."[116] Hence, unlike Tillich, Rubenstein does not refer to the Holy Nothingness solely as a God of love in contrast to the biblical God of wrath. However, while creativity and destruction may make up the divine process following the Holocaust, Rubenstein excludes any notion of punitive destruction from it. In Rubenstein's post-Holocaust theology, suffering ceases to be seen as "the payment of a debt exacted by an angry Master" and is now seen simply as the necessary and "natural termination of organic existence."[117]

Rubenstein's God is therefore not a causative agent, and consequently human beings are responsible for evil. In effect, he is really distinguishing between an angry, purposeful God and a God who is somewhat indifferent, more appropriately linked to the impersonal realm of fate.[118] Yet even this latter type of theology is more desirable to Rubenstein because it relinquishes the view that the Holocaust was a form of divine punishment. Ultimately, Rubenstein's bifurcation of divinity affixes to both Jewish and Christian theism a monolithic image of the biblical God as an all-powerful despot that was articulated to some extent in rabbinic literature and given even more voice in Christian anti-Jewish writings.

Rubenstein's Protofeminist Critique of Judaism

In his post-Holocaust reconstruction of the divine image, Rubenstein offers a radical protofeminist critique of the rabbinic, misogynist perception of God. In the process, however, he exhibits what would later be considered anti-Jewish motifs of Christian and post-Christian feminism. In her article "Rabbinic Powerlessness and the Power of Women," Jocelyn Hellig discusses the "thread of feminism" underlying Rubenstein's work, which she argues is not always obvious, yet continuously present.[119] In constructing his post-Holocaust theology, Rubenstein refers to the Canaanite Goddesses Astarte and Anat and he uses maternal images like "ground," "source," "abyss," "matrix," and "sacred womb" in contrast to more patriarchal images of distance and control.[120] While the Canaanite polytheistic and pagan elements of his theology later fade, Rubenstein continues to refer to his post-Holocaust God using feminine motifs.

Using psychoanalysis earlier in his career, Rubenstein criticized the biblical and rabbinic, phallocentric perception of God that contributed to repression and misogyny. Rubenstein associated his own marital problems with the problems he observed between Jewish men and women since antiquity as a result of their powerless exilic situation. He specifically linked his lack of a secure masculine identity to the inability of Jewish men throughout history to protect their women from physical assault or sexual abuse committed by their foreign conquerors. Yet, at the same time, he observed that these Jewish women were always socially and economically dependent on their emasculated Jewish husbands.[121] As a result of this Jewish male tension between power and powerlessness, Rubenstein observed the following problem developing:

> The men could only assert, and truth to tell, exaggerate, their masculine prerogatives *within* the community, never in the larger world. All of the masculine bias which Jews had inherited from ancient Palestine was intensified in the Diaspora. The Jewish God was a masculine God. The Jewish religion stressed the prerogatives of the male in two domains of fundamental importance over which Jews had any measure of independence, worship and learning.[122]

Rubenstein claimed that this insecure situation was the foundation for Jewish hostility toward women expressed in rabbinic *Aggadah* and halakhic repression of the emotional and sensuous elements of existence. The former can be seen in the rabbinic legends about Eve, Leah, Dinah, and the daughters of Zion. According to Rubenstein, the Rabbis followed the Scripture in placing greater blame on Eve and the serpent than on Adam for the primal crime of eating the forbidden fruit in the Garden of Eden. Moreover, they viewed Eve as immodest and lascivious, and they saw these characteristics as prototypical for her gender.

In *The Religious Imagination*, Rubenstein compares the primal crime of Genesis to the primal parricide portrayed by Freud in *Totem and Taboo*. However, his use of Freudian psychoanalysis is ironic in the sense that Freud has been criticized for exactly the patriarchal, misogynist position that Rubenstein ostensibly opposes. In fact, Rubenstein acknowledges that in his portrayal of the primal crime of parricide, Freud says nothing about the role of women. Rubenstein finds it inconceivable that such an important conflict regarding the possession of women could have occurred without their participation. He argues that the rabbinic portrayal of the primal crime in Genesis "may have had an antifeminine bias, but it at least suggested that no member of the original family was entirely without a measure of responsibility."[123]

The Rabbis portray Leah in one *midrash* as a harlot because she "goes out" to meet Jacob. They view Dinah's behavior like that of Leah, to be flirtatious, and the rape of Dinah is viewed as a punishment for her "wanton conduct" with foreign men. Finally, whereas in Isa. 3:16 the daughters of Zion are merely described as haughty, the Rabbis interpret that they seek lovers among the conquerors. According to Rubenstein, these last two cases especially illustrate the anxiety of Jewish men in relation to women as a result of political powerlessness.[124] Here Rubenstein's psychoanalysis of rabbinic patriarchy uncovers misogyny yet seems to overstate Jewish powerlessness. His powerlessness argument does not address the argument made by Jewish feminists that Jewish women were treated better than their counterparts for centuries with regard to legal rights in marriage and divorce.[125] Even in regard to talmudic education, there were voices of opposition to the exclusion of women, especially in the Tosefta and Palestinian Talmud, where menstruating and parturient women were able to study the Written and Oral Torah. This presupposes that women in general were able to study.[126]

Rubenstein claimed that as a response to the destruction of the Second Temple, the Rabbis, like himself, had to contain their rage in the face of a powerful enemy by submitting to the discipline of Jewish law commanded by a masculine Sky God. They were forced to control any emotional spontaneity and sexual encounter through halakhic restraints. Rubenstein even went so far as to see the Rabbis through the guise of the sexually repressed character Alexander Portnoy in Phillip Roth's Portnoy's Complaint. In fact, he argued, "Neither the religiously sanctified laws of sexual encounter nor the image of women encouraged the development of mature sexuality."[127] As we have seen, Rubenstein submitted that while repressing the sensuous or earthly elements of existence, the Rabbis emphasized the abstract and intellectual in conjunction with their belief in a transcendent, punitive God. God was seen as an abstract, unfathomable essence, a supernatural, transcendent Lord of history who controls nature and gives permission to people to change and subordinate it according to their desires.[128]

To counter this religious expression leading to the Holocaust, Rubenstein initially advocates a religion that celebrates the return to earth and bodily gratification. God as the maternal Ground of Being is now immanently present within nature and is united with the cosmos in a heterogeneous reality. Using psychoanalysis, Rubenstein argues that the reunification of humanity with its Ground of Being is manifest in the urge of humanity to return to its primal origins and free itself from the bonds of culture and history. This liberation is reflected in human sexuality that "achieves an importance possessed by no product of 'civilized' strivings." He emphasizes that only in the religion of nature is it possible for human beings to return to eros from the state of "guilt, inhibition, acquisition, and synthetic fantasy" in which they had been throughout history.[129]

Yet, the matriarchal religion of nature is not only based on eros but also on hate, life and death, growth and decay. However, Rubenstein asserts that following the Holocaust, "nature's inevitabilities are seen as part of the tragic course of existence itself rather than as God's retaliation against human sinfulness."[130] As we have seen, Rubenstein views the post-Holocaust age of the death of the historical God as a time in which heteronomous authority has collapsed.[131] In this instance, Rubenstein anticipates some of the anti-Jewish motifs later attributed to post-Christian feminists who portrayed Judaism as the antithesis of Goddess-centered religion. First, both Rubenstein and several post-Christian feminists argue that Hebrew and later Jewish monotheism repress sexuality, whereas matriarchal religions celebrate it.[132] By linking Jewish monotheism with a repression of sexuality, Rubenstein and the post-Christian feminists are clearly presenting a monolithic portrait of Judaism that fails to take into account the profound ambivalence toward sexuality that Jews have demonstrated through-out history.

In *Eros and the Jews*, David Biale traces a tension in Jewish thought from the biblical to the modern periods between procreation and sexual desire, reflecting the struggle between contradictory attractions of asceticism and gratification among competing Jewish cultures. Whereas Rubenstein uses *Portnoy's Complaint* as a guide to the history of Jewish sexual repression, Biale argues that this book reflects a set of myths and countermyths about Jewish at-titudes toward sexuality. On the one hand, Jews are perceived as having a posi-tive relationship to eros or even being hypersexual, while on the other hand, they are seen as ethically chaste, which is also interpreted by others as sexually re-pressed. Phillip Roth internalizes the antisemitic construction of the Jew as hypersexual and "neutralizes it; the Jew does not corrupt gentile America by his hypersexuality so much as he deeroticizes it with his comic fumbling."[133] Hence, both Roth and Rubenstein define their Jewish identities in dialogue with a Chris-tian culture that often prejudges it negatively. While Roth pokes fun at Jewish self-perception, Rubenstein offers a serious critique of it.

Next, Rubenstein prefigures an anti-Jewish polemic developed by Christian feminists when portraying the patriarchal, biblical-rabbinic God as an angry deity whose rigid laws were followed strictly and blindly, in contrast to a religion in which the submission to a maternal Ground of Being is necessary and benefi-cial. Moreover, by associating autonomy with a feminine image of God, he ex-presses a viewpoint shared by German feminists who argue that YHWH legitimizes authoritarianism that is anachronistic to feminist values of autonomy and individuality.[134] Finally, he anticipates another antithesis that appears in post-Christian feminist writings between a male Jewish God who is identified with abstract, ethereal culture and a pagan goddess who is identified with na-ture. In *Anti-Judaism in Feminist Religious Writings*, Von Kellenbach argues that this "nature-culture split" is ironic because it actually inverts the tradi-tional anti-Jewish Augustinian portrayal of Jews as a carnal people who under-stand only the material meaning of Scripture. In contrast, the Gentile and Jewish believers in Christ were considered by Paul to be "Israel according to the Spirit" because they understood the immaterial or spiritual meaning of scripture.[135]

Yet, despite his criticism for the repression by rabbinic patriarchy, Rubenstein offers a psychological analysis of rabbinic perceptions of divinity that uncovers an inner tension regarding the allegiance to masculine and feminine images of God in the rabbinic psyche. His portrayal of this tension defends Judaism from the anti-Jewish critiques of post-Christian feminists, while at the same time it anticipates their anti-Jewish myths. Rubenstein portrays the Mother Earth God-dess as exhibiting both destructive and creative characteristics. In fact, Rubenstein argues that the "mother goddess had two sides. She was a loving giver and sustainer of life. She was also an incomparably hideous and terrifying ogress. She inspires infinitely greater terror than the God of Judaism at His worst."[136] This terror was reflected in the rabbinic legends reflecting anxiety about being incorporated or consumed by the cannibal Mother in the form of fire, earth or, water.[137] Moreover, Rubenstein concludes that the *Aggadah* reflects a far greater number of instances in which the Rabbis illustrate a pre-Oedipal fear of the Mother Goddess than the Oedipal fear of castration by a tyrannical, Father God that is symbolized in the rite of circumcision.[138] In this instance, he avoids the tendency of post-Christian feminists to portray the male Jewish God as strong, aggressive, and militaristic versus the female goddess who is weak, peace loving, and healing.[139]

In addition, Rubenstein also recognizes a continued fascination as well as aversion toward Goddess worship by the Rabbis inherited from their biblical predecessors. This is illustrated in the attempt by religions of the Father God "to obliterate all traces of the older mother goddesses. The history of Judaism and Protestantism attests to the violence with which that project was carried out."[140] Yet, according to Rubenstein, the *Aggadah* illustrates how, despite the efforts of the Rabbis to repress her, the Mother Goddess is reflected in their worst fears as well as their deepest yearnings.[141] This corresponds to the fact that in the Hebrew Scriptures, attempts to repress Goddess worship actually reflect its continued persistence.[142] For example, in *Counter-traditions in the Bible*, Ilana Pardes has uncovered Ugaritic, Sumerian, and Egyptian Goddess-centered texts that parallel biblical myths of Eve, Zipporah, Miriam, Yocheved, Shifra, Puah, and Pharaoh's daughter.[143] This convergence of Goddess- and God-centered traditions confirms Rubenstein's psychological analysis.

However, Rubenstein focuses his critique of patriarchal religion solely on the Hebrew Scriptures and attributes the shift from matriarchal to patriarchal religion to Jewish monotheism. This resembles the post-Christian feminist portrayal of Judaism as the scapegoat for the destruction of Goddess worship and the mythical fall from matriarchy into patriarchy. Katharina von Kellenbach argues that patriarchy was established at least three centuries before the compilation of the biblical text, and therefore isolating "Hebrew monotheism as the ultimate step in the development of patriarchal religion is misleading and anti-Jewish in its consequence."[144] Moreover, while the cults of the Canaanite Goddesses Anat and Asherah became part of the Israelite cult of YHWH, the latter was too small "to have undermined the religious authority of the Egyptian Isis, Greek Aphrodite, Roman Venus and Assyrian Myllita."[145]

While in *The Religious Imagination*, Rubenstein cites the Jewish and later Protestant repression of Goddess worship, in *My Brother Paul*, he portrays Paul as recognizing the feminine aspect of divinity to some extent, despite the fact that his "view of the divine-human encounter was distorted by an overly masculine orientation he had probably inherited from rabbinic Judaism."[146] According to Rubenstein, Paul's religious images of "the warfare of the *brothers*, the atoning death of the *Son* and the gracious forgiveness of the *Father*" are all in-herited from the Rabbis.[147]

However, Rubenstein claims that in his portrayal of Christ as the Last Adam (1 Cor. 15.20–28), Paul was describing an eschatological return of the cosmos to its originating Sacred Womb through Christ. He perceives Paul to be saying that when human beings achieve a correct relationship with the Father, they will then be able to reunite with the Mother. Furthermore, he observes that Paul's images of cosmic exile and restoration reflect "a return to the maternal matrix and the lost omnipotence of the womb."[148] Here Rubenstein demonstrates to some extent what von Kellenbach describes Christian feminists as doing, dividing Paul into a feminist Christian self and a sexist Jewish self.[149] Although he does not discuss Paul's attitude toward women here, Rubenstein unwittingly presents Judaism as antithetical to feminist constructions of divinity in Christianity and subsequently as defec-tive or inferior. Paul's use of maternal divine imagery is associated with his Christian eschatology, while his use of masculine images is associated with a rabbinic, "overly masculine orientation," which Rubenstein ultimately must reject. He argues that in recognizing the feminine aspect of divinity, Paul overcame the rabbinic fear of women that manifested itself in repression of female deities, and he moved beyond his rabbinic colleagues toward an eschatological reunion with the Mother Goddess.[150]

Psychological Supersessionism? An Analysis of Pauline Christianity

In *My Brother Paul*, Rubenstein portrays Paul as a revolutionary Jewish mystic who liberated himself from a repressive rabbinic culture and facilitated the birth of Christianity. Rubenstein presents Pauline Christianity as psychologically more progressive than Judaism because of its recovery of what had been repressed in the rabbinic unconscious. While he claims to reject both "the normative Jewish and Christian solutions" to the problems of humanity, Rubenstein actually finds profound religio-psychological meaning in Christian motifs and sacraments, such as the baptism and the Eucharist. For him, they demonstrate the desire of the Christian community to permit "the resurfacing of the archaic wisdom of the unconscious among its believers to a far greater extent than did Judaism."[151]

However, the preceding statement from *My Brother Paul* appears to con-tradict earlier statements that he has made in regard to the psychological value of Judaism and Christianity. In *After Auschwitz*, Rubenstein argued that in re-gard to every significant human striving, "normative Judaism has always been as responsive to the covert and the unconscious as it has to the conscious and the rational."[152] Then, in *The Religious Imagination*, he insisted that neither Ju-daism nor Christianity is psychologically better or healthier than the other, but rather both contain "strong elements of both illness and health."[153] These conflicting statements confirm Rubenstein's ambivalence toward rabbinic Judaism and point to his ambiguous relationship with Christianity. It may be possible to reconcile these statements by reexamining Rubenstein's seemingly divergent path toward a post-Holocaust panentheistic theology. In desiring a return to the archaic worship of an immanent God of Nature, he found the prophetic components of both liberal Judaism and Protestant Christianity psychologically unhealthy and rejected them, because they only offer moral and rational exhortation to unrealistically improve human behavior. In contrast, priestly rituals recognize the unavoidable repetition of irrational human behavior in society and seek not to improve but more pragmatically to limit its destructiveness through controlled magic. He disagreed with modern Protestant and liberal Jewish thinkers who saw prophetic religion as an ethical advance over a more primitive and violent priestly form of religion, Rubenstein argued that the Holocaust is a perfect example of the failure of moral exhortation to improve the inherently violent nature of humanity.[154] Consequently, he found that to some extent, the priestly forms of both Judaism and Catholicism are equally healthy because they incorporate the most important purposes of the sacrificial cult as a unifying communal force and "an enormously efficacious instrument of moral and social control. It brought the ever-pressing problems of orality, aggression, and sadism into the domain of the sacred, where they could be regulated."[155]

In his essay "Atonement and Sacrifice in Contemporary Jewish Liturgy," Rubenstein points out that these shared sacrificial ideals are illustrated in the general concept of vicarious ritual atonement that lies at the heart of Yom Kippur for Jews and the Holy Communion ritual for Christians. He also finds other related examples of priestly rituals in the Jewish tradition that fulfill these purposes: the ritual of *kashrut* (Jewish dietary laws) that, like Holy Communion, calls attention to the problems of orality and cannibalism by making eating a sacramental act, and the *pidyon ha-ben* ritual, which involves the symbolic sacrifice of the first-born Jewish male. What is unique about these sacrificial rites is that they all originate from the pagan practices of ritual murder and ritual cannibalism, retaining their emotional and moral force while avoiding their gratuitous violence. Here Rubenstein praises the Rabbis for having the wisdom to sublimate the dangerous aspects of pagan rituals through a verbal reenactment of the concrete deed in liturgy and homiletics that would elicit many of the same communal responses that had previously only been made in response to the actual sacrifice.[156]

However, while Rubenstein complemented the Rabbis for sublimating traces of paganism in order to construct rituals that bring the community together in times of crisis, he criticized them for that very sublimation when he perceived it as preventing individuals like Paul and himself from attaining a closer relationship with God. According to Rubenstein, the Rabbis were responsive to unconscious human needs and emotions in terms of how they relate to each other under the watchful eye of a transcendent God. However, they were not as psychologically advanced as Paul when it came to constructing rituals that relate the individual directly to a more immanent God. Here Paul was ultimately blurring the conscious boundaries between God and humanity, something that the Rabbis were unable to countenance. Initially, in his attempt to construct a panentheistic theology after the Holocaust, Rubenstein was attracted to sublimated traces of paganism in both Judaism and Christianity. However, he would eventually discover the most pristine, unaltered image of the unity between God and world in the rituals of Pauline Christianity. By portraying Christianity as a psychological advance beyond Judaism, Rubenstein was unwittingly exhibiting a type of Christian supersessionism. According to him, rabbinic Judaism was superseded by a religion that rejected the legalistic obedience of a superego culture and furthered the process of liberating human consciousness from repression.[157]

In the beginning of *My Brother Paul*, Rubenstein emphasizes his solidarity with and empathy for Paul as a loyal Jew who could not find fulfillment in establishment Judaism. Rubenstein distinguishes himself from other Jewish interpreters of Paul at the time who had viewed him as "the ultimate enemy in early Christianity." Furthermore, he argues that the debate between Paul and the Rabbis had nothing to do with "whether Paul's theology was an 'advance' over first century Judaism," but rather whether Jesus was the messiah.[158]

Ironically, however, Rubenstein proceeds to view Paul's relationship to his fellow Jews with Christian anti-Jewish lenses, portraying Paul as rejecting a society that was characterized by "instinctual discipline," sublimating feelings in order to diminish anxiety over guilt and estrangement from God. Ultimately, Rubenstein promotes the very perception that he had apparently rejected, namely, that Paul initiated a "psychological triumph" of Christianity over Judaism that actually may warrant Jewish hostility toward him.[159] The "psychological triumph" was the fact that Paul had discovered a way to achieve an acceptable relationship with God that was based not on "obedient submission to the will of the Father" required by the Rabbis but on identification with the crucified older brother, Christ. According to Rubenstein, the Rabbis suppressed any identification with God, emphasizing God's total incommensurability with humanity. Moreover, they wanted to curb the gratification of infantile yearnings for omnipotence and immortality. Unfortunately, this only reinforced Jewish anxiety because the harder Jews tried to improve their relationship with God, the more they realized how great the distance remained between them.[160] In contrast, the "psychological triumph of the Cross was such that through it no man could be so fallen, degraded, or devoid of worldly accomplishment that he was unable to identify with divinity."[161] Through identification with Christ, Paul and later Christians were able to vicariously experience omnipotence and immortality, thus liberating themselves from rabbinic repression.

Paul achieved this identification in his encounter with the risen Christ on the road to Damascus. According to Rubenstein's psychoanalytic interpretation, this experience led to a temporary loss of Paul's normal ego functions, as his normal thinking process, or "secondary process," was supplanted by his id's level of mental functioning, or "primary process."[162] Rubenstein interprets this experience to be one of creative regression in which Paul was able to "return to that period in his mental development that preceded the separation of self and world, the division into subject and object." Subsequently, using "the imagery of the primary process," Paul was able to assert that "the Christian's ego boundaries had been dissolved into the larger unity of the body of Christ."[163] Rubenstein claims that what made Paul an "authentic religious genius" was his ability to use this imagery to recover "the emotional reality" unavailable to him as a Pharisee without permanent loss of his ego function, which greatly contributed to "the Christian psychological revolution."[164]

Rubenstein's psychoanalysis of Paul and the Christian rituals associated with him corresponds to a traditional Christian supersessionist claim that what is hidden or latent in Judaism becomes manifest in Christianity. Specifically, Paul envisions a dual structure of reality in which outer physical reality corresponds to and signifies an inner, higher, spiritual reality. This dichotomy is symbolized by Paul's use of the phrases "Israel according to the flesh" and "Israel according to the Spirit." Sparked by Rosemary Radford Ruether's indictment of Paul as anti-Jewish, a number of diverse reinterpretations of his writing have appeared since World War II, including Daniel Boyarin's view that Paul's dichotomy reflects an indigenous tension regarding the particularity and universality of the people Israel. Yet, even in Boyarin's reading of Paul, this dichotomy suggests a perhaps unintentional supersession of the "Israel of the flesh," ethnic Jews who retain their particularity, with its signifier, "Israel of the spirit," those Jews and Gentiles who enter into the universal community of Christ. This would later become the basis for the Augustinian supersessionist claim that the carnal Jews are blind to the spiritual meaning of their own Scriptures that prefigure Christ and the new chosen people, Christians.[165]

Rubenstein perpetuates the dichotomy between internal and external reality in the sense that Paul uncovers the archaic strivings hidden in the depths of the rabbinic psyche and enables them to become fully conscious. However, Rubenstein actually inverts what Paul saw as internal and external. For Rubenstein, bodily or sensuous instincts would correspond to Paul's inner, higher spiritual reality because they are primary process imagery repressed in the rabbinic unconscious. In contrast, rabbinic *Halakhah* is considered abstract or immaterial, yet it corresponds to Paul's external reality because it represents the secondary-process thinking at work on the conscious level. The Christian rituals of baptism and Eucharist facilitate this psychological supersession because they bring to consciousness internal, archaic needs sublimated by the external, punitive framework of the Rabbis. In regard to baptism, Paul gave theological expression to the subliminal, human understanding of water as the place of life in the womb in which one is born and reborn, as well as the tomb to which one returns at death. Moreover, baptism enables one to escape from a Jewish Father God who condemned all humanity to death for its sins, illustrating what can be understood as the "Divine Infanticide." Through the rebirth of baptism, one is provided with the hope for a new "noninfanticidal Parent." Finally, by equating baptism with circumcision, Paul uncovered the severity of intergenerational hostility between heavenly and earthly fathers and sons that, when unmasked, can also be understood as a repressed infanticidal impulse. He subsequently confirmed that one could not overcome the hostility of the Father God by a token removal of flesh in circumcision, but rather only through symbolic death and rebirth in baptism, which Christ underwent when facing the ultimate wrath of God.[166]

Rubenstein's discussion of baptism as a response to the Divine Infanticide mirrors his own experience, in the sense that he described the death of his son in 1950 as a Divine Infanticide. Following his son's death, he realized that no matter how well he observed the commandments, he would still die a mortal human being. It was as if he himself had died and was reborn in a "second womb." Although he did not have faith in a messianic redeemer like Paul, Rubenstein was able to overcome the hostility of the Father God by undergoing his own creative regression through therapy and envisioning a return to the maternal matrix.[167]

Using a Freudian interpretation, Rubenstein claims that the Eucharist brings to the surface the simultaneous archaic desire for identification with and deicidal displacement of the omnipotent Father God through ingestion.[168] However, he argues against Freud that in the ritual of Holy Communion, Christians do not repeat the primal crime of deicide against the Father God, but rather gain omnipotence and express deicidal hostility against the elder brother, Christ, without the direct involvement of the Father God.[169] In addition, for Paul and his early Christian followers, Christ became the perfect sacrifice who could not be destroyed in the act of consumption because he had already been slaughtered and resurrected. Rubenstein claims that Paul's identification of Christ with the loaf of bread as the sacrifice "can be seen as an example of how the muted and latent expressions of archaic sacrificial ritual in Judaism became explicit in Christianity."[170] Ultimately, Rubenstein intuits neopagan motifs in these Christian rituals that serve as prototypes for his own post-Holocaust panentheistic theology. Hence, he portrays a Christian psychological advancement over rabbinic Judaism by recovering the pagan roots of Christianity. Therefore, what is most important to Rubenstein in Pauline Christianity is actually its alleged pagan foundation.

Like Paul, Rubenstein appears to be paradigmatic of Jewish identity in the sense that he "represents the interface between *Jew* as a self-identical essence and *Jew* as a construction constantly being remade."[171] For much of their lives, both men expressed a tension between preserving their Jewish heritage and critiquing it from a Christian perspective, using the pagan tools of Greek wisdom. It is also clear, however, that both Paul and Rubenstein wanted to transcend Jewish and Christian boundaries and achieve a universal oneness with all humanity in a world immanently permeated by divinity. In the case of Rubenstein, this desire for universality is reflected in his rejection of Jewish and Christian "religio-historic myths" in order to develop a community of persons, instead of two religious societies centered around "dehumanizing myths." He argues that Jews and Christians are united in guilt following the Holocaust and should concentrate more on their shared human existence than on what their religious institutions promise and threaten. In this era after the death of God, Rubenstein conceives of the divine-human relationship as one in which God is the ocean and we are the waves. While each wave has its moment of distinction as a separate entity, it is never entirely distinct from the oceanic ground into which it is subsumed.[172] In this way, he illustrates his desire for dissolution of individual identity in the universal, primordial Ground of Being, while still maintaining human autonomy.

However, in rejecting heteronomous repression, Rubenstein seeks a scapegoat and proceeds to recapitulate the mythical distinctions between Judaism and Christianity that he had supposedly negated. Through psychoanalysis, he tries to pinpoint the source of his own sense of impotence that is shaped to a great extent by an ambivalent relationship with his Christian environment. In the process, he appears to project his own anxiety onto that of the Jewish people, branding rabbinic Judaism as the scapegoat for a repressed and self-punitive culture. Ultimately, his portrayal of rabbinic Judaism as the culprit reflects the profound yet perhaps undetected impact of Christian thought on his own perception of Jewish identity. In Rubenstein's critique of rabbinic Judaism, the impact of Christian thought is at times complete, while at other times it is more partial and implicit, but always prevalent. Rubenstein seems to read rabbinic texts with pre-Holocaust, German Lutheran, and Protestant lenses when portraying rabbinic Judaism as a legalistic culture whose members submissively obey an omnipotent, transcendent Lawgiver. His distinction between the transcendent, wrathful God of biblical and rabbinic Judaism and his own immanent, post-Holocaust God clearly approximates the negative image of the Jewish God reflected in the Marcionite theological dichotomy that Rubenstein also applies to Christian theism. Alternatively, while Rubenstein's proto-feminist critique of rabbinic Judaism lays the foundation for a feminist form of Judaism and may even empower Jewish women, there is still a subtle, yet pervasive Christian anti-Judaism at work. Finally, although rooted in paganism, Rubenstein's psychological subordination of rabbinic Judaism to Pauline Christianity reflects an underlying Christian claim of supersessionism.

In conclusion, I agree with Braiterman that "Rubenstein's resistance to tradition and modern readings of tradition constitutes his surest contribution to the post-Holocaust readings of tradition that have followed him."[173] However, I would argue that what distinguishes Rubenstein as a modern and contemporary Jewish thinker is the construction of his Jewish identity in dialectic with Christianity. By rejecting the heteronomous God of covenant and election, Rubenstein claims to be "out of the box" containing Judaism and Christianity.[174] However, his critique of Judaism is permeated by Christian motifs and anti-Jewish myths, suggesting that he indeed remains in the realm of Jewish-Christian dialectic. Like his predecessors Rosenzweig and Schoeps, Rubenstein tended at times to view Judaism from a Christian perspective. Each of these thinkers seemed to internalize anti-Jewish or antisemitic myths while utilizing them for different purposes. Rosenzweig transformed accusations of Jewish abnormality into affirmations of Jewish superiority, while Schoeps and Rubenstein seemed to accept Christian negative portrayals of Judaism and incorporated this opposition into their own critiques of rabbinic legalism. Nonetheless, while perpetuating Jewish-Christian opposition to some extent, all three of these theologians attempted to achieve a level of coexistence between the two cultures that had not existed prior to the twentieth century.

Rubenstein's radical reconstruction of Judaism in relation to Christianity after the Holocaust was extremely significant because it led other post-Holocaust theologians like Eliezer Berkovits and Irving Greenberg to reexamine Jewish theology in light of its encounter with Christianity throughout history leading up to and culminating in the Holocaust. These theologians were forced to challenge "theodic" justifications for God's relationship to evil with the "antitheodic" condemnations of God in the aftermath of the Holocaust leveled by Rubenstein. At the same time, they attempted to ascertain the role of Christianity in precipitating the theological quagmire in which they now found themselves, and they began to reassess their current standing with God vis-à-vis their Christian contemporaries. Although they were both forced to deal with the same theological dilemmas articulated by Rubenstein, Berkovits and Greenberg would each interpret them differently in light of Christianity.

Berkovits followed Rubenstein in rejecting the traditional Deuteronomic theodicy that all suffering is divine punishment for sin and openly questioning a "beneficent providence" after the Holocaust. Yet in support of the faithful survivors, Berkovits constructed a post-Holocaust theology that has a strong theodic thrust, in that it transfers much of the blame for the Holocaust from God to humanity and, more specifically, to Christian culture.[175] In *Faith after the Holocaust*, Berkovits appeared to construct a counterhistory of Judaism and Christianity by recasting Christian culture as the representative of a this-worldly "power history" in opposition to a powerless Israel that occupies a metaphysical "faith history." Just as we saw with Rosenzweig, his reconfiguration of Judaism and Christianity appears to be a mirror image of the Augustinian dualistic historiosophy based on the categories of the "City of God" and "City of Man." Berkovits ultimately reconstructed a post-Holocaust Jewish identity that demonstrates divine power through political powerlessness. He accomplished this by exploiting Christian models of suffering and inverting antisemitic myths regarding Jewish power. In this way, he was able to reconnect Jews to an absent God and rally them against an unregenerate Christian Other after the Holocaust.[176]

In contrast to Berkovits's anti-Christian polemic in *Faith after the Holocaust,* Greenberg's theological reconfiguration of Judaism and Christianity after the Holocaust would follow the model of Rubenstein more closely. Theologically, Greenberg would go further than Berkovits in simulating Rubenstein's anti-theodicy without abandoning traditional Jewish myths. While publicly branding Rubenstein an atheist, Greenberg's replacement of a theonomous covenant with one initiated by human autonomy after the Holocaust would resemble Rubenstein's rejection of an omnipotent, transcendent God in favor of a more immanent God who is manifest through human religious activity. Moreover, Greenberg would take up Rubenstein's cause of reintegrating Jews and Christians after the Holocaust, and, ironically, by constructing his Jewish theology in conversation with Christianity, would contribute to the Jewish-Christian dialectic. Whereas Rubenstein tended to negate Jewish identity in favor of a paganized Christianity, would appear to subsume Christianity in a post-Holocaust Jewish theology.

4

Between Dialectic and Dialogue

Irving Greenberg's Organic Model of the Jewish-Christian Relationship

For Irving Greenberg, like his contemporary Rubenstein, the Holocaust marked a theological watershed and consequently a significant turning point in Jewish-Christian relations. Yet while they both view the Holocaust as theologically and historically unique, they differ somewhat in their interpretations of this uniqueness and what response it requires. Whereas Rubenstein views the Holocaust as the punitive destruction of an omnipotent God, Greenberg sees God as actually abdicating his covenantal responsibility to protect the Jewish people from annihilation. Consequently, Rubenstein understands the Holocaust as the death knell for the historical God of Israel and an end to the myths of covenant and election. Greenberg agrees with Rubenstein that the Holocaust marks an end to the historical covenant between God and Israel as it was previously understood. However, Greenberg sees the Holocaust as a revelatory event that ushers in a new, "voluntary covenant" initiated by the Jewish people in response to a divine invitation to become more involved in the work of redemption.[1]

Moreover, Greenberg follows Rubenstein in arguing that the Holocaust affects not only Jews theologically but also Christians. Yet while Rubenstein claims that the Holocaust necessitates the abandonment of Jewish and Christian myths to facilitate dialogue, Greenberg interprets the Holocaust and the establishment of the State of Israel as "orientating events" that lead religious adherents to "reorient" themselves toward God and each other not by becoming more human but by becoming better Jews and Christians who are more aware of their interconnected identities. For Greenberg, the

Holocaust and the establishment of the State of Israel "illumine and fundamentally reinterpret the meaning and significance of the past 1900 years and the constellation of Judaism and Christianity."[2]

Reaching across Borders: A Biographical Sketch

Throughout his career, Irving Greenberg has broken down religious barriers both inside and outside of the Jewish community, striving to unify the American Jewish community and reintegrate it with Christian culture. His desire for good relations among Jews and between Jews and Christians grew largely out of his response to the horror of the Holocaust and its impact on both Jews and Christians. He has attempted to fulfill this desire through theological reflection as well as social activism. Greenberg was born in 1933 to European Jewish immigrants. His father was a kosher butcher and an Orthodox rabbi in Boro Park, New York. Greenberg himself was educated in the modern Orthodox day school system and became involved in a religious Zionist youth movement, Hashomer Hadati, that later became known as B'nei Akiva. While attending Brooklyn College, he entered Beth Joseph Rabbinical Seminary, an Orthodox yeshiva where he became fascinated with Rabbi Israel Salanter, the founder of the nineteenth-century eastern European, Orthodox Musar movement that focused on ethics as well as Torah study. The combination of his father's example and his exposure to the Musar movement at the yeshiva influenced Greenberg's lifelong tension between intellectual pursuits and grassroots community service. In 1953, he graduated from Brooklyn College while at the same time becoming ordained as a rabbi at Beth Joseph Seminary.

As an undergraduate at Brooklyn College and later as a graduate student at Harvard University, Greenberg would also become interested in the encounter of Judaism with the secular world of Western culture through his study of science and intellectual history. During these years, he became attracted to the work of a prominent Christian as well as a Jewish scholar who had also explored the tension between religion and secular thought: the neo-Orthodox Protestant thinker Reinhold Niebuhr and the great spokesman for modern Orthodoxy, Rabbi Joseph Soloveitchik. In 1957, Greenberg married Blu Genauer, who became a prominent Orthodox feminist. Under her influence, Greenberg became dedicated to breaking down the barriers between Jewish men and women, offering a serious critique of what he considers to be the "authoritarianism" of his own Orthodox leaders and their resulting failure to be more open to women's experience and their participation in the covenant.[3] In 1960, Greenberg received his doctorate from Harvard and began to articulate his positions on these issues as a history professor at Yeshiva University. In 1961–62, Greenberg studied intensively about the Holocaust as a visiting professor at Tel Aviv University in Israel and was transformed religiously and intellectually. As a result, Greenberg would devote his career to teaching about and developing a theological response to the Holocaust.

After his return to Yeshiva University, however, his general reemphasis on Jewish as well as Holocaust studies met some resistance and led him to temporarily devote his time to being a pulpit rabbi for the Riverdale Jewish Center in 1965. There he tried more successfully to integrate secular and religious studies as well as a study of the Holocaust and the State of Israel at a day school level. He also began to enter into dialogue with Protestant thinkers A. Roy Eckardt, Paul van Buren, and Franklin Littell, who were also dealing with these issues from a Christian perspective and subsequently attempting to reformulate their identities in relation to Judaism. His dialogue with Christian thinkers about the Holocaust and the need for a joint theological response led to the publication of his first and arguably most important essay on the Holocaust, "Cloud of Smoke, Pillar of Fire: Judaism, Christianity and Modernity after the Holocaust." This article was based on a paper he presented at the 1974 "International Symposium on the Holocaust" held at the Cathedral of Saint John the Divine in New York City.[4] He has continued to reconstruct the covenantal relationship between Judaism and Christianity throughout history in subsequent essays, most recently in the article "Judaism and Christianity: Covenants of Redemption," in *Christianity in Jewish Terms*.[5]

Greenberg has attempted to unify Jews across denominations and genders, reconcile religion and secularism, and redefine Jewish identity in relation to Christianity in response to the Holocaust. Yet as a result of his efforts to break down barriers, he has faced opposition at Yeshiva University and in the modern Orthodox community as a whole. Subsequently, he left his congregation and became the founding chairman of the Department of Jewish Studies at City College of the City University of New York in 1972. While at City College, Greenberg, together with Elie Wiesel and Steven Shaw, established the National Jewish Conference Center that later became known as the National Jewish Center for Learning and Leadership (CLAL), which Greenberg directed from 1974 to 1997. This institution facilitates adult and leadership education in the American Jewish community, promoting intra-Jewish dialogue and Jewish unity.[6]

Most recently, Greenberg has become the president of the Jewish Life Network, whose mission is to create new institutions that foster religious and cultural programs for American Jews, such as "The Partnership for Excellence in Jewish Education" and "Birthright Israel," a program sending diaspora Jewish youth to Israel. Accordingly, in his books *The Jewish Way: Living the Holidays* (1988) and *Living in the Image of God* (1998), Greenberg has attempted to apply his post-Holocaust theology of voluntary covenant to the everyday lives of individual Jews. In the former, he illuminates and justifies the concrete observance of Jewish holidays, *Halakhah*, and ritual innovations, while in the latter he discusses other practical dimensions of contemporary Jewish life, including learning, the role of women, the Jewish family, the current situation of modern

Orthodoxy, leadership training, the Holocaust, Israel, and Jewish unity.[7] Currently, he also serves as the chairman of the United States Holocaust Memorial Council, which oversees the United States Holocaust Memorial Museum in Washington, D.C., and general Holocaust education on behalf of the U.S. government and the American people. Ultimately, through his theological writings and even more through his social activism, Greenberg has had a tremendous impact on the American Jewish community as a whole, moving beyond Jewish parochialism and reaching across the borders of Jewish and Christian cultures.

Holocaust and the State of Israel: Reorienting Jewish and Christian Identities

In his reconfiguration of Judaism and Christianity, Greenberg condemned Christian complicity in the Holocaust and Christianity's anti-Jewish "teaching of contempt" throughout history, yet he warned against using the Holocaust as an excuse for Jewish triumphalism. He attempted to reconceptualize the relationship between Judaism and Christianity in a "new organic model" that would enable "both sides to respect the full nature of the other in all its faith-claims."[8] Greenberg developed this "new organic model" by engaging in dialogue with Christian thinkers A. Roy Eckardt and Paul van Buren, who responded to his call to reconstruct Jewish and Christian identities in response to the Holocaust. Using a framework similar to those developed by Eckardt and van Buren, Greenberg perceived Judaism and Christianity to be dialectically united under a dual covenant.[9]

Greenberg subsequently followed Eckardt in his own theological interpretation of the Holocaust and the establishment of the State of Israel, by viewing their relationship to each other using the terms "crucifixion" and "resurrection." Yet, like Eckardt, Greenberg inverted the meaning of the crucifixion, accepting it only as a model for total degradation rather than redemptive suffering.[10] Moreover, Greenberg reclaimed the biblical "suffering servant" in Isa. 53 as a Jewish figure, disassociating it from Christ in order to account for Jewish suffering in the Holocaust. Hence, while reconstructing Jewish identity in relation to Christianity, Greenberg still perpetuated the Jewish-Christian dialectic to an extent by painting a somewhat totalizing portrait of Christianity and inverting the traditionally anti-Jewish symbolic structure that Stephen Haynes describes as the "witness people myth." In the myth as it was originally constructed by Augustine, Jews were seen as witnesses to Christian authenticity and as proof of supersessionism. Therefore, they have to be preserved until the eschaton yet subjugated for their failure to believe in Christ. Following the Holocaust, however, Christian theologians like Eckardt and van Buren inverted the myth by no longer seeing Jews as symbols of Christian superiority but rather as symbols of Christian failure and self-abnegation. While Jewish fate is no longer seen as a sign of God's judgment on Israel for failing to accept Christ, it becomes a sign of impending divine judgment on the Church for its anti-Judaism.[11]

Ironically, we will see that by constructing a Jewish theology in conversation with Christianity, Greenberg tends to subsume Christianity into a Jewish framework. Greenberg develops his theological interpretation of the Holocaust and the establishment of the State of Israel through dialogue with Eckardt and van Buren, yet he unwittingly contributes to a Christian remythologization of Judaism following the Holocaust that tends to negate Christian difference in the process of overcompensating for a history of anti-Judaism. As a result, Christianity appears at times to be a mere outgrowth of Judaism whose sole function is to be "Judaism for the Gentiles."[12] Thus, while Greenberg attempts to reconfigure the Jewish-Christian relationship following the Holocaust, he ultimately redraws the boundaries on his terms without fully respecting Christian difference.

For Greenberg, the Holocaust and the establishment of the State of Israel were events that changed the self-understanding of Jews and Christians in relation to each other and challenged them to reconsider the very foundations of their faith traditions. Greenberg argues that because they share the notion of a God acting in history, Jews and Christians accept the idea that revelation is unfinished and can be affected by later events in history. He states that both Jewish and Christian religions have come to affirm the value of human life and its ultimate redemption based on their fundamental revelatory experiences of God in history.[13] These experiences "bring humans into contact with a reality beyond themselves; that is, they reveal that behind the mundane, everyday reality . . . is a ground that nurtures its life and value and gives it direction."[14] Hence, the revelatory event orients the adherents in the right direction on the path toward redemption. In the case of the Jews, this experience was the Exodus from Egypt, and for Christians, the events of Jesus' life, death, and resurrection.[15] Yet the Holocaust was the "most radical contradiction to the fundamental statements of human value and divine concern in both religions," while the establishment of the State of Israel revealed the need "to create and rehabilitate the divine image in a human community."[16]

Jewish Orientating Events

Greenberg explains that for the Jews, the Exodus has a dual significance. On the one hand, it is "a norm by which all of life and all other experience can be judged and oriented." Hence, the event itself makes two normative claims: First it affirms the existence of a caring God who "transcends human power." Second, human beings are to be viewed as God's creatures that are valuable and possess freedom.[17] However, because it is a historical event, the Exodus does not eradicate the evil in history. Instead, it becomes a model for an alternative conception of the world that is in dialectical tension with reality. Thus, while the present historical reality is acknowledged, the Exodus paradigm cannot be viewed as legitimate. Yet at the same time, history itself cannot be accepted as normative because it does not meet the ideal standards of the Exodus model and therefore must be overcome.[18]

Just as the Exodus model reflects a dialectic between ideal norms and the real world, the credibility of Jewish faith is dialectical as well. It is a testimony by the Jewish people of what the final redemption will confirm which is based on its own experience. Yet this ultimate truth is not reflected in current reality. Hence, faith is neither "pure abstraction," which is unaffected by contradictory events, nor is it "purely empirical," because it is not immediately refuted by historical disasters such as exile, persecution, and even the genocide of the Holocaust. Greenberg describes Jewish faith as a "testimony anchored in history, in constant tension with it, subject to revision and understanding as well as to fluctuation in credibility due to the unfolding of events."[19]

The tension between Jewish faith and history reached its peak following the two most cataclysmic events in Jewish history, the destruction of the Second Temple and the Holocaust. In each case, there was a reformulation of traditional self-understanding and a transformation of the relationship between God and Israel, yet still within the covenantal framework. In response to the first tragedy, the Rabbis reconceived God as a hidden "presence, as *Shechina*, not as automatic intervener who brings victory to the deserving." Moreover, according to Greenberg, "God had 'constricted' or imposed self-limitation to allow Jews to take on true partnership in the covenant." In fact, the Rabbis actually reaccepted or renewed the covenant of Sinai following the destruction of the Temple on the new terms of the covenant model reflected in the story of Purim, the festival of lots. Greenberg states that this covenant is also redemptive, "but it is built around a core event that is brought about by a more hidden Divine Presence acting in partnership with human messengers."[20]

Yet, as a result of the genocide of the Holocaust, the authority of the covenant was broken. Greenberg agrees with the post-Holocaust Jewish theologian Elie Wiesel's position that God did not adhere to the terms of the covenant, which stipulates that Jews will protect the Torah in return for God's protection of them. Moreover, God can no longer command allegiance to the covenant nor enforce it through punishment, because of the divine order to pursue a covenantal mission that was ultimately suicidal. According to Greenberg, in a moral relationship, one cannot command another to "step forward to die." In regard to divine punishment, Greenberg claims, "there is no risked punishment so terrible that it can match the punishment risked by continuing faithfulness to the covenant."[21]

Like other post-Holocaust Jewish theologians, Rubenstein, Fackenheim, and Wiesel, Greenberg views the Holocaust as a completely unique event in Jewish history in terms of its absolute evil that subsequently demands some type of theological reformulation.[22] Yet, in Greenberg's case, one could ask why other tragic events in which Jews were killed for protecting the Torah, that is, destruction of the Second Temple, the Crusades, the Spanish Inquisition, did not warrant an abrogation of their covenant. Moreover, what about the Jews who actually did commit suicide voluntarily for the purpose of martyrdom, or *kiddush hashem* (the sanctification of God's name)? Unlike Fackenheim, Greenberg does not raise the distinction between prior acts of Jewish martyrdom and the Holocaust in which Jews did not have a choice whether or not they wanted to die.[23]

In his critique of Greenberg, Steven Katz raises the question that if there ever was a valid covenant between God and Israel, then how could it be shattered by Hitler? Conversely, he asks, if Hitler was able to break the covenant, was it ever valid in the first place? Katz bases his questions on the assumption that divine revelations and promises are immune from human destruction by their very definition. He states that if "Hitler could break God's covenantal promises, God would not be God and Hitler would indeed be central to Jewish belief."[24]

Greenberg then makes a somewhat radical move by maintaining that following their release from covenantal obligations following the Holocaust, the majority of the Jewish people chose voluntarily to accept the covenant again. When comparing this voluntary covenant with the renewal of the covenant following the destruction of the Second Temple, Greenberg states that if "after the Temple's de-struction, Israel moved from junior participant to true partner in the covenant, then after the *Shoah*, the Jewish people is called upon to become the senior partner in action." He explains that God is now calling upon Israel and all of humanity to prevent another Holocaust and bring the redemption on their own with divine encouragement but not divine assistance.[25]

For Greenberg, the State of Israel was established in response to this divine revelation. The Jews heard God's call to action and responded by taking responsibility and creating their own state. Hence, they took power into their own hands to prevent another Holocaust from occurring.[26] Yet Greenberg is careful to say that the Holocaust was not necessary for the development of the voluntary covenant or the State of Israel. Drawing upon the modern Orthodox theologian Joseph Soloveitchik's discussion of covenant in "Lonely Man of Faith," Greenberg claims that the voluntary stage was implicit in the covenantal model from the beginning by virtue of its "*Juridic-Halakhic* principle of free negotiations, mutual assumption of duties, and full recognition of the equal rights of both concerned with the covenant." He argues that Israel can only gain full dignity when it takes full responsibility for its redemption and that of all humanity. Additionally, Greenberg bases the redistribution of power in the covenantal relationship on modern culture's empowerment of the human being. He perceives the development of Zionism in the nineteenth century as an attempt to bring about this empowerment of the human covenantal partner prior to the Holocaust. Yet neither secularists nor traditionalists were able to perceive this redistribution of power occurring in the covenantal relationship. Many modern secularists viewed human empowerment as a rejection of the divine-human relationship in favor of human liberation. However, Greenberg argues that this "misconstruction" of the divine-human relationship "is directly implicated in the emergence of pathological forms of total human power . . . which reach a climax in the *Shoah* itself." At the same time, many traditionalists continued to see the covenant as involuntary and opposed a higher degree of human responsibility for it. Ultimately, according to Greenberg, the Holocaust was "a tragedy which forces us to face up to an issue and a responsibility which was long coming."[27]

We can compare Greenberg's discussion of the Holocaust as "orientating experience" to Emil Fackenheim's portrayal of a "root experience" in *God's Presence in History* (1970). Influenced by Greenberg's concept of orientating experience, Fackenheim argues that the root experience is the foundation of Jewish faith in a God who is present in history.[28] He states that there are three characteristics of the root experience: dialectic between the present and the past, a public, historical character, and accessibility to the present.[29] Like Greenberg, Fackenheim claims that dialectical contradictions arise when trying to testify to the validity of the Exodus as a paradigm for faith. One contradiction that Fackenheim describes occurring in the root experience is between divine power and human freedom. Greenberg alludes to this in his description of the orientating experience yet does not call it a contradiction. Fackenheim and Greenberg both discuss the contradiction between divine involvement in the world and the existence of evil.[30]

However, Fackenheim appears to diverge from Greenberg in his distinction of "root experiences" from "epoch making events" such as the destruction of the First and Second Temples, the Maccabean revolt, the expulsion from Spain, and the Holocaust. According to Fackenheim, these tragedies "each made a new claim upon the Jewish faith. . . . They did not, however, produce a new faith."[31] In this earlier stage of his career, Fackenheim, argued that while the Holocaust is historically unique, it does not warrant a complete theological reformulation. Despite his claim regarding the historical conditionality of faith, he still portrayed a traditional, biblical image of a commanding divine presence arising out of the ashes of Auschwitz. However, at the same time, this "commanding voice" was actually a fleeting trace of divinity out of which emerged a series of seemingly contradictory obligations loosely centered on the Jewish duty to survive so as not to "hand Hitler posthumous victories." Later in *To Mend the World* (1982), Fackenheim's commanding voice had been reduced to its barest essence, the human affirmation to live with dignity in the face of utter degradation.[32]

For Greenberg, the horror of the Holocaust completely alters the Exodus paradigm in terms of divine omnipotence and subsequently revises the testimony of faith to be autonomous and not theonomous. In fact, Greenberg criticizes Fackenheim's and the Orthodox post-Holocaust theologian Berkovits's responses to the Holocaust as being too weak because their theological refor- mulation is too modest.[33] Alternatively, he argues that Rubenstein goes too far in his response, accusing him of being an atheist. Greenberg asserts, "Neither classical theism nor atheism is adequate to incorporate the incommensurabil- ity of the Holocaust . . . neither is credible alone—in the presence of the burn- ing children."[34]

Yet Rubenstein is clearly not an atheist in his construction of a post-Holo- caust paneatheistic theology, and Fackenheim is not a "classical theist" because his portrayal of "The Commanding Voice of Auschwitz" is actually fragmented and is arguably more of a personal response to the Holocaust than a divine im- perative. In fact, as Zachary Braiterman observes, Fackenheim's career-long en- counter with the Holocaust shatters his original fideistic faith in the divine human relationship, ultimately replacing it with a vision of cosmic rupture and disconti- nuity.[35] Both Greenberg and Fackenheim describe a revelation emanating from Auschwitz that is addressed to both religious and secular Jews whose authentic response led to the creation of the State of Israel.[36] Moreover, both agree that the events of the Holocaust and the establishment of the State of Israel have dissolved the dichotomy between secular and religious, inaugurating a new era of "secular holiness," in Fackenheim's words, or "holy secularism," as Greenberg describes it.[37] To demonstrate this secular reorientation of Jewish identity, Greenberg points to three factors: First, in the Holocaust, Hitler did not distinguish between reli- gious and secular Jews in his destruction of European Jewry. Second, the State of Israel has "shifted the balance of Jewish activity and concern to the secular enter- prises of society building, social justice and human politics." Third, the 'secular' activity of building the Jewish state" guarantees the existence of the Jewish people, whose survival reflects God's awesomeness. In this instance, Jewish secularity actually manifests a divine presence that has become far more subtle and elusive since the Holocaust, illustrating a greater human role in redemption.[38]

Greenberg refers to a "secular revelation" emanating from the State of Is- rael that reflects the moral and theological ambiguity of the post-Holocaust era and subsequently is "flawed, partial, real."[39] This revelation initiates a process of "dialectical secularization" because it opposes the "absolutization of the secu- lar" that led to the affirmation of human power by Hitler and the Nazis yet at the same time promotes the importance of secularity as the new locus of God's hidden presence in history.[40] However, this secular revelation may be "flawed, partial and real" not because of moral and theological ambiguity but because Greenberg's description of its divine origin and how it is communicated is ambiguous. Katz argues that Greenberg's God-idea generates more theological problems than it solves. According to Katz, Greenberg needs to clarify the onto- logical characteristics of God as a silent partner as well as the implications of this metaphysical principle on traditional Jewish concerns such as covenant, reward and punishment, morality, Torah, commandments, and redemption. Katz questions whether Greenberg's God is capable of being the author of moral value or the guarantor of salvation, and whether or not Jews can pray to such a God on Yom Kippur.[41]

Greenberg attempts to respond to these questions by explaining how this secular revelation may be understood in terms of halakhic practice and how this hidden God is also a force for morality. First, he argues against what he considers to be the fundamentalism of his own Orthodox community and its failure to apply "religious values and practices to all areas of secular life. But this can only be done when Orthodoxy works through in depth, the modern experience so that it speaks to this generation and in it."[42] Greenberg claims that a "secular halakhah" would lead Orthodoxy away from its ascetic tendencies toward "directed enjoyment," and this would have tremendous appeal to those Jewish youth who are abandoning tradition for secular culture. One example of this directed enjoyment would be to make ". . . sexuality the expression of a loving relationship and discovery of the uniqueness of the body and soul of another," instead of just emphasizing that men and women must regulate their sexual behavior through relationships and fidelity or that they must abstain from sexual intercourse during the period of menstruation.[43]

However, one could argue that Greenberg's theological concepts of voluntary covenant and secular halakhah have had less impact on Orthodox Jewish practice, than they have had on secular Jews who have tried to rediscover their Judaism following the Holocaust in nontraditional ways. In fact, Alan Berger claims that the voluntary nature of Jewish obligation is suggested in the literature of second-generation Holocaust witnesses "whose emphasis is on existential rather than halakhic modes of being Jewish." Moreover, because it transcends "denominational squabbles and petty triumphalism, this covenant provides a theological base for genuine pluralism and is intimately linked to Jewish survival."[44]

Berger observes that in the work of Lev Raphael and Art Spiegelman, the behavior of their characters, rather than any traditional theological formulations, exemplifies the voluntary covenant. In Raphael's book of short stories, *Dancing on Tisha b'Av*, his characters voluntarily accept the covenant by reading books on the Holocaust and getting involved in relationships with individuals who help them come to terms with their parents' Holocaust experience and their own identities. In Spiegelman's comic book, *Maus*, the stories of his father's survival in Auschwitz indicate a combination of religion and random chance, demonstrating the hiddenness of God and the role of humanity in the voluntary covenant. Berger concludes that while Raphael and Spiegelman abandon traditional forms of Jewish identity, the fact that they wish to remain Jews "underscores that the voluntary covenant is a significant mode of Jewish expression in culturally diverse America."[45]

In terms of morality, Greenberg claims that this "secular revelation" ethically reorients Jews toward Christianity and other religions at the same time that it reorients them toward God. Full responsibility for the covenant entails that individuals must be morally responsible for their own traditions and must re-examine their theological or ideological frameworks for any doctrines that demean or negate others. One can no longer defend these derogatory beliefs as the Word of God but must take responsibility to reconstruct them, even if it means arguing with God.[46]

In his article "The New Encounter of Judaism and Christianity" (1967), Greenberg wrote a bold critique of Judaism, stating that the past pressures of Jewish life had perhaps legitimized an antagonistic and stereotypical portrayal of the Gentile that "has become an important dimension of Jewish identification and Jewish self-definition."[47] Later, in "New Revelations" (1979), Greenberg claimed that the Holocaust reveals "the general Jewish tendency to underestimate Christianity's redemptive contribution to the world, due to the bad experience Jews have had with it." He explained that Jewish anger at Christian antisemitism "has obscured the ambivalence and importance of Judaism in Christianity which meant that Christians persecuted, but also kept alive and protected Jews."[48]

Moreover, he suggested that because of its medieval powerlessness and the stark contrast between hope and reality, the Jewish community "could only push Christianity away—or, patronizingly, argue that the righteous of the Gentiles have a share in the world to come or that they have the Noachide covenant to live by."[49] Now, following the voluntary reacceptance of their covenant and the reclaiming of their holy land, Jews are in a secure enough position to reexamine the significance of Christianity and refrain from the negation and condescension of Christians that go against the moral fabric of their tradition. They have learned the painful lessons of the Holocaust, having experienced the terrible consequences of such ethnocentric attitudes. Consequently, Jews cannot use the Holocaust as an excuse "to morally impugn every other religious group but their own" because this will lead to their own indifference to the Holocausts of others.[50]

Christian Orientating Events

Just as Exodus was the first orientating event for the Jews, Greenberg perceives the recognition of Jesus as the messiah by early Jewish Christians to be an orientating event for Christianity because it was a "messianic moment," illuminating the covenantal way toward redemption initiated by the Exodus event. He argues that by generating a messianic moment leading to the establishment of Christianity, Jewish Christians were demonstrating that the dynamics of the covenant were operating, thereby proving the vitality of Judaism.[51] According to Greenberg, the actions of the early Jewish Christians were actually consistent with Jewish self-understanding when they viewed Jesus' death as another orientating event illuminating the significance of his life and clarifying the meaning of redemption.[52] Faced with the death of their messiah and the fact that redemption had not yet come, the Christians were forced to deal with the dialectic between ideal norms and the real world reflected in the Exodus paradigm, yet now reaching its highest and most painful level. Many early Christians were tempted to deny that the messiah had actually come. Others chose a strategy to deal with the contradiction of a failed messiah by arguing that this tragedy is only a temporary aberration that will be overcome by an even more glorious, final redemption. This was later expressed in the Christian belief regarding the second coming of Christ.[53]

However, the majority of Christians remained faithful that the messianic moment they had experienced in Christ did take place, but they insisted that the redemptive change had occurred internally instead of externally, "invisible except through the eyes of faith and to those who experienced rebirth."[54] Hence, Christ's death is seen as a lesson that true redemption is otherworldly. Greenberg notes that even this reorientation toward God is consistent with the classical Jewish tradition in the sense that it illustrates the messianic idea of bringing about redemption in the Kingdom of God while being expressed in a different way. Yet he argues that by interpreting the Crucifixion as a symbol of otherworldly redemption, Christians made a hermeneutical error because they negated the real world of suffering and oppression in favor of a spiritual world, which goes against the fundamental Jewish claim of this-worldly redemption.[55]

Later, in his article "Judaism and Christianity: Covenants of Redemption" (2000), Greenberg makes a less triumphalist claim about Christian interpretations of the Crucifixion, arguing that while preserving the covenantal dialectic between the ideal and the real, the early church "leaned to one side of this dialectic, a skewing that was reinforced by its projection of Judaism as the devil's advocate, rather than as God's balancing voice."[56] Moreover, Greenberg places this early Christian theological development in its historical context by pointing out that early Christians began to "spiritualize redemption" in response to the Jewish claim that the world was "manifestly unredeemed." He also argues that in order to reduce the impact of Christian domination, the Rabbis "dismissed the significance of this world and of politics and military power."[57]

Greenberg even admits that the Christian supersessionist position grew out of a classical Jewish strategy of faith to deal with the dialectic of the Exodus paradigm. He explains that as for their fellow Jews, the destruction of the Second Temple was an orientating event for the Jewish Christians, who responded to it by redefining their relationship to God as well as to their Jewish contemporaries. For the Christians, the destruction of the Temple as well as the later Bar Kochba Revolt "confirmed that the Messiah was an internal liberator not a political savior. The repeated failure of the Jews to grasp this must be increasingly perceived as willful stubbornness—even wickedness."[58] Consequently, Greenberg observes that the calamities in 70 C.E. and 135 C.E. could have been interpreted as divine punishment and rejection of the Jews for their failure to accept Jesus as the messiah.[59]

However, Greenberg points out that Christians were wrong in their assessment that Judaism would disappear following the destruction of the Second Temple. Just as the Christians had responded to the tragedy by affirming a new covenant, the Jews responded by affirming a renewal of the covenant.[60] He argues that nineteen hundred years later, the unparalleled, revelatory events of the Holocaust and the establishment of the State of Israel have again reoriented Christians in relation to God and to the Jewish people. Like Eliezer Berkovits, Greenberg states that the Holocaust reveals "the demonic consequences" of the Christian "'teaching of contempt' tradition," which provided the antisemitic stereotypes for the arguably pagan antisemitism of the Nazis, enabling them to focus on Jews as scapegoats. Moreover, according to Greenberg, Christian anti-Judaism "created a residue of antisemitism in Europe which affected local populations' attitudes toward the Jews, or enabled some Christians to feel they were doing God's work in helping or in not stopping the killing of Jews."[61]

Yet, unlike Berkovits, who accused Christianity of being inherently militaristic, Greenberg decries "the privileged sanctuary of hate allowed to exist at the very heart of and in fundamental contradiction to the gospel of love which is the New Testament's true role and goal."[62] Claiming not to be triumphant, Greenberg implores Christians out of respect to fully repent for a history of hate and confront the anti-Judaism in their most sacred sources. He states, "Repentance is a sign of life and greatness of the soul. Those who deny are tempted thereby into repetition."[63] Greenberg does acknowledge the efforts of the Catholic Church at the Second Vatican Council in 1965 to open a dialogue with Jews in *Nostra Aetate*, "Declaration of the Relation of the Church to Non-Christian Religions." However, he argues that the document was both ambiguous and ambivalent, reflecting the conflicting views of various leaders of the Catholic Church toward Judaism. This is most clearly represented in the statement "Although the Church is the new people of God, the Jews should not be presented as repudiated or cursed by God, as if such views followed from the Holy Scriptures."[64]

Moreover, in his article "New Revelations" (1979), Greenberg notes that since Vatican II, "the atmosphere of warm expectation and romance surrounding dialogue has cooled."[65] The Jewish perception of an inadequate Christian response to the Six-Day-War and the Yom Kippur War set back efforts at dialogue. In addition, both Jewish and Catholic preoccupation with internal needs limited dialogue. While individual Christian scholars gained a much deeper understanding of Judaism, Greenberg observes, "there have been no theological great leaps forward at the institutional level."[66] Yet Greenberg challenges Christianity to acknowledge the "reappearance of revelation in our time." He claims that while *Nostra Aetate* was written with an awareness of the Holocaust and the establishment of the State of Israel, "the revelatory significance was not grasped, even by the Jews. Hence, the document temporizes on the brink. The stakes now are considerably higher."[67]

Greenberg points to a further component of the revelation emanating from the Holocaust, and that is the failure of the Church to speak out against the annihilation of Jews. While acknowledging that the Church did protest against the Nazis, Greenberg observes that the protests were mostly in defense of non-Aryan Christians. The only Jews who were defended by the Church were the converts to Christianity in Poland and Hungary, and these protests did not occur until 1943 and 1944, after the Vatican received detailed reports of burning children and mass gassings. He specifically cites the fact that while German bishops and confessional Protestants spoke out against the Nazi euthanasia policy, they said nothing about the mass murder of Jews.[68] He interprets the motivation of the Church as wanting to save children who believe in "Jesus Christ as Savior and Word Incarnate, "yet if those children do not believe, ". . . it is not *so* bad that Christians ought to risk speaking out." Greenberg concludes, "In short, the Holocaust reveals that the redemption and revelation of Christianity is inescapably contradicted by the constellation of its classic understanding of Judaism."[69] He argues that Christians must choose between redemption and revelation versus antisemitism. The ongoing validity of Christianity depends on an alternative understanding of Judaism, and is based on the testimony of "true Christians" who resisted Nazism and risked their lives to save Jews.[70]

There is another element of the revelation from the Holocaust that Greenberg states is directed to both Christianity and Judaism, and that concerns "a fundamental shift in the ethics of power." Overwhelming power corrupted the Nazis and broke the morality of many people, "leading them to sacrifice their most precious and beloved people and values, so that self-sacrifice and spiritual demonstration were obscured or suppressed."[71] Greenberg claims that this revelatory shift in the ethics of power has led to a "fundamental reorientation away from the traditional Christian and medieval Jewish glorification of suffering passivity."[72] Specifically, this desire for "a moral balance of power" explains the urgency of Jews to establish the State of Israel following the Holocaust.[73] To avoid the corrupting effect of power following the Holocaust, Greenberg advocates a "wide distribution of political, cultural, and theological power" to ensure the moral behavior and safety of the world. He makes the multicultural claim that the Jews need the presence of Christianity, other religions, and secular movements so that no group will attain societal domination. Greenberg asserts, "Thus the presence of many spiritual power centers will enable humanity to move toward the creation of the kingdom of God."[74] In his article "Pluralism and Partnership" (1999), Greenberg observes that modern technology and communication play an important role in bringing together individuals from different religious groups, enabling them to "recognize the power of the other religion as valued in its own right, yet experience their own religion's power equally."[75] In this pluralistic society, different religious groups not only recognize each other's existence but also seek to redefine themselves in order to affirm the ongoing legitimacy and dignity of other religions. Ultimately, Greenberg argues that religious pluralism must lead to a position of partnership in which God assigns different roles and contributions to different groups that are all dependent on one another to achieve *tikkun olam*, messianic repair of the world.[76]

Greenberg also claims that Christianity is affected by the secular revelation coming out of the State of Israel that carries with it "the moral danger and profound ambiguity of a secular state carrying a religious message."[77] He argues that "to keep this secular revelation from degenerating into idolatry," Christians will have to respond with their testimony of the evil in human nature, while the Jews will have to testify that the messiah has not yet arrived. In addition, Greenberg hopes that Christians as well as Jews will respond to this revelation with "the fullest spiritual maturity" in order to appreciate the State of Israel's unique theological position in the real world and help protect it from "the real dangers which its isolation poses to its very existence."[78] He realizes that there is great resistance by Christians as well as Jews to recognize further revelation, yet both communities must move beyond triumphalism by reorienting themselves to God.[79]

Moreover, he points out that the recognition of further revelation does not cancel the validity of the Gospel message. In fact, it clarifies Paul's affirmation that Jewish rejection of Christ paves the way for Gentile acceptance into the covenant. While Greenberg rejects the supersessionist hermeneutic, he does admit that for Christians, the later revelations, including that of Christ's resurrection, the Holocaust, and the State of Israel, illuminate and clarify the earlier revelation to Israel.[80] For him, the events of the Holocaust and the establishment of the State of Israel therefore engender a radical reconstruction of Jewish and Christian identities in relation to each other. Greenberg not only has deconstructed the modern, essentialist definitions of Judaism and Christianity but also has attempted a constructive reconfiguration of Jewish and Christian identities that takes into account the interconnection between history and theology.

Greenberg defines Jewish cultural identity contextually. For him, Jewish identity construction depends on the social and political forces following the Holocaust, especially the reconfiguration of Jewish power in the State of Israel. Indeed, Greenberg describes the need for a "postmodern biblical scholarship" after the Holocaust that recognizes "the profoundly historical nature of divine metaphor, language, and presence in history." Yet he argues that while religion must be connected to history, it cannot be subsumed completely into cultural categories, "lest it lose the power to oppose the extraordinary and total powers assumed by modern political and moral philosophies."[81] Finally, Greenberg recognizes that one can only define Jewish identity by understanding the discourse of Christianity.[82] His work appears to illustrate what the cultural theorist Homi Bhabha calls the "third space," in which all cultures are related: "This third space displaces the histories that constitute it, and sets up new structures of authority, new political initiatives, which are inadequately understood through received wisdom. . . . This process of cultural hybridity gives rise to something different, something new and unrecognizable, a new area of negotiation of meaning and representation."[83]

This third space does not simply represent a revision or inversion of the subject-object duality but rather "revalues the ideological bases of division and difference."[84] In his response to the Holocaust, it appears that Greenberg has attempted a revaluation of Jewish and Christian boundaries based on the assumption that there is a process of displacement and realignment already at work. Because he has challenged Jews and Christians to redefine their cultural identities following the Holocaust, Greenberg's work has been both criticized and supported by Jews while at the same time becoming a source of intense internal debate among Christians over their post-Holocaust identity construction. While many post-Holocaust Christian thinkers have rejected or ignored Greenberg's challenge of redefinition, those who have responded have demonstrated a tension between preserving tradition and restructuring Christian culture entirely.[85] Two theologians were in direct dialogue with Greenberg and illustrated this tension: A. Roy Eckardt and Paul van Buren. They both recognized that the Holocaust represents a challenge to their most fundamental religious claims.[86]

In *Long Night's Journey into Day*, Eckardt and his wife, Alice, refer specifically to Greenberg's statement, "Since even God should be resisted [were he to order a Holocaust], we are called to challenge such central sancta as the Gospels, the Church Fathers, and other sources for their contributions to the sustenance of hate."[87] Subsequently, the Eckardts criticize Catholic theologian Jürgen Moltmann's post-Holocaust theology for proclaiming that just as "inhuman legalism" fails to triumph over Christ, divine grace ultimately emerges victorious "over the works of law and power." Yet in the same context, he condemns the Nazi murder and gassing of Jews during the Holocaust. The Eckardts argue that Moltmann is unable to escape Greenberg's indictment of New Testament sources after the Holocaust because he does not recognize that the anti-Jewish charge of "inhuman legalism" actually leads to the murder and gassing of Jews during the Holocaust. Therefore, they conclude that his interpretation of the New Testament is actually "pre-Holocaust" rather than "post-Holocaust" because it fails to account for the role of Christian anti-Judaism in creating the climate for the Holocaust.[88]

In "Christian Theology and Jewish Reality," van Buren draws upon Greenberg's interpretation of the Holocaust and the establishment of the State of Israel as reorienting events for Christianity as well as Judaism. Van Buren argues that over and above the horror and novelty of these events, they are important in the sense that "they are events in the continuing history of that very people who are the protagonists in as well as the authors of the Scriptures held sacred by both Jews and Christians."[89] He asserts that this is the basis for perceiving the Holocaust and the establishment of the State of Israel as reorientating events that force Jews and Christians to reinterpret their traditions and come to a new self-understanding.[90]

Yet, rather than reconstructing Christian theology from the ground up, these post-Holocaust Christian theologians have continued to use traditional Christian theological categories to develop a positive understanding of Judaism and their relationship to Jews. In both cases, Jews remain mythical witnesses to God in a Christian *Heilsgeschichte*, and the suffering of the Jews in the Holocaust along with their restoration in the State of Israel are divine markers for Christian fate. Stephen Haynes argues that despite the attempt by these theologians to overturn the antisemitic tradition that they inherited, they "actually recapitulate the symbolic structure of the witness-people myth." Ultimately, Jewish history, survival, and the Jewish people themselves become "superlative symbols of Christian failure."[91] These Christian Holocaust theologians exemplify Martin Jaffee's description of public Holocaust discourse in which Christians recommend solidarity with Jews "as a theological norm for the church as a whole in its effort to atone for the crimes of Christendom against the Jewish people."[92] Jaffee states that the Christian participant in Holocaust discourse typically undergoes a "spiritual self-annihilation, a confessing openness to one's own guilt that mirrors in subtle ways themes of classical Christian theology." For the Christian, "the Jew stands symbolically in God's place," as the judge of Christian credibility who can provide forgiveness or judgment.[93]

The work of these Christian Holocaust theologians indicates an inversion of the witness-people myth in which Christians assume the traditional Jewish role of the subjugated other who can return to the Christian self only through atonement and conversion. Drawing upon Rosemary and Herman Ruether's criticism of van Buren, Haynes refers to some Christian Holocaust theologians as antisemites "turned inside out" because of their apparent subordination of Christian identity to Judaism.[94] By attempting to level the playing field between Judaism and Christianity after the Holocaust, they actually end up negating Christianity somewhat in the process and preserving an unequal relationship. Hence, they contribute to a reverse supersessionist model in which Judaism becomes the more dominant religion with greater legitimacy. Ironically, in their effort to reconstruct Christian theology in dialogue with Judaism, these Christian Holocaust theologians perpetuate the very dialectic that they wish to reject.

Greenberg's Covenantal Framework: Dialogic or Dialectic?

We see this tension between dialectic and dialogue in the work of Irving Greenberg, whose dialogical reformulation of Jewish and Christian identities after the Holocaust tends to sacrifice Christian uniqueness. Yet, in his reexamination of Jewish and Christian histories, Greenberg has significantly uncovered the ongoing interconnection between Jewish and Christian cultures. He has accomplished this by developing what he calls an "organic model" of the Jewish-Christian relationship that portrays the historical conditionality of Jewish and Christian faiths in relation to each other. This model is based on the affirmation of a "profound inner relationship" between Judaism and Christianity that Greenberg argues has been mostly denied to preserve the integrity of both religions. The organic nature of Jewish and Christian faiths can only be understood in the context of Greenberg's post-Holocaust affirmation of a dialectical faith. The validity and vitality of this faith are determined by "the willingness to confront, to criticize, and to correct" one's religious position in light of the dialectic between ideal norms and the destructive events of the real world. He even states that the religion most adept at self-correction will prove itself to be most true.[95] Greenberg admits that when struggling with ethical dilemmas and self-criticism generated by the Holocaust, he received crucial guidance from the Christian thinkers Eckardt and van Buren. Greenberg was deeply affected by the fact that they were able to challenge the inherited anti-Jewish positions of Christianity yet remain rooted in their tradition. He had been hesitant to "wrestle with inherited traditional positions" because of his love for Jewish tradition, yet fear of being seen as an outsider. Ultimately, he proclaimed that if these Christian thinkers "could hold themselves to the standard of patriarch Jacob, who became Israel by struggling with God and humans, perhaps I as a Jew could do it within my own tradition as well."[96] Hence, in light of the Holocaust, Greenberg tried to articulate a dialogical model of the Jewish-Christian reality that would serve as a permanent corrective to the dialectical model of the past. Using a similar model to those developed by Eckardt and van Buren, Greenberg describes a single, unfolding covenant of redemption that is at the heart of the Jewish-Christian relationship.[97]

There has been some debate regarding the classification of different post-Holocaust Christian scholars based on their perception of the Jewish-Christian covenantal relationship. There are generally considered to be two schools of thought, the "single-covenant" and "double-covenant" approaches. These two approaches emerged out of the post–Vatican II milieu in which both Catholics and Protestants had to face the challenge of preserving classic Christian theological claims about the new direction that God would take in the world with Christ while at the same time making clear that the novelty of Christ in the divine plan does not annul the original covenant between God and Israel. The Catholic post-Holocaust theologian John Pawlikowski has raised the question as to whether it is still productive for Christian theologians to continue to use the terms "old covenant" and "new covenant" when discussing the Jewish-Christian relationship after the Holocaust and Vatican II. In *Reinterpreting Revelation and Tradition: Jews and Christians in Conversation*, he describes the initial efforts of Catholic scholars following the Second Vatican Council to promote the Pauline portrayal of the Jewish-Christian relationship first articulated in chapters 9–11 of Paul's Letter to the Romans. This New Testament passage later became the basis for the restatement of the Jewish-Christian relationship in *Nostra Aetate*. In this scenario, Jews are included in the biblical covenant after the coming of Christ, yet the nature of their compatibility with Christians remains a "mystery" in the divine plan of human salvation. Additionally, their inclusion in the covenant is contingent upon their acceptance of Jesus as the Christ.[98]

Pawlikowski points out that about ten years after Vatican II, Catholic theologians basically abandoned the "mystery" model and, along with Protestant theologians, have since advocated either the single- or double-covenant approaches. The single-covenant model portrays Jews and Christians as basically sharing one ongoing covenant established at Sinai. The proponents of this model, including Eckardt, van Buren, and even the pope to some degree, assert that the events involving Christ marked the entrance of the Gentiles into the covenant between God and the Jewish people. Whereas some see Christ having an impact on Jews as well as Gentiles, others "argue that the Christian appropriation and reinterpretation of the original covenantal tradition, in and through Jesus, applies primarily to non-Jews."[99]

The double-covenant theory addresses this ambiguity by emphasizing the distinctiveness of Jewish and Christian traditions that emerges gradually beginning in the first century C.E. while at the same time acknowledging their continuing bonds with each other. While clearly locating Jesus in a Second Temple Judean milieu, these Christian scholars insist that because of his ministry, teachings, and overall personality, there was an unprecedented development in the divine-human relationship. Pawlikowski further notes that both Jewish and Christian scholars have observed a greater fluidity in the first century C.E. than previously acknowledged that points to a greater divergence of Jewish groups, including "Christian Jews." While rooting themselves in the biblical tradition, these emerging Jewish and Christian cultures were essentially postbiblical phenomena. He argues that these factors make it impossible to describe the linear development of a single biblical covenant between Jews and Christians.[100] Ultimately, the single- and double-covenant models offer only a partial solution to the current dilemma facing Christian theologians vis-à-vis Judaism. While the single-covenant approach preserves a stronger sense of connection between Judaism and Christianity in light of the Holocaust, it fails to account for the unique revelation of Christ. Alternatively, the double-covenant theology tends to perpetuate to some extent the classical Christian displacement or subjugation of Judaism, thereby ignoring the alleged Christian complicity in the Holocaust.[101] Nonetheless, both approaches indicate a movement away from overt Christian triumphalism toward a more dialogical relationship with Judaism.

In his earlier book, *Christ in the Light of the Christian-Jewish Dialogue*, Pawlikowski places the work of Paul van Buren and A. Roy Eckardt in the single-covenant school but admits that some attributes of their theologies may place them outside of that category. Pawlikowski admits that van Buren's theology might be better placed in the double-covenant school because he stated that God's revelation to the Gentiles through Jesus as Christ is somewhat different than that of the Jews.[102] In fact, James Wallis argues, "van Buren presents Judaism and Christianity in many ways as two autonomous and equally valid religious communities existing alongside one another." Yet he also acknowledges that van Buren moved Christianity back into a Jewish context by abandoning traditional Christian doctrines of Incarnation, Atonement, and the Trinity.[103] However, Pawlikowski asserts that van Buren's work should still be included in the single-covenant school because of his insistence that God's way is one and Judaism and Christianity have been given "valid and complementary glimpses into the same life and love of the Creator God."[104] Pawlikowski more recently notes that toward the end of his life, van Buren had not succeeded in explaining adequately "the uniquely Christian appropriation of the covenant with Israel in and through Christ." He began to articulate the idea that God became more "transparent' to humanity" through the revelation in Christ in a way that surpassed the Sinaitic revelation to Israel, yet he did not pursue this notion further before his death. Ultimately, Pawlikowski concludes that van Buren cannot be included in the double-covenant school because he portrayed the Christ event only as an opportunity for Gentiles to enter the covenant with Israel and not as a vehicle toward an enhanced understanding of the divine-human relationship.[105]

In the case of Eckardt, Pawlikowski states that he first promoted a dialectical, covenantal relationship but later expressed the view that Christianity should allow the Jewish community to move in whatever direction it desires. Eckardt stated that his earlier promotion of the single covenant was a response to Christian supersessionist claims. If Christianity were to abandon its supersessionist position, then Eckardt could see the two communities separating yet maintaining love for one another. He even went so far as to say that the original theological category of covenant was no longer valid in light of the Holocaust, and now only a covenant of "divine agony" exists. However, in his later work, Eckardt reaffirmed his support for the single-covenant theory.[106] According to Pawlikowski, both van Buren and Eckardt ultimately portrayed Christianity as Judaism for the Gentiles, because they failed to sufficiently distinguish between the Jewish version of the one covenant and its Christian expression. In regard to their covenantal frameworks, he asks, if "the only difference between the Messianic vision of Christianity and Judaism respectively is that the Gentiles now understand the plan of human salvation, then why bother with a separate faith community?" He subsequently argues that based on these models, one might as well reincorporate the Church into the synagogue, at least theologically.[107] Because of these ambiguities, Haynes's description of a dual covenant is most helpful to understand these thinkers who attempt to reconstruct a single yet pluralistic covenantal relationship.[108]

While emphasizing the organic, historical nature of Jewish and Christian faiths, Greenberg maintains that "both Judaism and Christianity are outgrowths of and continuous with the biblical covenant."[109] In "Judaism and Christianity: Covenants of Redemption," Greenberg explains that God originally initiated a permanent and universal divine covenant with humanity through Noah in order to move the world toward perfection while still preserving human freedom. This divine-human partnership ensures human authority "within a framework of relationship and accountability to God."[110] Yet God later became concerned that centralizing or unifying human power and freedom in the pursuit of perfection could lead to the infliction of unchecked evil that one finds in movements of "utopian totalitarianism." Subsequently, God initiated a particular covenant with the family of Abraham that Greenberg claims would be the first in a series of smaller covenants with national groups that would "open up the possibility of experimental, varied pathways toward perfection." This Abrahamic covenant was renewed and extended to the entire people Israel who were chosen to be God's "avant-garde" in the human contribution to redemption.[111]

In a mystical vision, Greenberg explains that the entire world is permeated with divinity, but God's presence is eclipsed by evil and will become manifest only in the messianic age. "In the interim, Israel is the holy place/nation/time where God's presence is more visible, and consequently, life is (more) triumphant there than elsewhere." Yet Israel must live up to its commitment to become a nation of priests in order to become a "signpost" of redemption for the nations.[112] For Greenberg, however, God would later choose a new avant-garde group of Christians growing out of the "family and covenanted community of Israel" to spread the message of redemption to the Gentiles in their own language and images. In fact, he inverts the Pauline metaphor of the olive tree in Romans 11 by claiming, "it was God's purpose that a shoot of the stalk of Abraham be grafted onto the root of the Gentiles. Thus non-Jews could be made aware that they were rooted in God also, and they could bear redemptive fruit on their tree of life."[113] Greenberg argues that Christianity's emergence out of Judaism is logical because it represented an "expression of divine pluralism, God seeking to expand the number of covenantal channels to humanity without closing any of them." However, Christianity had to become autonomous in order to preserve the distinctively Jewish covenantal task, "while enabling deeper exploration of the polarities that characterize the covenantal dialectic."[114]

Like Eckardt, Greenberg argues that this covenant does not simply express the unified relationship of two cultures but rather illustrates the "dialectical tensions built into the covenantal structure."[115] Just as Eckardt described conflicting yet complementary temptations by the covenant partners, Greenberg portrays two communities, each needing the other "in order to correct and exemplify the fullness of the divine-human interaction."[116] Both Eckardt and Greenberg portray the temptation of Judaism toward human participation in the covenant versus Christianity's temptation toward grace and transcendence. In addition, they both describe the temptation of Judaism to naturalize divine claims to the point of defeating them, while emphasizing that Christianity needs to take

worldly holiness more seriously. Greenberg concludes that to uphold the totality of the covenant, there must be a multiple number of communities working
toward perfection with mutual criticism to maintain high standards. He suggests that this may be "why the divine strategy utilized at least two covenantal
communities."[117]

For Greenberg, this covenant is really a divine-human pledge to work toward the unfulfilled dream of "a final unification of history and the divine ideal
reality." He argues that neither religion claims that this final stage of history is
already a fact, but commits itself to making this vision into a fact.[118] Like van
Buren, Greenberg claims that later "events along the way to the perfection can
unfold the meaning of this covenant."[119] Greenberg describes the destruction
of the Second Temple and the Holocaust as two historical, revelatory events that
served as Jewish-Christian intersections. At these points in history, the two
cultures utilized the dialectical hermeneutic of faith to redefine their identities
in relation to God and each other within their shared covenant. Following the
destruction of the Second Temple, Jews and Jewish Christians were convinced
that their covenant was unfolding in different ways.

While claiming the supersession of the old covenant, Jewish Christians op-
erated out of the classic biblical model of divine intervention when they interpreted
God to have become flesh in Christ, "intervening to overthrow the facticity of
present reality and reveal the true way to redemption." In this sense, Greenberg
calls Christianity "a commentary on the original Exodus."[120] He contrasts the
Christian claim of a new covenant based on a more manifest divine presence with
the rabbinic reacceptance of the covenant at a higher level of human responsibility, in which God is more hidden and humans are more mature partners.
Greenberg claims that Christianity is actually closer to the biblical covenantal
model than Judaism, yet not in a triumphalist sense.[121] Following the Holocaust,
the dual covenant unfolded again for both Judaism and Christianity, as both were
forced to redefine their relationship with God and each other. Greenberg suggests
that while Jews have entered into their third stage of voluntary covenant characterized by a holy secularism, Christians will have to enter into their second stage
of covenant, characterized by "greater 'worldliness' in holiness."[122] He believes
that Jews should respond to Christianity's second stage by moving beyond mere
tolerance and pragmatic pluralism, ultimately recognizing the legitimacy of an
unfolding of the covenant that "does not destroy or deny the unfailing—indeed,
the equally unfolding—life of the Jewish covenant."[123]

Greenberg illustrates the dialogical and organic nature of these two covenantal communities by utilizing the motifs of crucifixion and resurrection developed in dialogue with Christian theologians, in order to redefine Jewish identity
in the wake of the Holocaust and the establishment of the State of Israel. He
argues that in this post-Holocaust period, secularism and scientism have basically negated the credibility of covenant faith. As a result, the strongest "confir-
mation of religious hope is that crucifixion and resurrection have occurred in

this generation—in the flesh of the covenanted people."[124] He then qualifies the preceding statement by pointing out two problems associated with these theological categories. First, he argues that when the Christian thinker Jurgen Moltmann uses the crucifixion and resurrection motifs, "the Holocaust is coopted to reinforce the crucifixion as credible Christian symbol." This is a misuse of the crucifixion/redemption model that does not take into account its past anti-Jewish associations.[125] In addition, Greenberg points out another problem arising out of the use of these theological categories shared with Christians, "the danger of dignifying the Nazi Final Solution as a necessary step on the way to salvation."[126]

In response to this type of indirect Nazi glorification, Greenberg views the crucifixion using what he considers to be Holocaust categories, developed by A. Roy Eckardt. Greenberg shares Eckardt's position that the crucifixion must no longer be seen as redemptive but rather as "total degradation," which must not be tolerated. He argues that in light of a history of supersessionism, Christians have misunderstood the crucifixion. In the wake of the Holocaust, when one thinks of God being crucified in the flesh, one could argue that God would not survive and actually lose faith. Consequently, if God could not survive the cross, then no human would be expected to survive.[127] Greenberg states that in this sense, the suffering servant motif must be reinterpreted, especially by Christians who have glorified it. He maintains that in light of the burning of children in the Holocaust, the "redemptive nature of suffering must be in absolute tension with the dialectical reality that it must be fought, cut down, eliminated."[128] He appears committed to breaking down the false barriers between Judaism and Christianity by reinterpreting the idea of covenant and developing a shared theological discourse with Christian thinkers. However, he continues to mythologize the Jew in relation to Christianity, inverting the witness people myth and devaluing Christianity to an extent. Throughout his writing, Greenberg appears to vacillate between referring to the Jewish people in supernatural and superlative terms and emphasizing their humanness.

In his essay "Cloud of Smoke" (1974), he approximates the Christian interpretation of the suffering servant motif as a reference to vicarious suffering for the entire world. Greenberg states that his interpretation of the suffering servant is "closer to Berkovits's emphasis on the Jew as witness. Through its suffering, Israel testifies to the God who promises ultimate redemption and perfection in an unredeemed world."[129] As a result, Israel draws the anger of all those who claim to already possess absolute perfection, whether in the form of spiritual perfection with Christianity or social and political perfection with Stalin or Hitler.[130] Yet Greenberg attempts to demystify Berkovits's interpretation of the suffering servant motif by describing it as "a kind of early warning system of the sins intrinsic in the culture but often not seen until later." In terms of the Holocaust, the genocide of the Jews was an "advance warning of the demonic potential for modern culture."[131]

However, in his essay "The Third Great Cycle" (1981), Greenberg echoes Berkovits's mythological description of the Jews' fate in the Holocaust by stating that "the decision to kill every last Jew was an attempt to kill God, the covenantal partner known to humanity through the Jewish people's life and covenant."[132] As we have seen, Greenberg claims that the source of this demonic hatred of the Jews by the Nazis is the Christian teaching of contempt tradition. Yet he claims that if Christians find the courage to recognize the reappearance of revelation emanating from the Holocaust, "at one stroke this undercuts the entire structure of the 'teaching of contempt.'"[133] His interpretation of the suffering servant motif appears to be an inversion of the witness people myth because in it, Jews are portrayed as a witness people but not as witnesses to Christ. Alternatively, they are witnesses to God and the divine covenant. Moreover, Greenberg seems to perpetuate the idea developed by Christian Holocaust theologians that the fate of the Jew after the Holocaust is a sign of God's impending judgment on the Church for a history of antisemitism culminating in the Holocaust. In fact, just as Jaffee argued, the Jewish people appear to take on the role of God who is the judge of Christian credibility and will forgive Christians if they undergo "spiritual self-annihilation."[134]

At the same time, it is not Christ but rather the Jewish people who represent the collective suffering servant, suffering for the sins of humanity in the Holocaust. Greenberg attempts to illustrate this passive mentality of suffering by drawing upon the myth of Jewish powerlessness constructed by the eighteenth-century *maskilim*, or Jewish enlighteners, who tried to negate their nationalistic status in order to be accepted into their host countries.[135] However, he perceives the very legacy of Jewish powerlessness, culminating in the Holocaust, as a justification for Jewish power in the State of Israel. He acknowledges that this desire for an ethical redistribution of power is "the subterranean source of the enormous proliferation of liberation movements."[136] The Jewish liberation theologian Marc Ellis, in his radical critique of Zionism, disagrees with Greenberg, accusing him of adopting an "obfuscating religious language for American and Israeli *Realpolitik*."[137] Richard Rubenstein argues that Ellis's critique of Zionism in *Toward a Jewish Theology of Liberation* could be construed as antisemitic because he draws heavily from the work of Christian liberation theologians whose views of Judaism are clearly shaped by Christian supersessionist claims, which Ellis himself rejects.[138] Two Christian theologians, Rosemary and Herman Ruether, support Ellis's critique of Greenberg, accusing Greenberg of promoting a Western colonialist position toward the Palestinians.[139]

Rubenstein agrees with Greenberg's position on Jewish power after the Holocaust, stating that it is "a pragmatism new to Jewish experience." Both argue that Palestinian self-government can be accepted only if it does not endanger Israel's security.[140] In "The Third Era of Jewish History," Greenberg maintains with Eckardt that the State of Israel should not be held to a higher moral standard than other nations when it comes to using power, especially since it faces an ongoing threat to its existence.[141] Similarly in "Judaism and Christianity: Covenants of Redemption," Greenberg reaffirms the humanity of the people Israel and warns against idealizing their status as a "model people." He admits that sometimes "Israel looks out only for itself and fails to teach; at times, its behavior contradicts its witness. At such times, Israel is a model of what not to do."[142] Yet he, like Eckardt, still refers to the State of Israel in theological terms, as if to say that it has divine power behind it. He states that "the great Biblical sign of the ongoing validity of the covenant—the affirmation of God and hope— is the restoration of Jewry to Israel."[143] As discussed earlier, he even refers to the establishment of the State of Israel as redemptive and sees it a source for a secular revelation.

This tension clearly represents what David Biale describes as the dialectic between perceptions of power and powerlessness in Jewish history. Both sides in this debate have taken the problematic position of identifying Jewish history with powerlessness culminating in the Holocaust, while ignoring the oscillation between the two extremes throughout history. Each position views Israel's political position through Holocaust lenses, either exaggerating its powerless past or inflating its power to compensate for it. Biale argues that the unique burden of Jewish history is to "see both past and present realistically without forgetting or suppressing the memory of the Holocaust."[144] He asserts that the tension between perceptions of Jewish power and powerlessness is indicative of a new secular version of divine election. The biblical doctrine of chosenness justified military revolts against the empires by a weak nation and rationalized Jewish powerlessness in exile. The secular version of Jewish uniqueness arises out of political power in the Jewish state while at the same time representing the powerlessness of the Holocaust. In *Power and Powerlessness in Jewish History*, Biale explains the rationale behind this secular form of chosenness and its implications:

> The Jews have suffered a unique fate and therefore the struggle for
> Jewish survival draws its meaning and justification from this
> uniqueness. . . . Israel is a continuation of the unique Jewish fate of
> antisemitism, but it is also a miraculous manifestation of power. . . .
> Between the Jew as victim and the Jew as military hero, the ideal of
> the Jew as a normal human being has begun to disappear.[145]

This inability to portray Jews as normal human beings in relation to Christians leads to an inversion of the witness people myth and perpetuates the dialectic between Judaism and Christianity. Despite his efforts to emphasize Israel's imperfection in relation to the rest of the world, Greenberg's theological portrayal of the Jews tends to subordinate Christians to an auxiliary status of the Jewish people who are in fact identified with God. Ironically, by drawing upon the single covenant approaches of van Buren and Eckardt, Greenberg at times subsumes Christianity into a Jewish covenantal framework. In this framework, Christianity is described as broadening the Jewish covenant to include the Gentiles by taking the biblical, covenantal model of divine intervention to its extremes with the belief in an incarnate God. Greenberg then argues that the rabbinic model was a more mature mode of religion because the rabbis entered into their second stage of covenant, while the Christian, sacramental mode of religion was more appropriate for the Gentiles who were in the first stage of their covenantal relationship with God. He anticipates the potentially negative reactions to this claim in both Jewish and Christian communities by recognizing that Jews might argue against linking Christianity more closely than Judaism to biblical faith, while Christians might see this as a denial of the ultimacy of the Christ event. In fact, in his response to Greenberg's essay, "Judaism and Christianity: Covenants of Redemption," Christian thinker R. Kendall Soulen asserts that Christians cannot be completely satisfied with Greenberg's claim that Christianity represents only a "spin off" of the Jewish covenant with God. Specifically, he argues that according to Christians, resurrection of the crucified messiah has significance not just for Gentiles but for everyone.[146] Thus while Greenberg is sympathetic to Christian concerns, his portrayal of the Jewish-Christian relationship still provides the impression of a subordinate Christian role in a Jewish framework.

In another instance, Greenberg makes a claim about the Christian interpretation of the crucifixion that might be misconstrued as condescending by arguing that Christians made a hermeneutical error when they interpreted the crucifixion to mean that salvation is otherworldly in light of the Jewish emphasis on this-worldly redemption. While he later rephrases this claim in a more conciliatory way, Greenberg still makes inconsistent and inaccurate generalizations regarding Christianity and Judaism. First, he makes the totalizing contrast of Christianity as otherworldly versus Judaism as this-worldly and then makes the inaccurate claim that the Rabbis retreated from political involvement and this-worldly concerns after Christianity became the religion of the empire. Both of these statements fail to take into account the diversity of voices in each community on this issue and the more complex nature of their identity construction throughout history.[147]

In another essay, he makes the radical claim that in light of their past triumphalism leading to the Holocaust, Christians have misunderstood the crucifixion as being redemptive when it is really represents total degradation.[148] By referring to the Holocaust as a Jewish crucifixion, he appears to be saying, along with Eckardt, that the Holocaust, not the Christ event, represents the true crucifixion in terms of the degree of nonredemptive suffering. In discussing the second covenantal stage of Christianity following the Holocaust, Greenberg actually refers to Christianity as entering into its "rabbinical era," because of the need for a "greater 'worldliness' in holiness." This would entail a more secular reading of Jesus' life, revealing that "the process of redemption was less advanced than Christians assumed." Greenberg insists that while not taking away from the divinity of Jesus, one must view his life as "relatively indistinguishable from that of other teachers and would-be redeemers," and his resurrection must be "subject to historical interpretation as a natural event or as not having happened."[149] This secular reconstruction of the Gospel narrative would help contribute to the development of a Christianity that would be more historical, making "the move from being out of history to taking power, i.e., taking part in the struggle to exercise power to advance redemption." He concludes that this new form of Christianity would be a religion that is "both absolute yet nonimperialistic, one that could embrace the world without losing its soul."[150]

Thus, while trying to recognize Christian otherness, Greenberg appears to be circumscribing Christianity within his own prescribed Jewish boundaries and classifying it according to Jewish categories. He recognizes the necessity of Christian autonomy apart from Judaism, yet like van Buren, he never allows Christianity to fully stand on its own. For Greenberg, Christians must become autonomous not because of any self-declared Christocentric or Trinitarian theology but rather to preserve the biblical covenantal model and probe its dialectic further. Moreover, he seems to strip Christians of their own self-proclaimed identity to an extent by reappropriating the symbols of crucifixion and resurrection in a Jewish context while at the same time diluting their Christological symbolism in a secular framework. By de-Christologizing Jesus, Greenberg appears to be guilty of exactly what he accused Martin Buber of doing in *Two Types of Faith*, assimilating Christianity to Jewish ideas. He claims that Buber's affirmation of Christianity is patronizing, arguing that the "Christianity that Buber loves turns out to be suspiciously like the Judaism that Buber loves."[151] However, Greenberg's affirmation of Christianity may also appear patronizing for the same reason.

While Greenberg rejects Christian otherworldliness as being non-Jewish, he later asserts that following the Holocaust, the Church would begin to exercise its responsibility toward advancing this-worldly redemption. Here he seems to be arguing that after the Holocaust, Christians would reassume their Jewish task of redeeming or Judaicizing the world. This ultimately brings up the question raised by Pawlikowski regarding van Buren's and Eckardt's single-covenant approaches. If the only difference between Jewish and Christian messianic visions is that Gentiles now understand the divine plan of human salvation, then why maintain separate faith communities? Why not reincorporate Christianity into Judaism, at least theologically? Greenberg's single covenant reflects the problems resulting from his desire to maintain Christian absoluteness while making it nonimperialistic. The end result is a form of Judaicized Christianity or, more appropriately, what Pawlikowski describes as Judaism for the Gentiles. Ironically, by utilizing the same covenantal framework as Eckardt and van Buren, Greenberg contributes to the spiritual self-abnegation of Christianity in a Jewish totality. Hence, in Greenberg's single covenant framework, Christianity may "embrace the world," but it could be losing its soul.

Nonetheless, by constructing an organic model of the Jewish-Christian relationship, Irving Greenberg is one of the first twentieth-century Jewish theologians to attempt a reconfiguration of Jewish and Christian identities that takes into account their historical and theological interdependence. In response to what he considers to be the orientating events of the Holocaust and the establishment of the State of Israel, Greenberg has reconstructed the foundation of Jewish and Christian identities by linking their development to historical events that are seen as revelatory. In an era of secular holiness, he challenges Jews as well as Christians to redefine their own identities and their relationship with each other in a way that reflects the human dignity associated with a revised image of God.

Greenberg's self-proclaimed challenge of redefinition is met by mixed reactions in both the Jewish and Christian camps, which reflects his unique position in a neutral zone between Judaism and Christianity. He shares this "third space" with Eckardt and van Buren, whose work he influences and by whom he is influenced. Their symbiosis leads to dialogue in the form of a mutual, single covenant while at the same time perpetuating an ongoing dialectic of attraction and repulsion through their unconscious inversion of the witness people myth. Perhaps the real problem lay in the very foundation of their theological frameworks. Because they perceive the Jew as having a divine status, both Greenberg and his counterparts inevitably place Christianity in a subordinate position. As a result, these theologians are unable to present a truly decentered Jewish-Christian framework in which both Jews and Christians are equidistant from God as their center.

To conclude, in his effort to revalue Jewish and Christian boundaries following the Holocaust, Greenberg's work may be a bridge between modern and postmodern constructions of Jewish identity in relation to Christianity. Modern Jewish thinkers like Rosenzweig have tended to reify Jewish and Christian boundaries while at the same time revealing their already existing contiguity. Schoeps, Rubenstein, and Greenberg have emphasized the malleability of Jewish and Christian borders while still perpetuating Jewish-Christian opposition either through an internalization of anti-Jewish myths, in the case of Schoeps and Rubenstein, or by totalizing the Other, in the case of Greenberg.

Alternatively, Greenberg illustrates the postmodern tendency to deconstruct the totalizing narratives of Jewish identity in dialectic with Christianity and portray the development of theologies in the context of cultural interaction. He even approximates the postmodern claim that theologies are situationally constructed in response to historical events. However, Greenberg is unable to overcome the essentialist, mythological definition of Jewish identity that is shared by his modern Jewish and Christian colleagues. As a result, he appears at times to unwittingly silence the Christian voice in the very dialogue that he proposes. Yet, ultimately, Greenberg does legitimize and lay the groundwork for a postmodern Jewish-Christian totality in which self and other remain intact.

Epilogue

Jewish-Christian Relations in a Multicultural Society

As postmodern writers and thinkers remind us, we live within intertextuality. Texts and methods of interpretation often conflict. They may even attempt to annihilate one another. Texts sometimes complete one another. . . . Methods sometimes complement one another. . . . We begin to suspect that consciousness itself is radically intertextual. . . . Otherness has entered, and it is no longer outside us among the "others." The most radical otherness is within. Unless we acknowledge that, it will be impossible for us to responsibly participate in, or meaningfully belong to our history.

—David Tracy, *Plurality and Ambiguity*

The works of Rosenzweig, Schoeps, Rubenstein, and Greenberg have been constructed out of the intersections of Jewish and Christian texts and methods of interpretation, illustrating the radically intertextual and arguably intercultural nature of modern Jewish self-consciousness. The juxtaposition of these Jewish and Christian intertexts demonstrates a shared religious and cultural discourse that these modern Jewish thinkers have drawn upon to deal with common theological issues prior to and following the Holocaust: secularization, spiritual alienation, revelation, redemption, suffering, and theodicy. In the process, they have charted the course of Jewish self-definition in history by locating themselves in relation to Christian culture. Consequently, when studying modern Jewish history, I suggest that we can no longer distinguish between Jewish-Christian relations and Jewish identity formation itself. Just as Jewish studies scholars are beginning to take into account the influence of gender in all aspects of Jewish culture, one could argue that Jewish-Christian dialectic may be considered a significant factor in modern Jewish identity construction, while arguably having a strong impact in other periods of Jewish history since the destruction of the Second Temple.[1]

The Jewish thinkers discussed in this work have participated in the historical navigation of Jewish identity in the midst of fluctuating Christian waters. One could argue that this demonstrates a postmodern understanding of "religion as a sextant, the instrument that sailors use to calculate their own position relative to a changing night sky . . . what the sextant indicates will always take account of the relative time and location of the navigators themselves."[2] Here religion is no longer considered a reified "cultural baggage" that is transported from one location and time period to the next while remaining unchanged. Instead, it may be defined relationally, continually shaped by its contextual bearings. In a multicultural society, religious, ethnic, and national identities precariously overlap with one another, as individuals choose whom to identify with and even when to reify their own self-perceived cultural identities.[3]

Throughout much of their history, Jews have challenged the conventional opposition between a majority monoculture and a minority "multiculture" because of their liminal status as both insiders and outsiders to the dominant cultures in which they lived, whether Roman, Christian or Islamic.[4] While Jews have clearly integrated into the societies in which they have lived, they have never fully become part of the dominant cultures of those nations. In fact, David Biale has argued, "Jews succeeded in surviving for so many centuries as a marginalized group precisely because they were able to establish themselves close to centers of power and negotiate between competing elite and popular forces."[5]

The Jewish theologians discussed in this work have demonstrated this ambivalence between insider and outsider roles in their dialectic between fascination for and aversion to Christian theological and cultural discourse. These modern Jewish thinkers have continued the historical process of cultural negotiation by engaging in a counterhistory of Christian scholarship most clearly articulated by the nineteenth-century Wissenschaft des Judentums. In her essay "Jewish Studies as Counterhistory," Susannah Heschel compares the nineteenth-century Jewish counterhistories to the methods employed by today's multiculturalists who not only want to give voice to marginalized groups in society but also want to destabilize the hegemonic authority of the academy and expose its use of power.[6] She specifically focuses on the work of Abraham Geiger as an early example of a multicultural challenge to the Western Christian canon. In his 1860 account of Jewish history, Geiger argued that Jesus was not the semidivine figure who established Christianity in opposition to a legalistic first-century Judaism but rather an ordinary Pharisee who promoted the democratization and liberalization of Judaism. In fact, Geiger claimed that Christian beliefs in Jesus' virgin birth, incarnation, and resurrection were later theological inventions influenced by pagan philosophy.[7]

Heschel claims that for Geiger and other Jewish historians of the Wissenschaft des Judentums, retelling the story of Christian origins from a Jewish perspective was self-empowering, while at the same time rendering Jewish identity dependent on Christian theology. Geiger's work, and to some extent modern Jewish thought as a whole, "demonstrates a Jewish desire to enter the Christian myth, become its hero, and claim the power inherent in it."[8] Heschel compares Geiger's reenvisioning of Christian origins to the gaze of the nude women in Edouard Manet's painting *Olympia* (1863) because Geiger reversed the position of the Christian from an observer of Judaism to the one who is observed by Jews. By reinitiating the gaze of Western Christian scholarship to Jewish culture, Geiger was inverting the power relations of the viewer and the viewed. Just as Christian scholars had objectified Judaism as a devalued "Other" in order to preserve Christian hegemony, Geiger transformed Judaism into the subject gazing at a Christian culture that became the object of Jewish representation.[9]

In this work, I have examined four twentieth-century theologians who have to some degree or another constructed their own counterhistories by entering the Christian myth and reclaiming its power for themselves and for Jewish culture as a whole. Through their engagement with Christian thought and culture, these thinkers have re-created Jewish as well as Christian theologies. Rosenzweig attempted to recover a sense of Jewish vitality and proximity to God in a post–World War I period of growing secularization and Jewish assimilation by inverting Augustinian theological motifs and caricatures of Judaism. Although not as polemical as Geiger, Rosenzweig reversed the power relations between Judaism and Christianity by constructing a counterhistory in which Christians must contribute to a Jewish mission of world redemption. He, too, offered a multicultural challenge to Christian domination while at the same time demonstrating his reliance on Christian discourse to construct Jewish identity.

Schoeps tried to reclaim the immediacy of the Divine Word expressed in the Protestantism of Luther and the early Barth, in an attempt to transform both Christian and Jewish cultures of World War II Germany. Although he entered the Christian myth, his intent was not to undermine it but to use it to confront Nazi paganism. In contrast to Rosenzweig, Schoeps did not attempt to reify his Jewish identity over against Christianity but instead embraced his liminal status as both insider and outsider to Christian culture. Unfortunately, this self-proclaimed liminality led to his marginalization in both Jewish and Christian camps.

Rubenstein blamed the Christian as well as Jewish myths for creating the historical climate of the Holocaust, yet he ultimately desired to acquire the power of the Christian myth for himself and the Jewish people following the *Shoah*. Whereas Geiger tried to discredit Christianity by claiming it originated from pagan influences, Rubenstein attributed the strength of Christian sacraments to their pagan roots and viewed them as a psychological advance over a repressive and self-punitive rabbinic culture. In his counterhistory of Christian culture, Rubenstein used the power of the Christian myth to criticize and overcome what he perceived to be a submissive Jewish culture and the transcendent, wrathful God of Jewish and Christian histories. Ultimately, he wanted to offer strength and consolation to both Jews and Christians after the Holocaust, united by guilt in a world filled with the immanent presence of a nonpunitive God.

In a spirit of reconciliation following Vatican II, Greenberg attempted to reconfigure Christian as well as Jewish histories in a dialogical relationship. However, to accomplish this reconfiguration, he entered the Christian myth and reclaimed the power of theological motifs valued by Christians, such as the crucifixion and resurrection, in a Jewish post-Holocaust theology. Moreover, he unwittingly reversed the power relations between Judaism and Christianity by attempting to make Christianity more rabbinic or this-worldly after the Holocaust. Instead of respecting the faith claims of Christianity, Greenberg appeared to subordinate and incorporate them in a Jewish framework.

These twentieth-century Jewish thinkers have contributed to the development of modern Jewish thought not only by enlarging Jewish historical and theological narrative but also "by attempting a rebirth of the Christian mythic potential under Jewish auspices."[10] Their counterhistories of Christian thought provide evidence for what I have called a process of dialectical symbiosis, in which Jewish and Christian thinkers have drawn upon a common theological and cultural language as a source for mutual antagonism and dialogue. In fact, one could argue that their religious identities are in some measure interdependent. Moreover, their works enhance the politics of multiculturalism by demonstrating the importance of restoring the voices of marginalized cultures and by providing a historical precedent with which to understand the complex relationship between dominant and subordinate cultures. While these examples of Jewish-Christian dialectic invariably present a Jewish reversal of the Christian gaze, multiculturalism can benefit from the "establishment of a variety of gazes that will unsettle and throw into question the complacency of academic categories and analyses."[11]

However, this analysis also problematizes the politics of multiculturalism by throwing into question the multiculturalist claim that particularity and universalism are conflicting goals. These Jewish thinkers present a constructive dialectic between these two contradictory ideals by attempting to forge a particular Jewish counteridentity that is ultimately dependent on the universal Christian identity from which they distinguish themselves.[12] While attempting to resist, denigrate, and later reconcile with Christianity, these Jewish thinkers have clearly interacted with and shared a theological and cultural discourse with Christianity. The Jewish-Christian dialectic therefore demonstrates a more complex relationship between subcultures and dominant cultures. Here the ideas of the dominant culture are neither passively internalized by the subculture nor entirely distinct from them; rather, they are actively negotiated at the boundaries between the two cultures and shaped to fit the circumstances of the subculture.

I would submit that the particular Jewish construction of multiple identities vis-à-vis Christianity described in this work is emblematic of a more universal, postmodern understanding of religious identity as being formed out of an intersection of cultures rather than one culture. Instead of viewing cultures as internally consistent wholes, the Jewish-Christian dialectic presents us with a picture of religious cultures that are fragmentary and indeterminate, possessing porous boundaries that are constantly being aligned and realigned in response to shifts in the religious practices of neighboring cultures. In *Theories of Culture*, Kathryn Tanner employs the methods of cultural studies to analyze Christian theology and comes to the conclusion that religious identity is based more on how one uses shared cultural materials rather than "the distribution of entirely discrete cultural forms to one side or the other of a cultural boundary. . . . Different ways of life establish themselves, instead, in a kind of tussle with one another over what is to be done with the materials shared between them."[13] Consequently, Tanner describes Christian identity as being established at a cultural boundary "of use" in the sense that Christians construct their identities through the use of cultural forms shared with "other religions (notably Judaism). . . . Christianity is a hybrid formation through and through."[14]

These modern examples of Jewish-Christian dialectic validate from the Jewish perspective what Tanner affirms regarding Christianity's relationship with Judaism and other religions: religious uniqueness is not preserved within a boundary but is produced through cultural interaction at the boundary where theological statements are made. Normative theological positions often appear to be a "transformative and reevaluative commentary" on the claims of another culture with which the religious group interacts, in the sense that "theological statements mouth the claims of other cultures while giving them a new spin."[15] Hence, instead of necessarily defending religious uniqueness, theological apologetics, polemics, and dialogue actually construct religious identity out of a shared religious and cultural discourse. Ultimately, the Jewish-Christian dialectic provides Jews, Christians, and other religious groups with an illustration of the complexity of a multicultural society in which different groups coexist and define themselves through conflict and negotiation.

Notes

INTRODUCTION

1. "What they're saying . . ." *Arizona Jewish Post*, 11 August 2000, p. 3.

2. On this issue, see Cheryl Greenberg, "Pluralism and Its Discontents: The Case of Blacks and Jews," in *Insider/Outsider: American Jews and Multiculturalism*, ed. David Biale, Michael Galchinsky, and Susannah Heschel (Berkeley: University of California Press, 1998), 80–83.

3. In response to this social ambiguity, David Biale raises the question of whether it is appropriate for Jewish scholars to claim to represent Jewish identity objectively as a "subaltern" voice in response to a hegemonic Christian culture. See Biale, "Between Polemics and Apologetics: Jewish Studies in the Age of Multiculturalism," *Jewish Studies Quarterly* 3, no. 2 (1996): 177, 184. On this issue, see also Susannah Heschel, "Jewish Studies as Counterhistory," and Sara Horowitz, "The Paradox of Jewish Studies in the New Academy," in *Insider/Outsider*, 103–4, 112–13, 119–29.

4. This survey, "Anti-Semitism in America: 2002," was conducted by the Anti-Defamation League and Martilla Communications in late April and early May 2002, shortly after the Israeli army's controversial incursion into the Jenin refugee camp. See "U.S. anti-Semitism on rise after 9/11, per new survey by ADL," *Arizona Jewish Post*, 14 June 2002, p. 1.

5. David Biale, Michael Galchinsky, and Susannah Heschel, "Introduction: The Dialectic of Jewish Enlightenment," in *Insider/Outsider*, 5.

6. Kathryn Tanner, *Theories of Culture: A New Agenda for Theology* (Minneapolis, Minn.: Fortress Press, 1997), 63, 107–15.

7. Steven Wasserstrom, *Between Muslim and Jew: The Problem of Symbiosis under Early Islam* (Princeton, N.J.: Princeton University Press, 1995), 9.

8. Ibid., 3.

9. Ibid., 224.

10. Amos Funkenstein, *Perceptions of Jewish History* (Berkeley: University of California Press, 1993), 170

11. Daniel Boyarin, *Dying for God: Martyrdom and the Making of Christianity and Judaism* (Stanford, Calif.: Stanford University Press, 1999), 5–6

12. Ibid.

13. Heschel, "Jewish Studies," 102, 108. Cf. Funkenstein, *Perceptions*, 36, 48.

14. Funkenstein, *Perceptions*, 48–49.

15. See my discussion of Augustine's *City of God* in chapter 1 of this work. A more extensive discussion of it occurs in Stephen Haynes, *Reluctant Witnesses: Jews and the Christian Imagination* (Louisville, Ky.: Westminster John Knox Press, 1995). Funkenstein discusses *City of God* and *Toldot Yeshu* as counterhistories in *Perceptions*, 38–39.

16. Heschel, "Jewish Studies," 110.

17. Paul Mendes-Flohr, *German Jews: A Dual Identity* (New Haven, Conn.: Yale University Press, 1999), 13–14, 76; Moses Mendelssohn, *Jerusalem or on Religious Power and Judaism*, trans. Allan Arkush (Hanover and London: University Press of New England, 1983), 13–35.

18, Mendes-Flohr, *German Jews*, 76–77.

19. Ibid., 77.

20. Heschel, "Jewish Studies," 102–03. Cf. Funkenstein, *Perceptions*, 282.

21. Hermann Cohen, *Religion of Reason Out of the Sources of Judaism*, trans. Simon Kaplan (Atlanta: Scholars Press, 1995), 239–40. Cf. Funkenstein, *Perceptions*, 282.

22. Funkenstein, *Perceptions*, 282.

23. Mendes-Flohr, *German Jews*, 77–86.

24. Marc Saperstein, "Christian Doctrine and the State of the Question" (paper presented at the Remembering for the Future 2000 Conference on the Holocaust, Oxford, 19 July 2000), 1–2. Cf. Jules Isaac, *Jésus et Israël* (Paris: Editions Albin Michel, 1948), 351–52, 508.

25. Saperstein, "Christian Doctrine," 2. Cf. James Parkes, *The Conflict of the Church and Synagogue: A Study in the Origins of Antisemitism* (London: Soncino Press, 1934), 374.

26. James Parkes, *Judaism and Christianity* (Chicago: University of Chicago Press, 1948), 167. Cf. Saperstein, "Christian Doctrine," 2.

27. James Parkes, *Antisemitism* (Chicago: Quadrangle Books, 1964), 60. Cf. Saperstein, "Christian Doctrine," 3, 20 n. 7.

28. In light of a history of antisemitism culminating in the Holocaust, many Christian theologians have now actively endeavored to redefine their identity in relation to Judaism. Both Catholic and Protestant theologians have begun to recognize the otherness of Jewish identity in and of itself instead of viewing Jewish survival as enigmatic and branding the Jew as a "witness" to the authenticity of Christian identity. As a result, these theologians have had to penetrate to the very core of their identities, replacing a theology of identity based on opposition and supersessionism with one based on mutual recognition. To accomplish this, Christian scholars have recast traditionally perceived Jewish theological categories such as covenant and messianism in a Jewish-Christian context.

In "Post-Conciliar Initiatives toward Recognition of the Salvific Reality of Judaism: A Theological Challenge of 'Nostra Aetate'" (Ph.D. diss., Catholic University of America, 1993), James E. Leibig analyzes the significance of the *Nostra Aetate* declaration at Vatican II and its theological ramifications for a reassessment of Judaism and its relation to the Catholic Church. Another Catholic thinker, John Pawlikowski, explores a number of Catholic and Protestant thinkers who have examined this issue in *What Are They Saying about Christian-Jewish Relations?* (New York: Paulist Press, 1980); he gives his own constructive theology in *Christ in the Light of Christian-Jewish Dialogue* (New York: Paulist Press, 1982). Glenn Earley explores the methodology of Post-Holocaust Christian thinkers when evaluating Judaism in "The Radical Hermeneutical Shift in post-Holocaust Christian Thought," *Journal of Ecumenical Studies* 18, no. 1 (1981): 16–32. Stephen Haynes explores the approaches toward Judaism of Karl Barth, Jürgen Moltmann and Paul van Buren in *Prospects for Post-Holocaust Theology* (Atlanta: Scholars Press, 1991). A Jewish historian, Alan Davies, explores the field of post-Holocaust Christian theology in "The Holocaust and Christian Thought," in *Jewish-Christian Encounters over the Centuries: Symbiosis, Prejudice, Holocaust, Dialogue*, ed. Marvin Perry and Frederick M. Schweitzer (New York: Peter Lang, 1994), 341–67.

29. This analysis would be incomplete without a brief discussion of the writings of five other Jewish thinkers who have made significant attempts to clarify the Jewish-Christian relationship in history and promote religious coexistence throughout the twentieth century: Leo Baeck, Martin Buber, Will Herberg, Abraham Joshua Heschel, and Michael Wyschogrod. Like the authors discussed in this work, these modern Jewish scholars have engaged Christian culture while at the same time keeping their perceived theological distance. Moreover, the argument could certainly be made that their theologies have been predicated to various extents upon that engagement with Christianity.

Caught in the throes of antisemitism leading up to and following the Holocaust, German liberal thinkers Leo Baeck and Martin Buber each expressed ambivalence toward Christianity as a legitimate religion whose adherents have a valid connection to God while also attacking Christian belief as a degenerated form of Judaism that is dogmatic and exclusivist. They accomplished this by creating a distinction between the Jewish Jesus who served God and his fellow human beings ethically versus the Pauline Jesus who became the deified Christ through whom everyone must come to God. Thus, both Baeck and Buber contributed to the modern Jewish counterhistory of Christian culture described previously by reclaiming for Jews the power of the Christian myth involving Jesus while at the same time disassociating it from Pauline Christianity. Baeck argued that whereas Jesus and the Gospels represent the ethical monotheism of Judaism based on the active observance of divine commandments, Pauline Christianity is a romantic religion promoting absolute dependence on God. For Buber, Jesus was part of the Pharisaic Jewish community in his thorough devotion to and trust in a God who could be experienced without mediation. Yet Paul undermined this immediacy by concealing the imageless God with the imaged God, Christ, who became an object of faith for each individual Christian. This distinction between Jesus and Paul was based on Buber's overall dichotomy between two types of faith, the Jewish *emunah*, or "trust," arising out of an immediate relationship between God and Israel, versus the Christian *pistis*, an "acknowledgment" of Christ as the object of faith.

See Sandra Lubarsky, *Tolerance and Transformation: Jewish Approaches to Religious Pluralism* (Cincinnati: Hebrew Union College Press, 1990), 29–31, 35–41, 88–99; Fritz Rothschild, ed., *Jewish Perspectives on Christianity: Leo Baeck, Martin Buber, Franz Rosenzweig, Will Herberg, and Abraham Joshua Heschel* (New York: Continuum, 1996), 46–108, 122–55; David Novak, *Jewish-Christian Dialogue: A Jewish Justification* (Oxford: Oxford University Press, 1989), 75, 80–86.

In the wake of the barbaric Stalinist purges and the Nazi Holocaust, the American Jewish thinker Will Herberg became disillusioned with the Marxist ideology he had championed from the 1920s to the early 1930s and was transformed by his encounter with the Protestant theology of Reinhold Niebuhr. Niebuhr's theology revealed to him the inherent sinfulness of his generation that was manifest in the evil regimes of Marxism and Nazism and led him to recover a relationship with the absolute God. Like Franz Rosenzweig before him, Herberg became convinced that he could rediscover revelation only through Christianity, yet he decided to first explore his Jewish tradition. When studying at the Jewish Theological Seminary in the 1940s, Herberg was introduced to classical rabbinic sources, as well as the modern Jewish theologies of Buber and Rosenzweig; like his German predecessor, Herberg returned to Judaism and constructed his own existential Jewish theology in conversation with Christian thought and culture. In fact, some in the Jewish community complained that his theology was more Christian than Jewish. Just as Rosenzweig portrayed Judaism and Christianity as complementary yet contradictory vehicles of divine redemption, Herberg described them as being dialectically united under a double covenant constituted by Jewish faithfulness to God and a Christian mission to the Gentiles. See Herberg, "Judaism and Christianity: Their Unity and Difference," in *Jewish Perspectives on Christianity*, 240–55; David G. Dalin, "Will Herberg," in *Interpreters of Judaism in the Late Twentieth Century*, ed. Steven T. Katz (Washington, D.C.: B'nai B'rith Books, 1993), 115–21.

Like their colleague Irving Greenberg, two Jewish scholars from traditional backgrounds, Abraham Joshua Heschel and Michael Wyschogrod, became caught up in the ecumenical fervor of the 1960s and subsequently worked hard to articulate their understandings of the meaning and vitality of Judaism to the Catholic Church and other Christian denominations. Heschel, who came from a European Hassidic dynasty but received his doctorate in philosophy, believed that the Jews had an unprecedented opportunity to dialogue with Christians who for the first time in two thousand years were interested in learning about Judaism. In fact, Heschel represented the American Jewish Committee in its negotiations with the Catholic Church prior to and during the Second Vatican Council. In his essay "No Religion Is an Island" (1965), Heschel emphasized essential doctrinal differences between Judaism and Christianity while also drawing upon more relativistic biblical and rabbinic portrayals of the divine-human relationship that describe a universal God who desires religious diversity and whose truth is not exclusive to any religious group. See Heschel, "No Religion Is an Island," in *Jewish Perspectives on Christianity*, 309–24; John C. Merkle, "Introduction," in *Jewish Perspectives on Christianity*, 267–77; Edward K. Kaplan, "Abraham Joshua Heschel," in *Interpreters of Judaism in the Late Twentieth Century*, 131, 140, 143; Randi Rashkover, "Jewish Responses to Jewish-Christian Dialogue," *Cross Currents* 50, nos. 1–2 (spring/summer 2000): 212–13.

The Orthodox Jewish thinker Michael Wyschogrod has followed Heschel's example by becoming active in interreligious organizations, serving as consultant on various Vatican committees as well as to the Presbyterian Church and coediting books on the Jewish-Christian relationship with Christian scholars. Like Heschel, he believes that today Christians are more likely to have a positive image of Judaism than in any other period of history, and he sees it as a religious responsibility to explain traditional Judaism to Christians without significant distortion. Yet, in his book *The Body of Faith* (1983), Wyschograd ironically constructs a Jewish theology in dialectic with Christianity. Similar to Rosenzweig in *The Star of Redemption*, Wyschogrod accepts the Christian anti-Jewish caricature of the Jews as a bodily people but inverts its negative valence by arguing that Jewish carnality should not be understood in terms of "sensuality" or "worldliness," but rather as the material locus of God's blessing and presence. In fact, Wyschogrod approximates Baeck and Buber's anti-Christian polemic when arguing that the Jews' emphasis on the body has saved them from the Hellenistic influences infecting Christianity, specifically the Gnostic bifurcation of spirit and matter. See Wyschogrod, *The Body of Faith: God in the People Israel* (San Francisco: Harper and Row, 1983), 176–77; Scott Bader-Saye, "Post-Holocaust Hermeneutics: Scripture, Sacrament, and the Jewish Body of Christ," *Cross Currents* 50, no. 4 (winter 2000/2001): 469; David R. Blumenthal, "Michael Wyschogrod," in *Interpreters of Judaism in the Late Twentieth Century*, 399–401.

These five Jewish thinkers have all made important contributions to the emerging Jewish-Christian dialogue in the twentieth century, and one could argue that they have also participated in the modern Jewish-Christian dialectic to various extents as illustrated by their continuing ambivalence toward Christian culture. There are two basic reasons for their exclusion from this study: First, in contrast to this analysis, their writings on the whole do not suggest a historical progression leading up to and following the Holocaust as a central point. The writings of Baeck and Buber are clearly linked to one another because both men were writing in Germany in the early years of World War II and were forced to leave because of the Nazi Holocaust. Their writings may be further linked with those of Herberg because of their engagement with Christian culture in light of a general concern with theological anti-Judaism and racial antisemitism in the twentieth century, while the works of Heschel and Wyschogrod may be linked because of their response to Vatican II. However, while their writings all surround the Holocaust chronologically, none of the thinkers following the Holocaust construct their theologies directly in response to that event. Alternatively, this analysis revolves to a large degree around the Holocaust as a historical turning point in Jewish-Christian relations. In their responses to the historical events leading up to and climaxing in the Holocaust, the Jewish thinkers discussed in this work drew upon a shared discourse with Christianity to confront the theological and cultural challenges they faced.

Second, the pragmatic time and space constraints of this work simply preclude the discussion of any other Jewish theologians regardless of the quality and importance of their writings. However, it is exactly for this reason that these works mandate a possible further investigation in any future projects.

30. See Biale's discussion of the use of cultural studies to better understand Jewish history in "Between Polemics and Apologetics," 181.

31. Frederic Jameson, "On *Cultural Studies*," in *The Identity in Question*, ed. John Rajchman (New York: Routledge, 1995), 271.

32. Ivan Marcus, *Rituals of Childhood: Jewish Acculturation in Medieval Europe* (New Haven, Conn.: Yale University Press, 1996), 11–12; Marcus, "Jews and Christians Imagining the Other in Medieval Europe," *Prooftexts* 15 (1995): 210.

33. Lawrence Grossberg, "Cultural Studies: What's in a Name? (One More Time)," in *Bringing It All Back Home: Essays on Cultural Studies* (Durham, N.C.: Duke University Press, 1997), 253–54.

34. See Lawrence J. Silberstein, "Mapping, Not Tracing: Opening Reflection," in *Mapping Jewish Identities* (New York: New York University Press, 2000), 4–5.

35. On the critique of essentialist definitions of Jewish identity, see ibid., 10–13, 27–28.

36. Grossberg, "Cultural Studies," 254–58.

37. Henry A. Giroux, "Resisting Difference: Cultural Studies and the Discourse of Critical Pedagogy," in *Cultural Studies*, ed. Lawrence Grossberg, Cary Nelson, and Paula A. Treichler (New York: Routledge, 1992), 202.

38. Etienne Balibar, "Culture and Identity (Working Notes)," trans. J. Swenson in *The Identity in Question*, 188.

39. Grossberg, "Cultural Studies," 258–61.

40. Trinh T. Minh-Ha, *When the Moon Waxes Red: Representation, Gender and Cultural Politics* (New York: Routledge, 1991), 74–77.

41. Henry A. Giroux, *Border Crossings: Cultural Workers and the Politics of Education* (New York: Routledge, 1992), 28–30.

42. Ibid., 30.

43. Biale, "Between Polemics and Apologetics," 183.

44. Grossberg, "Cultural Studies," 262–66.

45. Ibid., 266.

46. Ibid., 266–67.

47. Ibid., 267–68.

48. Mary McClintock Fulkerson's "intertextual" theological paradigm acknowledges that theological meaning may be conceived outside of a closed semiotic system through the interrelationship of different texts or semiotic systems. Because social and cultural realities are textualized along with written texts, the relation between a community in its particular cultural formation and the biblical text may be referred to as intertextual. See Fulkerson, *Changing the Subject: Women's Discourses and Feminist Theology* (Minneapolis, Minn.: Fortress Press, 1994), 160–61, 165–66, 362–64.

49. Novak, *Jewish-Christian Dialogue*, 141–42, 148–51.

50. See Tikva Frymer-Kensky, David Novak, Peter Ochs, and Michael Signer, "Dabru Emet: A Jewish Statement on Christians and Christianity," *New York Times*, 10 September 2000, sec. 1, p. 23. This document also appears in *Christianity in Jewish Terms*, ed. Tikva Frymer-Kensky, David Novak, Peter Ochs, David Fox Sandmel, and Michael Signer (Boulder, Colo.: Westview Press, 2000), xvii–xx.

51. Frymer-Kensky et al., *Christianity in Jewish Terms*, xi–xiii.

52. Ibid., xii; Peter Ochs and David Fox Sandmel, "Christianity in Jewish Terms: A Project to Redefine the Relationship," *Cross Currents* 50, no. 4 (winter 2000/2001): 453.

53. Frymer-Kensky et al., *Christianity in Jewish Terms*, xi; Ochs and Sandmel, "Christianity in Jewish Terms," 454–55.

54. Frymer-Kensky et al., *Christianity in Jewish Terms*, 367–68. David Novak made this observation in his contribution to a jointly written essay, "What of the Future? A Jewish Response," in the epilogue to *Christianity in Jewish Terms*, where the editors reflect on the impact of this work on the future of Judaism and Jewish-Christian relations.

55. Ochs and Sandmel, "Christianity in Jewish Terms," 448.

56. Ibid.

57. See Sandmel's comments in Tikva Frymer-Kensky, David Novak, Peter Ochs, David Fox Sandmel, and Michael Signer, "What of the Future? A Jewish Response," in *Christianity in Jewish Terms*, 367.

58. David Novak, "Introduction: What to Seek and What to Avoid in Jewish-Christian Dialogue," in *Christianity in Jewish Terms*, 2.

59. Ibid., 2–6.

60. Ochs and Sandmel, "Christianity in Jewish Terms," 454–55.

61. Biale, "Between Polemics and Apologetics," 184. In his discussion of this new type of apologetic, Biale provides examples from the work of two Jewish feminists, Tikva Frymer-Kensky, *In the Wake of the Goddesses: Women, Culture and the Biblical Transformation of Pagan Myth* (New York: Free Press, 1992), and Ilana Pardes, *Countertraditions in the Bible: A Feminist Approach* (Cambridge, Mass.: Harvard University Press, 1992). Frymer-Kensky presents a more apologetic interpretation of a biblical theology that "finesses the issue of divine gender by constructing a god who is beyond human attributes." Alternatively, Pardes offers more of a deconstruction of a biblical text that "simultaneously yields patriarchal and anti-patriarchal messages" (Biale, "Between Polemics and Apologetics," 181–82).

62. Biale, "Between Polemics and Apologetics," 182. Cf. Franz Rosenzweig, "Apologetisches Denken," in *Kleinere Schriften* (Berlin: Schacken, 1937), 31–42. See also Daniel Boyarin, *Carnal Israel: Reading Sex in Talmudic Culture* (Berkeley: University of California Press, 1993), 20.

63. Boyarin, *Carnal Israel*, 20–21. Cf. Biale, "Between Polemics and Apologetics," 182–83.

64. Biale, "Between Polemics and Apologetics," 183.

65. Ibid.

66. Boyarin, *Carnal Israel, Reading Sex in Talmudic Culture* (Berkeley: University of California Press, 1993), 19–21.

67. Ibid., 21.

68. Jonathan Boyarin and Daniel Boyarin lay out the parameters for the new Jewish cultural studies in "Introduction/So What's New?" in *Jews and Other Differences: The New Jewish Cultural Studies* (Minneapolis: University of Minnesota Press, 1997), xii.

69. Ibid.

70. Boyarin, *Dying for God*, 8.

71. Ibid., 8–11.

72. For a discussion of this dialectic between two opposing discourses about culture, see Gerd Baumann, *The Multicultural Riddle: Rethinking National, Ethnic, and Religious Identities* (New York: Routledge, 1999), 90–95, 138–40.

CHAPTER I

1. For a discussion on the Wissenschaft des Judentums as a German-Jewish subculture, see Amos Funkenstein, *Perceptions of Jewish History* (Berkeley: University of California Press, 1993), 257–58.

2. Paul Mendes-Flohr, *German Jews: A Dual Identity* (New Haven, Conn.: Yale University Press, 1999), 66–73.

3. See Rosenzweig's letter to Rudolf Ehrenberg, 31 October 1913, trans. Nahum Glatzer in *Franz Rosenzweig: His Life and Thought* (New York: Schocken Books, 1961), 28.

4. For a brief biographical sketch on Rosenzweig and his intellectual connection to Friedrich Meinecke and Hermann Cohen, see Robert Gibbs, *Correlations in Rosenzweig and Levinas* (Princeton, N.J.: Princeton University Press, 1992), 5; Funkenstein, *Perceptions*, 258–60.

5. See Stephane Moses' synopsis of *The Star of Redemption* and its connection to World War I in *System and Revelation: The Philosophy of Franz Rosenzweig*, trans. Catherine Tihanyi (Detroit: Wayne State University Press, 1992), 23–26.

6. Funkenstein describes *The Star of Redemption* as "one of the last great instances of this self-reflection" initiated by the Wissenschaft des Judentums. See *Perceptions*, 258.

7. Mendes-Flohr argues, "It was precisely the re-centering of the Jew in Judaism that Rosenzweig discerned to be the supreme task of the Jewish Renaissance, which reached full flower in the years of the Weimar Republic" (Mendes-Flohr, *German Jews*, 86). Yet, by establishing the Free Jewish School, Rosenzweig was acknowledging, if only implicitly, the legitimacy of the "and" that connected *Judentum* and *Deutschtum*. Instead of proclaiming or cultivating this "and," Rosenzweig respected the German cultural affiliations of his Jewish students, while enabling each to decide his or her own "way of living with the 'and.'" On this, see Mendes-Flohr, *German Jews*, 86–87.

8. For brief details on Rosenzweig's final years, see Gibbs, *Correlations*, 6; Funkenstein, *Perceptions*, 260.

9. See Funkenstein, *Perceptions*, 294–95, and Rosenzweig's letter regarding the relationship between *Gesetz* (law) and *Gebot* (commandment) to Martin Buber written on 16 July 1924 and translated in *On Jewish Learning*, trans. Nahum N. Glatzer (New York: Schocken Paperback, 1965); Rosenzweig, *The Star of Redemption*, 2d ed., trans. William W. Hallo (Notre Dame, Ind.: Notre Dame University Press, 1985), 176–77.

10. Funkenstein, *Perceptions*, 295–97.

11. Ibid., 269.

12. For a discussion of Rosenzweig's growing antipathy toward relativism and historicism and his near conversion to Christianity, see Moses, *System and Revelation*, 33–34.

13. Ibid., 34. Cf. Franz Rosenzweig, *Brief*, edited by Edith Rosenzweig with the cooperation of Ernst Simon (Berlin: Schocken Verlag, 1935), 55.

14. Rosenzweig, *The Star*, 3–6, 19–20, 109–11, 157–62, 254–57. Cf. Moses, *System and Revelation*, 25.

15. Moses, *System and Revelation*, 34.

16. Ibid.

17. Ibid., 34–35.

18. See Eugen Rosenstock-Huessy, ed., *Judaism Despite Christianity: The "Letters on Christianity and Judaism" between Eugen Rosenstock-Huessy and Franz Rosenzweig*, (University: University of Alabama Press, 1969), 72–74, 118–23; Rosenzweig, *Brief*, 81; Rosenzweig's letter to Rudolf Ehrenberg, 31 October 1913, trans. Alexander Altmann in "About the Correspondence," in *Judaism Despite Christianity*, 32–33. Cf. Glatzer, *Franz Rosenzweig*, xiv–xv, 24; Paul Mendes-Flohr, "Rosenzweig and the Crisis of Historicism," in *The Philosophy of Franz Rosenzweig* (Hanover, N.H.: University Press of New England, 1988), 143–44; Ronald Miller, *Dialogue and Disagreement: Franz Rosenzweig's Relevance to Contemporary Jewish-Christian Understanding* (Lanham, Md.: University Press of America, 1989), 36–37.

19. Franz Rosenzweig, *Almanach des Schocken Verlags auf das Jahr 5699* (1938): 60, trans. Nahum Glatzer in *Franz Rosenzweig*, xix–xx.

20. Rosenzweig to his mother, 23 October 1913, trans. Nahum Glatzer in *Franz Rosenzweig*, 27.

21. Rosenzweig to Rudolf Ehrenberg, 31 October 1913, trans. Nahum Glatzer in *Franz Rosenzweig*, 341–42.

22. Funkenstein, *Perceptions*, 252, 297; Alasdair I. C. Heron, *A Century of Protestant Theology* (Philadelphia: Westminster Press, 1980), 75–76; Karl Löwith, *From Hegel to Nietzsche: The Revolution in Nineteenth-Century Thought*, trans. David E. Green (New York: Columbia University Press, 1991), 377–88.

23. Franz Rosenzweig, "Atheistische Theologie," in *Franz Rosenzweig: Der Mensch und sein Werk, Gesammelte Schriften*, vol. 3, *Zweistromland: Kleinere Schriften zu Glauben und Denken*, ed. Reinhold Mayer and Annemarie Mayer (Dordrecht: Martinus Nijhoff, 1984), 691–93. Cf. Funkenstein, *Perceptions*, 265, 297; Miller, *Dialogue and Disagreement*, 32–34; Löwith, *From Hegel to Nietzsche*, 378–79.

24. Rosenzweig, "Atheistische Theologie," 693. Cf. Miller, *Dialogue and Disagreement*, 33–34.

25. Rosenzweig, *The Star*, 156–64, 167–71, 173–85. Cf. Miller, *Dialogue and Disagreement*, 34, 58–76; Moses, *System and Revelation*, 105–19.

26. Funkenstein, *Perceptions*, 297; Bruce L. McCormack, *Karl Barth's Critically Realistic Dialectical Theology: Its Genesis and Development, 1909–1936* (Oxford: Clarendon Press, 1995), 227–31. McCormack argues that in his second commentary to Romans, Barth responded to apparent misreadings of the first edition that transformed his theocentric understanding of divine eschatology into an anthropocentric understanding of God that calls into question divine subjectivity in revelation. As a result, Barth constructed a "radically futurist 'consistent' eschatology according to which the Kingdom of God is understood as that which brings about 'the dissolution of all things, the cessation of all becoming, the passing away of this world's time'" (McCormack, 207–8) Another factor that led to his revision of Romans 1, was the influence of Franz Overbeck, whose historical-philosophical category of *Urgeschichte* provided Barth with a hermeneutic with which to reconceptualize Christian eschatology. In *Christentum und Kultur*, Overbeck used the term to denote the originating history of living things in their

original essences, specifically in regard to the Church, and all historical development after that period is considered a falling away from that pristine essence. Barth transformed the historical term into a purely theological category that refers to an unhistorical, unknown origin of the world and humanity to which humans return after death. See Franz Overbeck, *Christentum und Kultur: Gedanken und Anmerkungen zur modernen Theologie*, ed. Carl Albrecht Bernoulli (Basel: Benno Schwabe, 1919), 6, 20–23; Karl Barth, "Unsettled Questions for Theology Today," in *Theology and Church*, trans. Louise Pettitbone Smith (London: SCM Press, 1962), 55–73.

27. Rosenzweig, *The Star*, 328. Cf. Glatzer, *Franz Rosenzweig*, 334–35.

28. For Rosenzweig's attitude toward Zionism as a deification of the state, see "Atheistische Theologie." For more specific references to Zionism, see "Der Jude im Staat," and "Liberalismus and Zionismus," in *Zweistromland*, 553–58; *Franz Rosenzweig: Der Mensch und sein Werk, Gesammelte Schriften*, vol. 2, *Brief und Tagebücher*, pt. 1, 1918–1929, ed. R. Rosenzweig and E. Rosenzweig Scheinmann (The Hague: Martinus Nijhoff, 1979), 2:774; Rosenzweig, *Brief*, 708; Rosenzweig *The Star*, 299–300, 328–35.

29. Rosenzweig, *The Star*, 331–32, 342. Cf. Funkenstein, *Perceptions*, 292.

30. Stephane Moses, "Franz Rosenzweig in Perspective: Reflections on His Last Diaries," in *The Philosophy of Franz Rosenzweig*, 193; Steven Katz, "On Historicism and Eternity: Reflections on the 100th Birthday of Franz Rosenzweig," in *Der Philosoph Franz Rosenzweig: Internationaler Kongress-Kassel 1986*, vol. 2, *Das neue Denken und seine Dimensionen*, ed. Wolfdietrich Schmied-Kowarzik (Munich: Verlag Karl Alber Freiburg, 1988), 750; Funkenstein, *Perceptions*, 297–98.

31. Moses, "Franz Rosenzweig in Perspective," 193.

32. Franz Rosenzweig, "Globus: Studien zur weltgeschichtlichen Raumlehre," in *Zweistromland*, 313–48. Cf. Mendes-Flohr, "Rosenzweig," 148–49.

33. Rosenzweig, "Realpolitik," in *Zweistromland*, 265. Cf. Mendes-Flohr, "Rosenzweig," 147.

34. Rosenzweig, "Globus," 330, 334–35. Cf. Mendes-Flohr, "Rosenzweig," 149–50, 153–54, 239 nn. 54–55.

35. Rosenzweig, *Der Mensch und sein Werk: Gesammelte Schriften*, vol. 2, *Brief und Tagebücher*, pt. 1, 543–44; translated by Miller in *Dialogue and Disagreement*, 107. Cf. Mendes-Flohr, "Rosenzweig," 154.

36. Rosenzweig, *The Star*, 298–300, 328–35, 338–43, 378–79, esp. 334–35. Cf. Mendes-Flohr, "Rosenzweig," 157; Funkenstein, *Perceptions*, 291–92.

37. Funkenstein, *Perceptions*, 293.

38. *The Babylonian Talmud* [henceforth, BT] (London: Soncino Press, 1961), *Nedarim* 32a, *Shabbat* 156a; Yehuda Halevi, *The Kuzari: An Argument for the Faith of Israel*, trans. Hartwig Hirschfeld (New York: Schocken Books, 1964), 1:4, 42, 95–96, 115; Yehuda Loew ben Bezalel, *Netzah Yisrael* (Tel Aviv, 1964), 9–11; :Loew, *Sefer Tifferet Yisrael* (Jerusalem, 1970), 9; Loew, *Sefer Gevurot Hashem* (Jerusalem, 1971), 147. Cf. Funkenstein, *Perceptions*, 293–94.

39. Rosenzweig, *The Star*, 379; Halevi, *The Kuzari*, 4:28, pp.226–27. Cf. Funkenstein, *Perceptions*, 148–49.

40. Funkenstein, *Perceptions*, 298–300. Cf. Mendes-Flohr, "Rosenzweig," 140–55; Peter Brown, *Augustine of Hippo* (Berkeley: University of California Press, 1967), 309.

41. Brown, *Augustine*, 301–2; Mendes-Flohr, "Rosenzweig," 140–43. Cf. Funkenstein, *Perceptions*, 296–97.

42. John H. S. Burleigh, *The City of God: A Study of St. Augustine's Philosophy* (London: Nisbet, 1949), 9–30; Funkenstein, *Perceptions*, 38. Funkenstein claims that counterhistories actually constitute a "specific genre of history written since antiquity" based on a polemical premise. Funkenstein describes the method of counterhistories as "the systematic exploitation of the adversary's most trusted sources against their grain. . . .Their aim is the distortion of the adversary's self-image of his identity through the deconstruction of his memory" (Funkenstein, *Perceptions*, 36). Along with Augustine's *City of God*, Funkenstein refers to Manetho's negative account of Jewish history and *Sefer Toldot Yeshu*, a parody of Jesus' life, as examples of purposeful attempts to negate the other through counterhistories. Yet he acknowledges that not all counterhistories reflect an attempt to negate the other, citing Herodotus's image of Egypt and Tacitus's image of the Germans. See Funkenstein, *Perceptions*, 36–40. See also the introduction of this work for an extended discussion of counterhistory.

Moreover, in *Gershom Scholem: Kabbalah and Counter History* (Cambridge, Mass.: Harvard University Press, 1982), 7–8, David Biale argues that counterhistory is also a genre of literature that develops within Jewish culture itself in order to deconstruct master narratives. He claims that this is illustrated in the work of Gershom Scholem, who affirmed the vitality of a secret kabbalistic tradition covered up by the "mainstream history" composed by the Wissenschaft des Judentums. In fact, Biale himself uses this methodology in *Power and Powerlessness* to uncover a history of Jewish power hidden by a modern myth of Jewish powerlessness. See Biale, *Power and Powerlessness in Jewish History* (New York: 1986; Schocken Books, 1987).

43. Augustine, *The City of God*, trans. Marcus Dods (New York: Random House, 1950), 15:5. Cf. Jill Robbins, *Prodigal Son/Elder Brother: Interpretations and Alterity in Augustine, Petrarch, Kafka, Levinas* (Chicago: University of Chicago Press, 1991), 21–48. For a discussion of Christian typological exegesis and specifically Augustine's work, see Funkenstein, *Perceptions*, 98–105.

44. Brown, *Augustine*, 313–29.

45. Augustine, *City of God*, 15:1, 26, 18:49. Cf. Funkenstein, *Perceptions*, 298–99.

46. Brown, *Augustine*, 314. He explains Augustine's perception that, like the Jews, the Christians live in this earthly world as if they are in exile in Babylon, while longing to return to the heavenly Jerusalem.

47. Augustine, *City of God*, 17:3, 29:17. Brown states that *The City of God* is not about a withdrawal from the world but is rather "a book about being otherworldy in the world" (Brown, *Augustine*, 324–25).

48. Augustine, *City of God*, 18:46. Cf. Stephen Haynes, *Reluctant Witnesses: Jews and the Christian Imagination* (Louisville, Ky.: Westminster John Knox Press, 1995), 28–32. Haynes maintains that the set of beliefs and assumptions about Jews contained in the witness people myth has never been an element of church dogma and is not even a clear doctrine in Augustine's writings. Yet it has developed in both religious and secular forms throughout history. See also Funkenstein, *Perceptions*, 176.

49. Edward Flannery, *The Anguish of the Jews: Twenty-three Centuries of Antisemitism* (New York: Paulist Press, 1985), 53.

50. Augustine, *City of God*, 18:46. Cf. Robbins, *Prodigal Son/Elder Brother*, 39–40.

51. Augustine, *City of God*, 4:34. Cf. Haynes, *Reluctant Witnesses*, 29; Funkenstein, *Perceptions*, 176, 299.

52. Rosenzweig, *The Star*, 329–30, 331–32. Cf. Funkenstein, *Perceptions*, 299 n. 58.

53. Rosenzweig, *The Star*, 299.

54. Richard A. Cohen, *Elevations: The Height of the Good in Rosenzweig and Levinas* (Chicago: University of Chicago Press, 1994), 14.

55. Rosenzweig, *The Star*, 332.

56. Funkenstein, *Perceptions*, 299–300.

57. Brown, *Augustine*, 314, 324.

58. Moses, *System and Revelation*, 179.

59. Rosenzweig to Rudolf Ehrenberg, 31 October 1913, trans. Nahum Glatzer in *Franz Rosenzweig*, 341–42; Rosenzweig, *The Star*, 300, 328–29. Cf. Funkenstein, *Perceptions*, 264.

60. Rosenzweig, *The Star*, 341–42, 415–16. Cf. Cohen, *Elevations*, 14, 18–21; Gibbs, *Correlations*, 105–6; David Novak, *Jewish-Christian Dialogue: A Jewish Justification* (Oxford: Oxford University Press, 1989), 108.

61. Mendes-Flohr, "Rosenzweig," 156.

62. Ibid.

63. Leora Batnitzky, *Idolatry and Representation: The Philosophy of Franz Rosenzweig Reconsidered* (Princeton, N.J.: Princeton University Press, 2000), 149–50.

64. Ibid., 153–54, 164.

65. See Novak, *Jewish-Christian Dialogue*, 109–10. Cf. Rosenstock-Huessy, *Judaism Despite Christianity*, 121, 139–40.

66. See Cohen, *Elevations*, 13–14.

67. Novak, *Jewish-Christian Dialogue*, 110.

68. See Rosenstock-Huessy's charge against Rosenzweig and Rosenzweig's response in *Judaism Despite Christianity*, 122–23, 131–32.

69. Cohen, *Elevations*, 13–14.

70. Ibid., 13–14, 21; Novak, *Jewish-Christian Dialogue*, 108–13.

71. Rosenzweig, *The Star*, 307. Cf. Cohen, *Elevations*, 18–19.

72. Rosenzweig, *The Star*, 306–7. Cf. Cohen, *Elevations*, 19–20.

73. Rosenzweig, *The Star*, 306.

74. Cohen, *Elevations*, 21.

75. Rosenzweig to Hans Ehrenberg, 13 June 1918, trans. Miller in *Dialogue and Disagreement*, 109–14. Cf. Funkenstein, *Perceptions*, 301.

76. Miller, *Dialogue and Disagreement*, 83–116, esp. 115–16. Cf. Cohen, *Elevations*, 14 n. 10. In regard to van Buren, Alan Davies and David Novak argue that his *Discerning the Way* is a revision of Rosenzweig's "two covenant theory." Yet Stephen Haynes points out that while Rosenzweig has clearly influenced van Buren's thought, van Buren himself argued that Rosenzweig has no theory regarding two covenants and did not use this terminology to refer to the relationship between Israel and the Church. Instead, Rosenzweig described the relationship between Israel and the Church in terms of a star and its rays. See Haynes, *Prospects for Post-Holocaust Theology* (Atlanta: Scholars Press, 1991), 169–70, 210 n. 34.

Alternatively, using Rosenzweigian terms, Eckardt described the Jewish-Christian relationship as complementary yet oppositional. Moreover, Eckardt argued that a "Christian theology of the Jewish-Christian relationship is called to proclaim from the Christian side what Franz Rosenzweig has expressed from the Jewish side: Judaism is the 'star of redemption,' Christianity the rays of that star" (A. Roy Eckardt, *Elder and Younger Brothers: The Encounter of Jews and Christians* [New York: Charles Scribner's Sons, 1967], 145, 160).

77. Batnitzky, *Idolatry and Representation*, 155–56.

78. Ibid., 158.

79. John T. Pawlikowski, *Christ in the Light of the Christian-Jewish Dialogue*, (New York: Paulist Press, 1982), 14, 17–18. See my discussion of these thinkers in chapter 4 of this work.

80. Rosenstock-Huessy, *Judaism Despite Christianity*, 136. Cf. Novak, *Jewish-Christian Dialogue*, 112, 177 n. 72; Batnitzky, *Idolatry and Representation*, 157.

81. Rosenzweig, *The Star*, 414–15.

82. Rosenstock-Huessy, *Judaism Despite Christianity*, 113.

83. Rosenzweig, *The Star*, 341–43. Cf. Funkenstein, *Perceptions*, 300. In *Idolatry and Representation*, Batnitzky points out that for Rosenzweig, the eternality of Jewish blood is purely a philosophical construct and not a racial distinction. However, this philosophical construct is actually intended to "undo the priority of philosophical constructs" in the sense that the bodily existence of the Jewish people is far more important than any idea and actually marks the limit of philosophy itself. See *Idolatry and Representation*, 73–75.

84. Rosenzweig, *The Star*, 329. Cf. Cohen, *Elevations*, 9.

85. See Rosenzweig to Rudolf Ehrenberg, 4 November 1913, in *Franz Rosenzweig: Der Mensch und sein Werk, Gesammelte Schriften*, vol. 1, *Brief und Tagebücher*, 142. This portion of the letter was translated by Batnitzky in *Idolatry and Transformation*, 261 n. 35.

86. See Glatzer's translation of this letter in *Franz Rosenzweig*, 345. Cf. Cohen, *Elevations*, 9.

87. Cohen, *Elevations*, 9.

88. Rosenzweig's commentary to Yehuda Halevi's poem "Out of My Straits," translated by Glatzer in *Franz Rosenzweig*, 335–36. Cf. Cohen, *Elevations*, 24; Rosenzweig, *Ninety-two Poems and Hymns of Yehuda Halevi*, ed. Richard A. Cohen, trans. Thomas Kovach, Eva Jospe, and Gilya Gerda Schmidt, (Albany: State University of New York Press, 2000), 169.

89. Batnitzky, *Idolatry and Representation*, 91. Cf. Richard Wagner, "Judaism in Music," in *Judaism in Music and Other Essays*, trans. W. Ashton Ellis (Lincoln: University of Nebraska Press, 1995).

90. Rosenzweig, *The Star*, 334. Cf. Batnitzky, *Idolatry and Representation*, 91.

91. Batnitzky, *Idolatry and Representation*, 93. Cf. Gordon C. F. Bearn, "Wittgenstein on the Uncanny," *Soundings* 17, no. 1 (spring 1993): 33.

92. Funkenstein discusses the history of Jewish theodicies in *Perceptions*, 203–6. Cf. Cohen, *Elevations*, 9–10.

93. Funkenstein, *Perceptions*, 204–5. Cf. Gershom Scholem, *Major Trends in Jewish Mysticism* 3d ed. (New York: Schocken Books, 1971), 244–86.

94. Funkenstein, *Perceptions*, 205–6.

95. Rosenzweig, *The Star*, 306–7, 314. Cf. Cohen, *Elevations*, 19. It was the medieval commentator Rashi who first appropriated the Christian interpretation of the suffering servant as suffering for the sake of the sins of the world and not for its own sins, subsequently redeeming the entire world through its afflictions. However, his portrayal of the suffering servant as the entire nation of Israel dates back to Hellenistic and rabbinic sources. See Amos Funkenstein, *Signonot Be-Parshanut Ha-Mikra Biymei Ha-Benayim*, [*Styles in Medieval Biblical Exegesis: An Introduction*] (Tel Aviv: Ministry of Defense, 1990).

In *Idolatry and Representation*, Batnitzky argues that Rosenzweig's use of the suffering servant motif may be traced directly to that of Hermann Cohen, who interpreted it to mean that the Jewish people, because of their role as witnesses to the one God, act as potential martyrs, suffering "vicariously for the faults and wrongs which still hinder the realization of monotheism" (Cohen, *A Religion of Reason Out of the Sources of Judaism*, trans. Simon Kaplan [Atlanta: Scholars Press, 1995], 268). Batnitzky further claims that the core of Cohen's argument for Jewish uniqueness as the bearers of ethical monotheism becomes a central theme of *The Star of Redemption*. See Batnitzky, *Idolatry and Representation*, 59.

96. Rosenzweig, *The Star*, 306, 345–46, 349–50. In addition, see his letter to Rosenstock in *Judaism Despite Christianity*, 130–32. Cf. Cohen, *Elevations*, 19–20.

97. Rosenzweig, *The Star*, 415–16; Augustine, *City of God*, 18:46. Cf. Funkenstein, *Perceptions*, 300–301.

98. Rosenstock-Huessy, *Judaism Despite Christianity*, 114. Cf. Batnitzky, *Idolatry and Representation* 89, 156.

99. Batnitzky, *Idolatry and Representation*, 89–90. Here she observes that by valorizing Christian images, Rosenzweig is going against the typical modern Jewish polemic against Christian visual representation of divinity expressed most conspicuously by Moses Mendelssohn, Heinrich Graetz, Hermann Cohen, and Leo Baeck. However, Rosenzweig is consistent with those thinkers in his portrayal of Judaism as resisting art for the sake of preserving pure monotheism.

100. Funkenstein, *Perceptions*, 300–301.

101. Rosenzweig, *The Star*, 416.

102. Ibid., *The Star*, 415; Augustine, *City of God*, 18:46.

103. Rosenzweig's commentary to Yehuda Halevi's poem "Out of My Straits," translated by Glatzer in *Franz Rosenzweig*, 335–36. Cf. Cohen, *Elevations*, 24; Rosenzweig, *Ninety-two Poems and Hymns of Yehuda Halevi*, 169.

104. Funkenstein, *Perceptions*, 305.

105. Batnitzky, *Idolatry and Representation*, 103.

106. Friedrich Wilhelm Joseph Schelling, *Philosophy of Art*, trans. Douglas W. Stott (Minneapolis: University of Minnesota Press, 1989), 35. Cf. Batnitzky, *Idolatry and Representation*, 102.

107. Rosenzweig, *The Star*, 305. Cf. Batnitzky, *Idolatry and Representation*, 103.

108. On the issue of organically constructed subjectivity, see Henry A. Giroux, *Border Crossings: Cultural Workers and the Politics of Education* (New York: Routledge, 1992), 165.

CHAPTER 2

1. For biographical information on Rosenzweig, see chapter 1 of this work. Hans Joachim Schoeps discusses his assimilated Jewish upbringing in *Die letzten dreissig Jahre, Rückblicke* (Stuttgart: Ernst Klett Verlag, 1956), 72. Cf. John V. H. Dippel, *Bound upon a Wheel of Fire: Why So Many Jews Made the Tragic Decision to Remain in Nazi Germany* (New York: Basic Books, 1996), 35–36. For his critique of historicism, see Schoeps, *Jüdischer Glaube in dieser Zeit: Prolegomena zur Grundlegung einer systematischen Theologie des Judentums*, in *Gesammelte Schriften*, ed. Julius H. Schoeps (Hildescheim: Georg Olms, 1990), 63–64.

2. Schoeps, *Jüdischer Glaube*, 64. Cf. Alexander Altmann, "Zur Auseinandersetzung mit der 'dialektischen Theologie,'" *Monatschrift für Geschichte und Wissenschaft des Judentums* 79 (1935): 360. There has been an ongoing debate regarding the supposed transition in Barth's thought from a dialectical theology that developed in reaction to liberal Protestantism in 1918, to a theology based on an "analogy of faith," in which there is an analogous relationship between the act of divine revelation and the human act of faith through which that revelation is acknowledged. This is an analogy between divine self-knowledge and human knowledge of God through human concepts and words. The debate among historians of Barth is based on Hans Urs von Balthazar's book *Karl Barth: Darstellung und Deutung seiner Theologie* (1951), in which he lays out two possible periodizations for Barth's theological development. The more popular model posits a radical break between Barth's dialectical and analogical periods in 1931 with the publication of his study on Anselm's *Proslogion*, in which Barth argues that divine revelation is not simply a momentary, existential encounter of God as the "Wholly Other" over against humanity, but in it, God actually provides humanity with a sense of divine intelligibility through the Word made flesh in Christ which can be understood rationally on the human level.

Von Balthazar's second model of Barth's theological progression presents a more gradual turn toward analogy in 1927 with his analysis of Barth's *Christliche Dogmatik*, in which the latter outlined the conditions for a genuine Christian theology based solely on the actuality of divine self-revelation in Jesus Christ and its reception in faith empowered by the Holy Spirit. According to Barth, theology cannot be based in any other discipline that might determine the nature of the object to be studied or the methods with which to study it. Even Christian dogmatics must refer back to their original divine ground in order to remove distortions and misrepresentations of the Divine Word so that it can be heard anew. See von Balthazar, *Karl Barth: Darstellung und Deutung seiner Theologie* [The Theology of Karl Barth] New York: Rinehart and Winston, 1971).

Recent Barth scholarship rejects the first model, while affirming varying versions of the second. In his *Karl Barth's Critically Realistic Dialectical Theology*, (1995), Bruce McCormack argues against the whole idea of a transformation in Barth's thought, claiming that the analogy of faith is itself inherently dialectical in the sense that the analogical relation between revelation and human language is predicated upon the dialectic of divine unveiling through the veil of human language. While Barth's dialectical method may have been subordinated to a dogmatic method later in his career, McCormack asserts that Barth remained a dialectical theologian even in *Church Dogmatics*. Yet McCormack argues against Jungel that unlike the other dialectical theologians with whom he is associated, Brunner, Bultmann, and Gogarten, Barth never identified the Kierkegaardian "dialectic of existence" as the fundamental problem of human life but rather viewed it as "a symptom of a deeper-lying problem (viz. Sin) which is only recognized when the answer to it is given in revelation." See Bruce L. McCormack, *Karl Barth's Critically Realistic Dialectical Theology: Its Genesis and Development, 1909–1936* (Oxford: Clarendon Press, 1995), 1–20, 239–40, n. 108. Cf. Alasdair I. C. Heron, *A Century of Protestant Theology* (Philadelphia: Westminster Press, 1980), 81–84.

3. Schoeps, *Jüdischer Glaube*, 75, 78; Gary Lease, ed., "Der Briefwechsel zwischen Karl Barth und Hans-Joachim Schoeps," in *Menora* (Munich: Piper, 1991), 111.

4. On Rosenzweig's conflicting views toward the Christian role in redemption, see chapter 1 of this work. For Schoeps's treatment of Christian participation in redemption, see Schoeps, *Die letzten dreissig Jahre*, 74–77; Schoeps, "Secessio Judaica-Israel in Ewigkeit," in *Bereit für Deutschland. Der Patriotismus deutscher Juden und der Nationalsozialismus* (Berlin: Haude and Spencer, 1970), 281–84; Schoeps and Hans Blüher, *Streit um Israel: Ein jüdisch-christliches Gespräch* (Hamburg: Hanseatische Verlagsanstalt, 1933), 15, 56, 62, 104, 110, 115–16, 118. Cf. Gary Lease, *"Odd Fellows" in the Politics of Religion: Modernism, National Socialism, and German Judaism* (Berlin: Mouton de Gruyter, 1995), 214–20.

5. Schoeps was criticized for his theology not being representative of Jewish thought by the Jewish thinkers Gershom Scholem and Alexander Altmann. In addition, the German cultural critic Hans Blüher even criticized Schoeps for recognizing Christian legitimacy too much! See Scholem, "Offener Brief an den Verfasser der Schrift, 'Jüdischer Glaube in dieser Zeit,'" *Bayerische Israelitische Gemeindezeitung* (15 August 1932): 241–44; cf. David Biale, *Gershom Scholem: Kabbalah and Counter History* (Cambridge, Mass.: Harvard University Press, 1982), 127–30; Altmann, "Zur Auseinandersetzung"; Schoeps and Blüher, *Streit um Israel*, 74, 80, 90. Cf. Lease, *"Odd Fellows,"* 217, 274, n. 382. Karl Barth also criticized Schoeps for not taking into account Christian theological categories enough. See Lease, "Der Briefwechsel," 115–20.

6. See Dippel's discussion of Schoeps's attraction to the Wandervogel movement in *Bound upon a Wheel of Fire*, 35–36. In addition, David Biale describes the Wandervogel movement in the context of Gershom Scholem's teenage years in Germany. See Biale, *Gershom Scholem*, 12–14.

7. Dippel, *Bound upon a Wheel of Fire*, 36; Paul Mendes-Flohr discusses the differences between *Gemeinschaft* and *Gesellschaft* in the introduction to his book *From Mysticism to Dialogue: Martin Buber's Transformation of German Social Thought* (Detroit: Wayne State University Press, 1989), 18.

8. Dippel, *Bound upon a Wheel of Fire*, 37–38.

9. Biale, *Gershom Scholem*, 12–14; Mendes-Flohr, *From Mysticism to Dialogue*, 110.

10. Dippel, *Bound upon a Wheel of Fire*, 36, 108.

11. Ibid., 37–38.

12. Lease, *"Odd Fellows,"* 226; Dippel, *Bound upon a Wheel of Fire*, 37. Cf. Hans Joachim Schoeps, "Zur freideutschen Fahne," *Die Wegwarte* 3 (October 1926): 14–15.

13. Lease, "*Odd Fellows*," 227. Cf. Hans Joachim Schoeps, "American Made in Germany—Es gibt eine freideutsche Position," *Die Freideutsche Position. Rundbrief an Jugendführer zur Besinnung und Stellungnahme* 1 (Spring 1929): 8. See also Dippel, *Bound upon a Wheel of Fire*, 39.

14. Lease, "*Odd Fellows*," 227–28.

15. Ibid., 231.

16. Ibid., 206–7, 231. Cf. Schoeps, *Jüdischer Glaube*, 76. See also note 24 in this chapter. I will later point out Lease's failure to fully take into account Schoeps's promotion of a racially based Jewish identity.

17. Salomon Ludwig Steinheim, *Die Offenbarung nach dem Lehrbegriffe der Synagogue*, vol. 1, *Ein Schiboleth* (Frankfurt am Main: Schmerber, 1835), 11, 358; Schoeps, *Jüdischer Glaube*, 70–73. Cf. Lease, "*Odd Fellows*," 195, 198, 270 n. 340.

18. Hans Joachim Schoeps, ed., *Salomon Ludwig Steinheim: Zum Gedenken* (Leiden: E. J. Brill, 1966), 34. Cf. Biale, *Gershom Scholem*, 128.

19. Dippel, *Bound upon a Wheel of Fire*, 68–69, 107.

20. Lease, "*Odd Fellows*," 228–30. Cf. Dippel, *Bound upon a Wheel of Fire*, 71.

21. Dippel, *Bound upon a Wheel of Fire*, 144–45, 178.

22. Lease, "*Odd Fellows*," 224–25.

23. For a larger discussion of Rosenzweig's attitude toward Zionism, see chapter 1 of this work. Schoeps equates Zionism with antisemitism in *Jüdischer Glaube*, 75–76, n. 224. In addition, see his response to Gershom Scholem's "Offener Brief," in *Ja-Nein-und Trotzdem: Erinnerungen, Begegaunger, Erfahrungen* (Mainz: Hase & Koehler Verlag, 1974), 49. Cf. George Mosse, "The Influence of the Völkish Idea on German Jewry," chap. in *Germans and Jews: The Right, The Left, and the Search for a "Third Force" in Pre-Nazi Germany* (New York: Howard Fertig, 1970); Biale, *Gershom Scholem*, 128; Dippel, *Bound upon a Wheel of Fire*, 58, 69.

24. Schoeps, *Jüdischer Glaube*, 76. Gershom Scholem also cited this passage as part of a larger footnote to his correspondence with Schoeps on 3 January 1937 in which he responds to the work that Schoeps sent him. While expressing the desire for dialogue with Schoeps, Scholem disapprovingly cites his construction of a Jewish identity patterned after Yehuda Halevi's portrayal of a racially based Jewish spiritual essence in *The Kuzari*. See Gershom Scholem, *Briefe I: 1914–1947*, ed. Itta Shedletzky (Munich: Verlag C. H. Beck, 1994), 262–63, 418–20 n. 5.

25. Schoeps, *Jüdischer Glaube*, 76 n. 225. Cf. Scholem, *Briefe I*, 420.

26. Ibid., 75 n. 224. Cf. Scholem, *Briefe I*, 419.

27. Ibid., 80 n. 230.

28. Lease, "*Odd Fellows*," 216–17.

29. Schoeps and Blüher, *Streit um Israel*, 55. Italics and brackets are mine.

30. Schoeps, *Jüdischer Glaube*, 80.

31. Ibid., 80, 87.

32. Ibid., 63, 74–76.

33. Schoeps's response to Scholem's "Offener Brief," in *Ja-Nein-Und Trotzedm*, 48.

34. Ibid., 48–49.

35. Schoeps, *Jüdischer Glaube*, 3.

36. Ibid., 69, 82.

37. Scholem, "Offener Brief," 242. Cf. Biale, *Gershom Scholem*, 128–29; Lease, "*Odd Fellows*," 208;

38. Altmann, "Zur Auseinandersetzung," 359–61; Altmann, "Theology in Twentieth-Century German Jewry," *Leo Baeck Institute Yearbook* 1 (1956): 210.

39. Schoeps, *Jüdischer Glaube*, 3, 73–75.

40. Altmann, "Zur Auseinandersetzung," 359; Altmann, "Theology in Twentieth-Century German Jewry," 210.

41. Martin Buber, *I and Thou*, trans. Walter Kaufman (New York: Charles Scribner's Sons, 1970), 149, 161. See also Biale's discussion of Buber's ahistorical portrayal of revelation in *Gershom Scholem*, 118–19.

42. Rosenzweig, *The Star of Redemption*, 2d ed., trans. William W. Hallo (Notre Dame, Ind.: Notre Dame Univesity Press, 1985), 163.

43. Ibid., 162–63, 178–85.

44. Lease, "*Odd Fellows*," 231.

45. Schoeps, *Jüdischer Glaube*, 76 n. 224. Cf. Scholem, *Briefe I*, 419.

46. Schoeps and Blüher, *Streit um Israel*, 104, 110. Cf. Lease, "*Odd Fellows*," 217.

47. Schoeps, *Jüdischer Glaube*, 76.

48. Lease, "*Odd Fellows*," 230–31.

49. Schoeps and Blüher, *Streit um Israel*, 45–47, 110. Cf. Lease, "*Odd Fellows*," 215–17.

50. Lease, "*Odd Fellows*," 227–31.

51. Schoeps, *Jüdischer Glaube*, 76 n. 224. Cf. Scholem, *Briefe I*, 419.

52. Schoeps and Blüher, *Streit um Israel*, 47–48. Cf. Lease, "*Odd Fellows*," 216.

53. Schoeps, "Der Nationalsozialismus als verkappte Religion," *Eltheto* 93 (March 1939): 93. Cf. Lease, "*Odd Fellows*," 181–82.

54. Lease, "*Odd Fellows*," 209, 231; Joachim H. Knoll, "In memoriam Hans-Joachim Schoeps: Der Mensch, sein Werk und sein Zeit," in *Deutsch-jüdische Geschichte im 19 und 20. Jahrhundert*, ed. Lodger Heid and Joachim H. Knoll, Studien zur Geistesgeschichte, vol. 15 (Stuttgart: Burg, 1992), 233–35.

55. On the Jewish criticism of Schoeps's political views, see Lease, "*Odd Fellows*," 225–26.

56. Paul Mendes-Flohr, "Rosenzweig and the Crisis of Historicism," in *The Philosophy of Franz Rosenzweig* (Hanover, N.H.: University Press of New England, 1988), 159.

57. Schoeps, *Jüdischer Glaube*, 4, 63–64, 84.

58. Schoeps, *Die letzten dreissig Jahre*, 72.

59. Schoeps, *Ja-Nein-Und Trotzdem*, 136. He provides another account of his encounter with Beyer in *Die letzten dreissig Jahre*, 72–73.

60. Karl Holl, *What Did Luther Understand by Religion?* ed. James Luther Adams and Walter F. Bense, trans. Fred W. Meuser and Walter R. Wietzke (Philadelphia: Fortress Press, 1977), 1–3. This book was based on a lecture that Holl gave at the University of Berlin in 1917.

61. Schoeps, *Ja-Nein-Und Trotzdem*, 136; Schoeps, *Die letzten dreissig Jahre*, 73.

62. Schoeps, *Jüdischer Glaube*, 77, 81–82; Holl, *What Did Luther Understand by Religion?* 41–43.

63. Schoeps, *Ja-Nein-Und Trotzdem*, 136.

64. Walter Bodenstein, *Die Theologie Karl Holls im Spiegel des Antiken und Reformatorischen Christentums* (Berlin: Walter de Gruyter, 1968), 206–7.

65. Schoeps, *Jüdischer Glaube*, 3, 5–6.

66. Schoeps, *Ja-Nein-Und Trotzdem*, 137.

67. Ibid., 139.

68. Holl, *What Did Luther Understand by Religion?* 41–45.

69. Schoeps, *Ja-Nein-Und Trotzdem*, 138.

70. Schoeps's response to Scholem's "Offener Brief," 48–49.

71. Schoeps, *Die letzten dreissig Jahre*, 73.

72. Schoeps, *Ja-Nein-Und Trotzdem*, 139.

73. Ibid.

74. See Hans Joachim Schoeps, *Paul: The Theology of the Apostle in the Light of Jewish Religious History*, trans. Harold Knight (Philadelphia: Westminster Press, 1961); Schoeps, *Jewish Christianity: Factional Disputes in the Early Church*, trans. Douglas R. A. Hare (Philadelphia: Fortress Press, 1969); Schoeps, *Philosemitismus im Barock: Religions-und geistgeschichtliche Untersuchungen* (Tübingen: Mohr, 1952).

75. Schoeps, *Paul*, 280–85.

76. Ibid.

77. See Lease, "Der Briefwechsel," 118.

78. Altmann, "Zur Auseinandersetzung," 359.

79. Altmann, "Theology in Twentieth-Century German Jewry," 209–10.

80. Altmann, "Zur Auseinandersetzung," 345–47, 359. Cf. Schoeps, *Jüdischer Glaube*, 63, 89.

81. Altmann, "Zur Auseinandersetzung," 347–49, 359. Cf. Schoeps, *Jüdischer Glaube*, 7–8.

82. Altmann, "Zur Auseinandersetzung," 359. Cf. Schoeps, *Jüdischer Glaube*, 3.

83. Altmann, "Zur Auseinandersetzung," 359–60. Cf. Karl Barth, *Die christliche Dogmatik im Entwurf, Erster Band: Die Lehre vom Worte Gottes* (Munich, 1927), 300; Schoeps, *Jüdischer Glaube*, 3, 75.

84. Altmann, "Zur Auseinandersetzung," 349–54, 360.

85. Scholem, "Offener Brief," 242–43. Cf. Biale, *Gershom Scholem*, 129.

86. Franz Rosenzweig, "The Builders," in *On Jewish Learning*, trans. Nahum Glatzer (New York: Schocken paperback, 1965), 90; Rosenzweig, *The Star*, 332. On Barth's dehistoricized eschatology, see chapter 1.

87. Altmann, "Zur Auseinandersetzung," 354–58, 360. Cf. Schoeps, *Jüdischer Glaube*, 66–67.

88. Altmann, "Zur Auseinandersetzung," 354–55, 360. Cf. Schoeps, *Jüdischer Glaube*, 5.

89. Lease, "Der Briefwechsel," 117.

90. Ibid., 119.

91. Schoeps, *Jüdischer Glaube*, 74.

92. BT, *Berakhot*, 61a–b. Cf. A. Cohen, *Everyman's Talmud* (New York: Schocken Books, 1975), 88–93.

93. Karl Barth, *The Epistle to the Romans*, 6th ed., trans. Edwyn C. Hoskyns (London: Oxford University Press, 1960), 173.

94. Schoeps, *Jüdischer Glaube*, 74, 82.

95. Barth, *The Epistle to the Romans*, 171–72, 175–76. Cf. McCormack, *Karl Barth's Critically Realistic Dialectical Theology*, 149–52.

96. Karl Barth, *Church Dogmatics*, vol. 3:1, *The Doctrine of Creation*, ed. G. W. Bromiley and T. F. Torrance, trans. J. W. Edwards, O. Bussey, and Harold Knight (Edinburgh: T. and T. Clark, 1958), 196, 200. Cf. Colin Brown, "Karl Barth's Doctrine of the Creation, *Churchman* 76 (June 1962): 100–101.

97. Barth, *The Epistle to the Romans*, 271–74. Cf. McCormack, *Karl Barth's Critically Realistic Dialectical Theology*, 155–56.

98. Schoeps, *Jüdischer Glaube*, 82.

99. Ibid.

100. Barth, *Church Dogmatics*, vol. 2:1, *The Doctrine of God*, ed. G. W. Bromiley and T. F. Torrance, trans. T. H. L. Parker, W. B. Johnston, Harold Knight and J. L. M. Haire, (Edinburgh: T. and T. Clark, 1964), 52. Cf. George Hunsiger, *How to Read Karl Barth: The Shape of His Theology* (Oxford: Oxford University Press, 1991), 79–80; Schoeps, *Jüdischer Glaube*, 75; Schoeps's, response to Scholem's "Offener Brief," 51.

101. Schoeps's response to Scholem's "Offener Brief," 50–51. According to Scholem, Schoeps's position on revelation did not correspond to what he considered to be the traditional Jewish understanding of revelation. Scholem claimed that "revelation, despite its total uniqueness, is still a medium. It is the absolute, meaning bestowing, but itself meaninglessness that is interpretable only through the continuing relationship to time in the tradition" (Scholem, "Offener Brief," 243). Scholem asserted that according to rabbinic Judaism, the Divine Word must be mediated by the oral tradition of commentary in order to be comprehensible and fulfillable. Otherwise it would be destructive. Hence, Scholem disputed the claims of theologians like Schoeps who posited that the Divine Word is "absolutely concrete. . . . Only in the mirrorings in which it reflects itself does revelation become practicable and accessible to human action as something concrete" (Scholem, "Revelation and Tradition as Religious Categories," in *The Messianic Idea in Judaism and Other Essays in Jewish Spirituality* [New York: Schocken Books, 1971], 296).

102. Schoeps, *Die letzten dreissig Jahre*, 74.

103. Schoeps's response to Scholem's "Offener Brief," 49–50, 52.

104. Holl, *What Did Luther Understand by Religion?* 71–72.

105. Ibid., 95, 100–101, n. 71.

106. Ibid., 101–8, esp. 104. Although, one could also argue that Schoeps was in?uenced by Steinheim's promotion of a political theocracy. In *Die Politik nach dem Begriffe der Offenbarung als Theokratie*, Steinheim argued that the goal of the state is to present a "higher order of things in the invisible world, i.e., the order of moral (ethical) harmony, of freedom." In freedom, humanity creates the state on earth, and as a result, transfers the higher order of freedom to this world. Because it represents the doctrine of revelation through its demonstration of freedom, the true state organically becomes a religious institution, a "religion of the state." According to Steinheim, this cannot be a "state religion" because it belongs to God and therefore cannot be controlled by the state. While throughout history, Christianity has been the state religion, the religious idea of a state in freedom has been hidden in Judaism and acted as a ferment in paganism. However, Steinheim

observed that in his lifetime, the German philosopher Hegel recognized that the state and religion have the same ethical basis. See Steinheim, *Die Politik nach dem Begriffe der Offenbarung als Theokratie* (Leipzig: Teubner, 1845), 2, 42, 50, 59–60, 97. Cf. Lease, "*Odd Fellows*," 198–200.

107. Holl, *What Did Luther Understand by Religion?* 74–78.

108. Ibid., 42–43, 53 n. 28, 86–91, 96–101.

109. "Editor's Introduction," in *What Did Luther Understand by Religion?* 10. Cf. Stephen R. Haynes, "'Between the Times': German Theology and the Weimar Zeitgeist," *Soundings* 74, nos. 1–2 (spring/summer 1991): 16–34; McCormack, *Karl Barth's Critically Realistic Dialectical Theology*, 116.

110. "Editor's Introduction," in *What Did Luther Understand by Religion?* 10–13. Holl responded to these points by arguing first that Luther always maintained a gradation between God and Christ and that his faith was never fully Christocentric. Thus, Luther never regarded "the forgetting of Christ" as a sin but only an example of a divine trial imposed by God directly. Next, Holl claimed that while God's forgiveness may appear in the form of an inference, Luther asserted, just as Schoeps did later, that the forgiveness he received from God can never be fathomed rationally, and in fact went against his conscience and ultimately God, whom his conscience testifies was against him. Finally, Holl disagreed with Gogarten's claim that Luther neglected secular matters because of his "'ethic of grace' based on faith rather than on love." Here Holl accused Gogarten of subjectively reading Luther with a Barthian presupposition that ethics is the "great disturbance." Instead, Holl maintained "that the God-ward side of Luther's ethic, faith, is always intrinsically connected with the world-ward side oriented to human beings, love." See Holl, *What Did Luther Understand by Religion?* 78–79, 81–82, 84, 114, 118–19.

111. Schoeps and Blüher, *Streit um Israel*, 104, 110; see the discussion about this between Franz Rosenzweig and Eugen Rosenstock-Huessy in Eugen Rosenstock-Huessy, ed., *Judaism Despite Christianity: The "Letters on Christianity and Judaism" between Eugen Rosenstock-Huessy and Franz Rosenzweig* (University: University of Alabama Press, 1969), 122–23, 131–32. See also Richard Cohen, *Elevations: The Height of the Good in Rosenzweig and Levinas* (Chicago: University of Chicago Press, 1994), 13–14.

112. Schoeps and Blüher, *Streit and Israel*, 104.

113. Ibid., 55, 110.

114. Schoeps, *Jüdischer Glaube*, 84, 87.

115. Lease, "Der Briefwechsel," 111; Schoeps, *Jüdischer Glaube*, 3.

116. Rosenzweig, *The Star*, 340–42; Schoeps, *Jüdischer Glaube*, 75; Schoeps, *The Jewish-Christian Argument: A History of Theologies in Conflict*, 3rd ed., trans. David E. Green (London: Faber and Faber, 1963), 162–63.

117. Schoeps and Blüher, *Streit um Israel*, 54–55. See Exod. 4:22–23, Deut. 8:5, 14:1, Jer. 45:11, 64:8, in *Tanakh: The Holy Scriptures* (Philadelphia: Jewish Publication Society, 1988).

118. Lease, "Der Briefwechsel," 119.

119. Yehuda Halevi, *The Kuzari: An Argument for the Faith of Israel*, trans. Hartwig Hirschfeld (New York: Schocken Books, 1964), 1:95. Cf. Amos Funkenstein, *Perceptions of Jewish History*, (Berkeley: University of California press, 1993), 200.

120. Schoeps and Blüher, *Streit um Israel*, 55.

121. Ibid.

122. Ibid., 62, 80, 90.

123. Ibid., 15.

124. Schoeps, *Die letzten dreissig Jahre*, 76–77.

125. Schoeps and Blüher, *Streit um Israel*, 15, 115–16.

126. Schoeps, *Die letzten dreissig Jahre*, 74–75.

127. Ibid.; Rosenzweig, *The Star*, 280, 283, 328–29, 350, 399–401, 421; Rosenstock-Huessy, *Judaism Despite Christianity*, 131–32.

128. It is important to note, however, that while modern liberal Jewish movements have appropriated Rosenzweig's work, his work is largely ignored among Orthodox Jewish thinkers, except for those on the left of the spectrum.

CHAPTER 3

1. Richard L. Rubenstein, *Power Struggle* (New York: Charles Scribner's Sons, 1974), 9–13; Rubenstein, *After Auschwitz: Radical Theology and Contemporary Judaism* (Indianapolis: Bobbs-Merrill, 1966), 153.

2. Richard Rubenstein, *After Auschwitz: History, Theology, and Contemporary Judaism*, 2nd ed. (Baltimore: Johns Hopkins University Press, 1992), 294.

3. Rubenstein, *After Auschwitz*, 147.

4. Ibid., 3, 19.

5. Ibid., 7–9.

6. Ibid., 9.

7. Ibid., 74.

8. Rabbi Taitelbaum was the leader of an anti-Zionist sect, Neturei Karta (Guardians of the City). In his book *Vayo'el Moshe* (*And It Pleased Moses*), Rabbi Taitelbaum concludes that the Holocaust was the inevitable consequence of and punishment for the sin of seeking divine redemption through human initiative. He based his position largely on a *midrash* from BT *Ketubot* 3a, which describes three oaths made between Israel, God, and the nations based on three appearances of a divine oath in the Song of Songs to the daughters of Israel not to force love before its time. The Rabbis interpreted this to mean that Israel should not rebel against its oppressors and subsequently not try to precipitate the coming of the messianic age, while the nations must agree not to oppress Israel too much. According to Taitelbaum, the Jews in the Zionist movement broke their oath to God to not try to force the coming of the messianic age by trying to achieve sovereignty in the State of Israel, and in turn the nations relinquished their oath to not oppress the Jews too much. For Taitelbaum, the Holocaust was not even the final catastrophe but only a prelude to an apocalyptic ending to the world that would serve as a punishment for the establishment of the State of Israel. See Amos Funkenstein, *Perceptions of Jewish History* (Berkeley: University of California Press, 1993), 307–8. See also the discussion of "passive messianism" later in this chapter.

9. Rubenstein, *After Auschwitz*, 54–55, 65.

10. Ibid., 56–57.

11. Ibid., 52.

12. Ibid., 56.

13. Rubenstein, *After Auschwitz*, 2d ed., 13.

14. Richard Rubenstein, "Luther and the Roots of the Holocaust," in *Persistent Prejudice: Perspectives on Anti-Semitism*, ed. Herbert Hirsch and Jack D. Spiro (Fairfax, Va.: George Mason University Press, 1988), 38; Rubenstein, *After Auschwitz*, 2d ed., 90–93. In *Perceptions*, Funkenstein argued that in addition to the mutual repulsion between Jews and Christians, there was an element of mutual fascination as well. See Funkenstein, *Perceptions*, 171–72. We will see that Rubenstein himself illustrates this dialectic between fascination and aversion for the Christian Other.

15. Rubenstein, *After Auschwitz*, 64, 74–75, 80.

16. Ibid., 75.

17. Rubenstein, *After Auschwitz*, 2d ed., 27.

18. Richard Rubenstein, *The Religious Imagination: A Study in Psychoanalysis and Jewish Theology* (Indianapolis: Bobbs Merrill, 1968), 147–49. Cf. Zachary Braiterman, *(God) After Auschwitz: Tradition and Change in Post-Holocaust Jewish Thought* (Princeton, N.J.: Princeton University Press, 1998), 101.

19. Rubenstein, *The Religious Imagination*, 136. Braiterman describes Rubenstein's portrayal of rabbinic Judaism in *The Religious Imagination* as a eulogy because he praises the Rabbis for imbuing Jewish tragedy throughout history with meaning "by interpreting it as punishment and by imbuing it with redemptive significance. He nevertheless argues that rabbinic response to disaster is no longer viable in the late twentieth century. . . . The rich world of aggadah, Rubenstein sadly concludes, is 'an irretrievable lost haven of human truth'" (Braiterman, [*God*] *After Auschwitz*, 101–2).

20. Jocelyn Hellig, "Richard L. Rubenstein," in *Interpreters of Judaism in the Late Twentieth Century*, ed. Steven T. Katz (Washington, D.C.: B'nai B'rith Books, 1993), 249. Cf. Rubenstein, *After Auschwitz*, 177.

21. Daniel Boyarin, *A Radical Jew: Paul and the Politics of Identity* (Berkeley: University of California Press, 1994), 41.

22. For Rubenstein's approach to religious ritual and myth, see "The Meaning of Torah in Contemporary Jewish Theology," in *After Auschwitz*, 2d ed., 234–46, "Symposium on Jewish Belief," and "The Symbols of Judaism and the Death of God," in the original edition of *After Auschwitz*, 146–47, 227–41.

23. On his reconstruction of the post-Holocaust God concept, see Richard Rubenstein, *Morality and Eros* (New York: McGraw-Hill, 1970), 190; Rubenstein, *After Auschwitz*, 2d ed., 295–96. On Marcionite Christianity, see Joseph B. Tyson, *The New Testament and Early Christianity* (New York: Macmillan, 1984), 385–87; and Helmut Koester, *History and Literature of Early Christianity*, vol. 2, *Introduction to the New Testament* (New York: Walter de Gruyter, 1987), 328–34.

24. Rubenstein, *After Auschwitz*, 2d ed., 207, 295–96. Rubenstein's emphasis on divine immanence and mystical nihilism is influenced by many other models: Pauline Christianity, paganism, Zoharic and Lurianic mysticism, Hegelian philosophy, Tillichian theology, and most recently Buddhism.

25. In "The Meaning of Torah in Contemporary Jewish Theology," Rubenstein describes rabbinic attempts to develop a mythology around the regal metaphors for God's relationship to Israel as a way to limit and anesthetize the awesomeness and

mysteriousness of the cannibal powers of the earth. Yet in "The Rebirth of Israel in Contemporary Jewish Theology," he argues that while the measurable punishments of the biblical God were more preferable to the arbitrary terror of the Mother Goddess, the Rabbis began to view the tragedies of Jewish history as the sole result of rebellion against an often tyrannical God and no longer as part of the inevitable self-unfolding of the universe. See *After Auschwitz*, 2d ed., 208–9, 244. Cf. Hellig, "Richard L. Rubenstein," 253.

26. Rubenstein compares rabbinic misogynist divine imagery with that of Paul in *My Brother Paul* (New York: Harper and Row, 1972), 162–73. Rubenstein further discusses rabbinic misogyny in *The Religious Imagination*, 47–52, 96–100, and *Power Struggle*, 165–66. For a critique of Rubenstein's protofeminism, see Jocelyn Hellig, "Rabbinic Powerlessness and the Power of Women," in *What Kind of God? Essays in Honor of Richard L. Rubenstein*, ed. Betty Rogers Rubenstein and Michael Berenbaum (Lanham, Md.: University Press of America, Inc., 1995), 124–29. The Jewish feminist theologian Judith Plaskow was the first to discuss the issue of the anti-Judaism of Christian feminist theologians in "Christian Feminism and Anti-Judaism," *Cross Currents* 33 (fall 1978): 306–9. In addition, see her "Feminist Anti-Judaism and the Christian God," *Journal of Feminist Studies in Religion* 7, no. 2 (fall 1991): 99–109. This essay was one of four papers presented at the 1989 conference of the European Society of Women for Theological Research that were reprinted as a special section on Christian feminist anti-Judaism in the *Journal of Feminist Studies in Religion* 7, no. 2 (fall 1991): 95–133. In addition, see Susannah Heschel, "Anti-Judaism in Christian Feminist Theology," *Tikkun* 5, no. 3 (May/June 1990): 25–28, 95–97. For a complete discussion of anti-Judaism in Christian feminism and post-Christian feminism, see Katharina von Kellenbach, *Anti-Judaism in Feminist Religious Writings* (Atlanta: Scholars Press, 1994).

27. See Rubenstein, *My Brother Paul*, 86, 105. Cf. Robert L. Moore, "Pauline Theology and the Return of the Repressed: Depth Psychology and Early Christian Thought," *Zygon* 13 (June 1978): 163–64.

28. Zachary Braiterman, "'Hitler's Accomplice?' The Tragic Theology of Richard Rubenstein," *Modern Judaism* 17, no. 1 (1997): 75; Braiterman, (*God*) *After Auschwitz*, 89.

29. Rubenstein, *Power Struggle*, 43–45.

30. Ibid., 23–26.

31. Ibid., 37–38.

32. Ibid., 42–43.

33. Ibid., 26–27, 134.

34. Rubenstein, interview by author, Bridgeport, Connecticut, 21 May 1997.

35. *The Oxford Dictionary of the Christian Church*, 3d ed., s.v. "Unitarianism"; *The New Schaff-Herzog Encyclopedia of Religious Knowledge*, 1964 ed., s.v. "Unitarians."

36. On this dilemma of second-generation American Jews, see Arnold M. Eisen, *The Chosen People in America: A Study in Jewish Religious Ideology* (Bloomington: Indiana University Press, 1983), 26–29. Cf. Leonard Dinnerstein, *Anti-Semitism in America* (Oxford: Oxford University Press, 1994), 128–29, 142–49.

37. Eisen, *The Chosen People in America*, 40–41.

38. Felix Levy, "The Uniqueness of Israel," in *His Own Torah: Felix A. Levy*

Memorial Volume, ed. Sefton D. Temkin (New York: Jonathan David, 1969), 161–73. Cf. Eisen, *The Chosen People in America*, 41–42, 194 n. 91.

39. See Benny Kraut, "The Ambivalent Relations of American Reform Judaism with Unitarianism in the Last Third of the Nineteenth Century," *Journal of Ecumenical Studies* 23, no. 1 (winter 1986): 58–68; Kraut, "A Unitarian Rabbi? The Case of Solomon H. Sonneschein," in *Jewish Apostasy in the Modern World*, ed. Todd M. Endelman (New York: Holmes and Meier, 1987), 272–308.

40. Rubenstein, *Power Struggle*, 45–46.

41. Ibid.

42. Ibid., 46–47; Rubenstein, *After Auschwitz*, 214–15.

43. Rubenstein, *After Auschwitz*, 224.

44. Kurt Lewin, "Self-Hatred among Jews," *Contemporary Jewish Record* 4, No. 3 (June 1941): 225. Cf. Eisen, *The Chosen People in America*, 30.

45. Eisen, *The Chosen People in America*, 30.

46. See Robert Goldenberg and Judith Plaskow, "Rabbi's Odyssey," review of *Power Struggle*, by Richard Rubenstein, *New Republic*, 5 October 1974, 26–27.

47. Jocelyn Hellig discusses Rubenstein's intellectual and spiritual path in "Richard L. Rubenstein," 249–51. Rubenstein himself provides a sketch of his career path in "A Twentieth-Century Journey," in *From the Unthinkable to the Unavoidable: American Christian and Jewish Scholars Encounter the Holocaust*, ed. Carol Rittner and John K. Roth (Westport, Conn.: Greenwood Press, 1997), 158–59.

48. Rubenstein, *My Brother Paul*, 10–13.

49. Rubenstein, *Power Struggle*, 94–95; Rubenstein, *My Brother Paul*, 8–11, 15–18.

50. Rubenstein, "A Twentieth-Century Journey," 158–59.

51. Hellig, "Richard L. Rubenstein," 251.

52. Rubenstein, "A Twentieth-Century Journey," 169.

53. Rubenstein, *The Religious Imagination*, 117–20, 163.

54. Ibid., 120–23.

55. Ibid., 120–24, 129–30.

56. Elliot B. Gertel, "Because of Our Sins," *Tradition* 15, no. 4 (spring 1976): 69, 73–74.

57. Rubenstein, *The Religious Imagination*, 124–26, 129.

58. Boyarin, *A Radical Jew*, 41.

59. Ibid.; E. P. Sanders, *Paul and Palestinian Judaism: A Comparison of Patterns of Religion* (Minneapolis, Minn.: Fortress Press, 1977), 33–59.

60. Rubenstein, *The Religious Imagination*, 165.

61. Ibid., 147.

62. Ibid., 140–42.

63. Rudolf Bultmann, *Primitive Christianity in Its Contemporary Setting*, trans. R. H. Fuller (New York: New American Library, 1974), 66. Cf. Sanders, *Paul and Palestinian Judaism*, 44.

64. Bultmann, *Primitive Christianity*, 70–71. Cf. Sanders, *Paul and Palestinian Judaism*, 45.

65. Rubenstein, *My Brother Paul*, 13.

66. Rubenstein, *The Religious Imagination*, 164–65; Rubenstein, *My Brother Paul*, 86. Cf. Moore, "Pauline Theology," 159–64.

67. Rubenstein, *The Religious Imagination*, 148, 170.

68. Rubenstein, interview by author, Bridgeport, Connecticut, 21 May 1997.

69. Ibid., Rubenstein, *Power Struggle*, 8–9.

70. Rubenstein, *The Religious Imagination*, 126–28, 36; Howard F. Stein, "Judaism and the Group Fantasy of Martyrdom: The Psychodynamic Paradox of Survival through Persecution," *Journal of Psycho-History* 6, no. 2 (fall 1978): 151–210, esp. 153–54, 157–59, 163–64, 199. Rubenstein criticizes Howard Stein for this type of reductionism, yet Rubenstein's psychohistoriography is more similar to that of Stein than he admits. Like Rubenstein, Stein tends to reduce all of Jewish history to a recurring psychic factor of self-hate. He also relates the transcendent God of Jewish theology to what he considers to be "Jewish personality's transcendent mind, not only removed from the world of passions, but which must vigilantly prevent the return of the oppressed" (Stein, 164). Moreover, Stein echoes Rubenstein's concern regarding the anxiety of following *Halakhah* in a legalistic manner, and Stein refers to La Barre's description of a compulsive observance of the commandments illustrating "a hidden ambivalence and surreptitious private revolt against one's own Jewish humanly impossible orthodoxy" (Stein, 163).

However, as Rubenstein clearly shows, Stein goes much further than him in his psychohistory of Judaism by arguing that Jewish history is characterized not only by self-hate but also by a "self-destructive fantasy that is the very substance of Jewish identity" (Stein, 199). Rubenstein ultimately calls Stein's article antisemitic, despite Stein's claim to the opposite. See Rubenstein, "Response to the Issue on Judaism and Psycho-History of *The Journal of Psycho-History*," *Journal of Psycho-History* 7 (spring 1979): 543–555, esp. 543–45, 553–54.

71. Rubenstein, *Power Struggle*, 171–72.

72. Richard Rubenstein, "Jewish Theology and the Current World Situation," *Conservative Judaism* 28, no. 4 (summer 1974): 9.

73. Ibid., 11.

74. Ibid., 11–12.

75. Rubenstein, *Power Struggle*, 172–76.

76. Rubenstein, "Jewish Theology," 13.

77. Ibid., 14.

78. Rubenstein, *The Religious Imagination*, 129–30.

79. Rubenstein, *Power Struggle*, 10–12.

80. Rubenstein, *The Religious Imagination*, 129.

81. Rubenstein, *Power Struggle*, 11; Rubenstein, *After Auschwitz*, 46; Rubenstein, "Varieties of God in the Psychologist's Frame of Reference," in *Psychology and Religion: A Contemporary Dialogue*, ed. Joseph Havens (Princeton, N.J.: D. Van Nostrand, 1968), 9. Cf. Klaus Rohman, "Radical Theology in the Making: Richard L. Rubenstein Reshaped Jewish Theology from Its Beginnings," in *What Kind of God?* 13–16.

82. Rubenstein, *After Auschwitz*, 245–46.

83. Braiterman, "'Hitler's Accomplice?'" 78; Braiterman, *(God) After Auschwitz*, 92.

84. Funkenstein, *Perceptions*, 309–10. Cf. David Biale, *Power and Powerlessness in Jewish History* (New York: Schocken Books, 1987), 143.

85. BT *Gittin* 55b-57a.

86. BT *Ketubot* 3a. Cf. Funkenstein, *Perceptions*, 307–10.

87. Biale, *Power and Powerlessness*, 36, 37; Funkenstein, *Perceptions*, 309

88. Biale, *Power and Powerlessness*, 23–24. See 213 n. 16. Cf. Arthur E. Green, "A Response to Richard Rubenstein," *Conservative Judaism* 28, no. 4 (summer 1974): 28–31. Here Green agrees with Rubenstein "that in many ways *Halakhah* did serve as the instrument of an overly repressive and self-destructive mentality for the Jew" (Green, 29). However, he argues that the root of this repression is not in Jewish exile alone but in an otherworldly Gnosticism that Jews share with Christians in Western religious society. Furthermore, Green disputes Rubenstein's historical portrayal of Yohanan ben Zakkai as submissive and servile, maintaining that he was "an important, positive model, as a cell builder of humanity in the hostile and destructive world" (Green, 29).

89. Braiterman, "'Hitler's Accomplice?'" 80. In making this claim, Braiterman brings various examples, including the famous *aggadah* in BT *Baba Mezia* 59b regarding the ritual purity of an oven that is the subject of a dispute between Rabbi Eliezer and a majority of Rabbis. After Rabbi Eliezer brings miracles to prove his position, the Rabbis override God's authority by claiming that the Torah is no longer in heaven, and eventually God laughs at the divine defeat to human initiative. Braiterman brings other rabbinic portrayals of human figures whose power equals that of God, i.e., Moses arguing with God about the golden calf; Jacob, Moses, Elijah, and Samuel inverting the order of creation; and Elisha and Elijah carrying out miracles equivalent to those of God. See Braiterman, *(God) After Auschwitz*, 93.

90. Braiterman, *(God) After Auschwitz*, 102–4.

91. Ibid., 101.

92. Ibid., 108–9.

93. Frederic Jameson, "On Cultural Studies," in *The Identity in Question*, ed. John Rajchman (New York: Routledge, 1995), 271.

94. Rubenstein, *After Auschwitz*, 2d ed., 295. Cf. Braiterman, "'Hitler's Accomplice?'" 82; Braiterman, *(God) After Auschwitz*, 95–97.

95. Rubenstein, *Power Struggle*, 161–63.

96. Rubenstein, *After Auschwitz*, 2d ed., 248.

97. Rubenstein, interview by author, Bridgeport, Connecticut, 21 May 1997.

98. For a discussion of rabbinic protest literature, see Braiterman, *(God) After Auschwitz*, 102–4.

99. Rubenstein, *After Auschwitz*, 2d ed., 174, 204, 207.

100. Braiterman, *(God) After Auschwitz*, 98–100.

101. Rubenstein, *Power Struggle*, 162; Rubenstein, *After Auschwitz*, 2d ed., 301–20.

102. Rubenstein, *After Auschwitz*, 2d ed., 302; Rubenstein, *Power Struggle*, 163.

103. Rubenstein, *The Religious Imagination*, 118–24, 142.

104. William E. Kaufman, *Contemporary Jewish Philosophies* (New York: Reconstructionist Press and Behrman House, 1976), 87.

105. Braiterman, *(God) After Auschwitz*, 47–54, 102–4.

106. Rubenstein, *After Auschwitz*, 136–37.

107. Rubenstein, *After Auschwitz*, 2d ed., 297.

108. Ibid., 294–97.

109. Rubenstein, *Morality and Eros*, 192.

110. Rubenstein, *After Auschwitz*, 2d ed., 303–4. Rubenstein describes the exile of the *Shekhinah* as being part of the Lurianic myth, but he neglects the fact that it is actually pre-Lurianic, already appearing in the *Zohar*.

111. Braiterman, *(God) After Auschwitz*, 105. Here Braiterman compares Rubenstein's Holy Nothingness to the kabbalistic notion of God as *Ayin* (Nothing) yet admits that "in reality, Rubenstein's thought has only the vaguest affinities with kabbalistic thought. Although intuitive and even insightful, his grasp of Kabbalah was neither well researched nor far reaching" (Braiterman, *(God) After Auschwitz*, 106).

112. Ibid., 109.

113. Gershom Scholem, *Major Trends in Jewish Mysticism*, 3d ed. (New York: Schocken Books, 1971), 273–74.

114. Rubenstein, *After Auschwitz*, 2d ed., 304; Rubenstein, *My Brother Paul*, 170.

115. Rubenstein, *My Brother Paul*, 170.

116. Rubenstein, "The 'Nothingness' of God," *Christian Century*, 21 February 1968, 232.

117. Rubenstein, *After Auschwitz*, 2d ed., 174, 204. Cf. Braiterman, *(God) After Auschwitz*, 100.

118. Braiterman, *(God) After Auschwitz*, 98.

119. Hellig, "Rabbinic Powerlessness and the Power of Women," 113.

120. Braiterman, "'Hitler's Accomplice?'" 80–81. Cf. Rubenstein, *After Auschwitz*, 2d ed., 3-01–02; Rubenstein, *My Brother Paul*, 163.

121. Rubenstein, *Power Struggle*, 164–65.

122. Ibid., 165–66.

123. Rubenstein, *The Religious Imagination*, 44–48, 57.

124. Ibid., 48–50.

125. See Rachel Adler, "The Jew Who Wasn't There," in *On Being a Jewish Feminist: A Reader*, ed., Susannah Heschel (New York: Schocken Books, 1983), 16. Cf. Hellig, "Rabbinic Powerlessness," 127.

126. Daniel Boyarin, *Carnal Israel: Reading Sex in Talmudic Culture* (Berkeley: University of California Press, 1993), 181. Cf. von Kellenbach, *Anti-Judaism in Feminist Religious Writings*, 69.

127. Rubenstein, *Power Struggle*, 166–68; Rubenstein, *The Religious Imagination*, 183. Cf. Hellig, "Rabbinic Powerlessness," 115.

128. Rubenstein, "Jewish Theology," 13; Rubenstein, *After Auschwitz*, 136–38; Rubenstein, *Power Struggle*, 167–68. Cf. Hellig, "Rabbinic Powerlessness," 122.

129. Rubenstein, *After Auschwitz*, 131–32, 136–37.

130. Ibid., 135, 137.

131. Rubenstein, interview by author, Bridgeport, Connecticut, 21 May 1997.

132. Von Kellenbach, *Anti-Judaism*, 103–4.

133. David Biale, *Eros and the Jews from Biblical Israel to Contemporary America* (New York: Basic Books, 1992), 1–10, 206–7, 229.

134. Von Kellenbach, *Anti-Judaism*, 101.

135. Ibid., 103; Boyarin, *Carnal Israel*, 1.

136. Rubenstein, *The Religious Imagination*, 95.

137. Ibid., 83–86, 88–91, 93–96. Rubenstein explains that the fear of incorpora-

tion is demonstrated in *midrashim* reflecting the greatest divine punishments for the Flood generation, Korah and his rebellious followers, Dathan and Aviram. They were all described by the Rabbis as having been "consumed by fire or a fiery substance in addition to having been incorporated in earth or water" (Rubenstein, *The Religious Imagination*, 85). See Hellig, "Rabbinic Powerlessness," 121–22.

138. Rubenstein, *The Religious Imagination*, 70, 80–81, 83–84.

139. Von Kellenbach, *Anti-Judaism*, 97–101, esp. 101; Marie-Theres Wacker, "Feminist Theology and Anti-Judaism: The Status of the Discussion and the Context of the Problem in the Federal Republic of Germany," *Journal of Feminist Studies in Religion* 7, no. 2 (fall 1991): 115–16.

140. Rubenstein, *The Religious Imagination*, 98.

141. Ibid.

142. In the *Early History of God*, Mark Smith points out that while there is little evidence to suggest that Asherah was a Goddess during the period of Israelite monarchy, the polemics in Judges 2:13, 10:6 and 1 Samuel 7:3–4, 12:10, possibly indicate a Judean cult to the Goddess Astarte in Jerusalem. In addition, he argues that although there is minimal evidence to prove that Asherah was a consort to YHWH, it is apparent that "the symbol outlived the cult of the goddess who gave her name to it and continued to hold a place in the cult" of YHWH. See Mark S. Smith, *The Early History of God: Yahweh and Other Deities in Ancient Israel* (San Francisco: Harper and Row, 1990), 88–94, esp. 90, 94. Cf. Heschel, "Anti-Judaism in Christian Feminist Theology," 26.

143. Ilana Pardes, *Counter-traditions in the Bible: A Feminist Approach* (Cambridge, Mass.: Harvard University Press, 1992), 45–46, 85–93.

144. Von Kellenbach, *Anti-Judaism*, 108.

145. Ibid.

146. Rubenstein, *My Brother Paul*, 162–64.

147. Ibid.

148. Ibid.

149. Von Kellenbach, *Anti-Judaism*, 63–66.

150. Rubenstein, *My Brother Paul*, 162–63.

151. Ibid., 20, 105. Cf. Moore, "Pauline Theology," 158–59, 163.

152. Rubenstein, *After Auschwitz*, 100.

153. Rubenstein, *The Religious Imagination*, 144.

154. Rubenstein, *After Auschwitz*, 94–96, 100–108.

155. Ibid., 103–4, 109.

156. Ibid., 95, 99–100, 104–5, 108–9, 110–11.

157. Rubenstein, *My Brother Paul*, 105, 112–13. Cf. Moore, "Pauline Theology," 158–59.

158. Rubenstein, *My Brother Paul*, 4, 19.

159. Ibid., 28–29, 36; Rubenstein, *The Religious Imagination*, 162–63. Cf. Robert L. Moore, review of *My Brother Paul*, by Richard L. Rubenstein, *Psychohistory Review* 5 (December 1976): 48.

160. Rubenstein, *My Brother Paul*, 23, 50–51; Rubenstein, *The Religious Imagination*, 162–63. Cf. Moore, "Pauline Theology," 159.

161. Rubenstein, *My Brother Paul*, 28–29.

162. Ibid., 46–48

163. Ibid., 31.

164. Ibid., 29–30. Cf. Moore, "Pauline Theology," 159–60.

165. Boyarin, A Radical Jew, 41, 201–6; Boyarin, Carnal Israel, 1; Augustine, The City of God, trans. Marcus Dods (New York: Random House, 1950), 16:35, 18:46–48.

166. Rubenstein, My Brother Paul, 68–69, 73–77. Cf. Moore, "Pauline Theology," 161–62.

167. Rubenstein, My Brother Paul, 17–18; idem, Power Struggle, 9–10, 117–18, 163–69.

168. Rubenstein, My Brother Paul, 84, 113. Cf. Moore, "Pauline Theology," 163.

169. Rubenstein, My Brother Paul, 84–85. Cf. Moore, "Pauline Theology," 162.

170. Rubenstein, My Brother Paul, 92, 99–101, 112. Cf. Moore, "Pauline Theology," 162–63.

171. Boyarin, A Radical Jew, 3.

172. Rubenstein, After Auschwitz, 2d ed., 299.

173. Braiterman, (God) After Auschwitz, 111.

174. Rubenstein, interview by author, Bridgeport, Connecticut, 21 May 1997.

175. Eliezer Berkovits, Faith after the Holocaust (New York: Ktav, 1973), 94. In (God) After Auschwitz, Braiterman argues against previous analyses of Berkovits's 1973 post-Holocaust work, Faith after the Holocaust, that overemphasize its theodic elements without taking into account the "antitheodic" language of protest that Berkovits directs against God. Braiterman makes the following claim: "Theodicy and anti-theodicy, trust and protest, formed the poles of a deep structure between which Berkovits' post-Holocaust writings alternated" (Braiterman, 114–15).

Berkovits demonstrates this oscillation between theodicy and antitheodicy by blaming western civilization and especially Christianity for the Holocaust in the first two chapters, while arguing against God in chapter 3. In chapter 4, he presents a powerful theodicy by denying the Holocaust's theological uniqueness and justifying human evil based on free will. Braiterman argues that while Berkovits alternates between theodicy and antitheodicy in the remaining chapters, he ultimately views the establishment of the State of Israel as a "theodic 'breakthrough'" in the sense that it represents the messianic payment of a divine debt for Jewish suffering in the Holocaust and thus vindicates God. It is this unequivocal language of theodicy together with that of chapter 4 which is the basis for the criticism of Berkovits by Katz, Cohn-Sherbok, Schweid, Berger, and Funkenstein. They criticize Berkovits not only for denying the uniqueness of the Holocaust but also for trying to place it in a pattern of redemption with the State of Israel. Specifically, Funkenstein argued that this response to the Holocaust and that of Fackenheim were "diluted versions of theodicy" that are offensive to survivors, while Katz maintains that Berkovits failed to recognize the importance of reassessing traditional theological approaches in light of the Holocaust. Yet Braiterman asserts that this criticism must be qualified by Berkovits's continued tension between theodicy and antitheodicy in his later works, Crisis and Faith (1976) and With God in Hell (1979), whose messianic fervor is tempered by the 1973 Yom Kippur War in Israel. See Braiterman, (God) After Auschwitz, 115–25. Cf. Funkenstein, Perceptions, 310–11.

176. This is taken from my larger discussion of Berkovits's anti-Christian

polemic in "Eliezer Berkovits's Post-Holocaust Theology: A Dialectic between Polemics and Reception," *Journal of Ecumenical Studies* 37, no. 1 (winter 2000): 28–45. I also discuss Berkovits's post-Holocaust theology in relation to that of Rubenstein and Greenberg in "Decentering Judaism and Christianity: Using Feminist Theory to Construct a Postmodern Jewish-Christian Theology," *Cross Currents* 50, no. 4 (winter 2000/2001): 474–87.

CHAPTER 4

1. Irving Greenberg, "Voluntary Covenant," in *Contemporary Jewish Religious Responses to the Shoah*, Studies in the Shoah Series, ed. Steven L. Jacobs (Lanham, Md.: University Press of America, 1993), 93–95.

2. Irving Greenberg, "New Revelations and New Patterns in the Relationship of Judaism and Christianity," *Journal of Ecumenical Studies* 16, no. 2 (spring 1979): 255. Cf. Paul van Buren, "Christian Theology and Jewish Reality: An Essay-Review," *Journal of the American Academy of Religion* 45, no. 4 (1977): 493.

3. For a discussion of Greenberg's approach to Jewish feminism, see Michael Oppenheim, "Irving Greenberg and a Jewish Dialectic of Hope," *Judaism* 49, no. 194 (spring 2000): 189, 193–94.

4. For a detailed discussion of Greenberg's biography, see Steven T. Katz, "Irving (Yitzchak) Greenberg," in *Interpreters of Judaism in the Late Twentieth Century*, ed. Steven T. Katz (Washington, D.C.: B'nai Brith Books, 1993), 59–62.

5. Irving Greenberg, "Judaism and Christianity: Covenants of Redemption," in *Christianity in Jewish Terms*, ed. Tikva Frymer-Kensky, David Novak, Peter Ochs, David Fox Sandmel, and Michael A. Signer (Boulder, Colo.: Westview Press, 2000), 141–58.

6. See Katz, "Irving (Yitzchak) Greenberg," 61–62.

7. See Oppenheim's discussion of these books in "Irving Greenberg and a Jewish Dialectic of Hope," 196, 200–201.

8. Irving Greenberg, "The Relationship of Judaism and Christianity: Toward a New Organic Model," *Perspectives/Quarterly Review* 4, no. 4 (winter 1984): 1–2.

9. Stephen Haynes, *Reluctant Witnesses: Jews and the Christian Imagination* (Louisville, Ky.: Westminster John Knox Press, 1995), 135. Cf. John T. Pawlikowski, *Christ in the Light of the Christian-Jewish Dialogue* (New York: Paulist Press, 1982), 11–18.

10. Greenberg, "New Revelations," 264–65. Steven Katz refers to Eckardt's influence on Greenberg in "Irving (Yitzchak) Greenberg," 62.

11. Haynes, *Reluctant Witnesses*, 28–33, 123, 139–40.

12. Ibid., 139–40. Cf. Pawlikowski, *Christ in the Light*, 14, 17–18. As I argued in chapter 1, Franz Rosenzweig believed that Christians possess their own divine revelation, portraying them as having the responsibility to eternalize or redeem the world through proselytization. However, this Christian-led redemption appears to really be a Judaicization of the world, because the world will become redeemed only when it becomes like the Jews who possess eternal truth. Thus Christianity essentially becomes a Judaism for the Gentiles. On this issue see Amos Funkenstein, *Perceptions of Jewish History* (Berkeley: University of California Press, 1993), 264–70,

300–301, esp. 268–69; David Novak, *Jewish-Christian Dialogue: A Jewish Justification* (Oxford: Oxford University Press, 1989), 108; Richard A. Cohen, *Elevations: The Height of the Good in Rosenzweig and Levinas* (Chicago: University of Chicago Press, 1994), 13–14, 21.

In fact, both van Buren and Eckardt were influenced by Rosenzweig's portrayal of the Jewish-Christian relationship. See note 76 in chapter 4 of this work.

13. Irving Greenberg, "Cloud of Smoke, Pillar of Fire: Judaism, Christianity, and Modernity after the Holocaust," in *Auschwitz: Beginning of a New Era? Reflections on the Holocaust: Papers Given at the International Symposium on the Holocaust Held at the Cathedral of Saint John the Divine, New York City, June 3–6, 1974*, ed. Eva Fleischner (New York: Ktav, 1974), 1.

14. Irving Greenberg, "Religious Values After the Holocaust: A Jewish View," in *Jews and Christians After the Holocaust*, ed. Abraham J. Peck (Philadelphia: Fortress Press, 1982), 63.

15. Ibid.

16. Greenberg, "New Revelations," 255–56, 263; Greenberg, "Cloud of Smoke," 3.

17. Irving Greenberg, "Judaism and History: Historical Events and Religious Change," in *Ancient Roots and Modern Meanings: A Contemporary Reader in Jewish Identity*, ed. Jerry V. Diller (New York: Bloch, 1978), 140.

18. Ibid., 140–41.

19. Ibid., 142–43.

20. Greenberg, "Voluntary Covenant," 83–88.

21. Ibid., 92–93. Cf. Elie Wiesel, "Jewish Values in the Post-Holocaust Future," in *Judaism* 16, no. 3 (summer 1967): 281.

22. Steven Katz, *Post-Holocaust Dialogues: Critical Studies in Modern Jewish Thought* (New York: New York University Press, 1983), 185–88.

23. See Emil Fackenheim, *God's Presence in History: Jewish Affirmations and Philosophical Reflections* (New York: New York University Press, 1970), 73–74. In this book, and in his forward to Yehuda Bauer's *Jewish Emergence from Powerlessness* (Toronto, 1979), Fackenheim lays out a series of eight propositions that characterize the historical uniqueness of the Holocaust. In his book *The Holocaust in Historical Context*, vol. 1, *The Holocaust and Mass Death before the Modern Age* (Oxford: Oxford University Press, 1994), Steven Katz agrees with Fackenheim's premise regarding the historical uniqueness of the Holocaust, yet he argues against drawing any unique theological conclusions from this.

However, David Biale disagrees with the very claim regarding the Holocaust's historical uniqueness as genocide, arguing that this has become part of a debate over comparative victimization in which Jews are defending the particularity of their identity based on the Holocaust, subsequently constructing a new secular form of chosenness. Biale maintains that Katz's repeated claims of moral and theological neutrality belie the fact that he is making some sort of extrahistorical argument for Jewish uniqueness. Moreover, according to Biale, his argument appears unhistorical in the very way he poses his question. No historian tries to establish the uniqueness of a historical event by painstakingly demonstrating how it cannot be compared with any other events. Biale claims that "for historians concerned with understanding the past for its own sake, 'uniqueness' is either trivial, meaningless, or a code word for an extra-historical agenda" (David Biale, "The Perils of Uniqueness," review of *The Holocaust in Historical Context*, vol. 1, by Steven Katz, *Tikkun* 10, no. 1 [January/February 1995]: 79–80, 88).

24. Katz, "Irving (Yitzchak) Greenberg," 83.

25. Greenberg, "Voluntary Covenant," 93–95.

26. Ibid., 95.

27. Ibid., 96–97.

28. Fackenheim, *God's Presence in History*, preface. Cf. Fackenhbeim, *The Jewish Thought of Emil Fackenheim: A Reader*, ed. Michael L. Morgan (Detroit: Wayne State University Press, 1987), 220–21 n. 2.

29. Fackenheim, *God's Presence in History*, 8–14.

30. Ibid., 16–19.

31. Ibid., 9. Katz observes that Fackenheim's distinction between "root experiences" and "epoch-making events" is illuminating but vague. Furthermore, Katz points out that Fackenheim supplies no criteria as to why the Holocaust is an epoch-making event and not a root experience. Hence, there are no rules to distinguish which category to associate with future events, and "without such criteria of assignment the distinction becomes purely stipulative, providing only *a priori* plausibility that turns out to be tautological" (Katz, *Post-Holocaust Dialogues*, 225–26).

32. Fackenheim, *God's Presence in History*; Fackenheim, *To Mend the World*, (Bloomington: Indiana University Press, 1994), 25, 217. Cf. Zachery Braiterman, *(God) After Auschwitz: tradition and Change in Post-Holocaust Jewish Thought* (Princeton, N.J.: Princeton University Press, 1998), 142–43, 148–49.

33. Greenberg, "Judaism and History," 158.

34. Greenberg, "Cloud of Smoke," 20.

35. Katz argues that Fackenheim's commanding voice is not revelation, as the Torah was believed to be revelation. Instead, the fragments of divine revelation that Fackenheim describes are really a human response to Auschwitz. See Katz, *Post-Holocaust Dialogues*, 219. In contrast, Michael Morgan argues that this divine imperative is "complexly human in its interpretation and execution but divine in its origin" (Michael L. Morgan, *Dilemmas in Modern Jewish Thought: The Dialectics of Revelation and History* [Bloomington: Indiana University Press, 1992], 103).

In *(God) After Auschwitz*, Braiterman provides a very careful and nuanced analysis of how Fackenheim's thought evolves during the course of his career from a systematic theology to a more fragmented theological minimalism following the Holocaust. See Braiterman, *(God) After Auschwitz*, 134–60, esp. 135.

36. Greenberg, "Voluntary Covenant," 93–95; Emil Fackenheim, "The Holocaust and the State of Israel: Their Relation," in *Auschwitz: Beginning of a New Era?* 212.

37. Greenberg, "Judaism and History," 159–60; Fackenheim, *God's Presence in History*, 79–92, esp. 81–82, 85–86.

38. Greenberg, "Judaism and History," 159.

39. Greenberg, "New Revelations," 263.

40. Greenberg, "Religious Values after the Holocaust," 78.

41. Katz, "Irving (Yitzchak) Greenberg," 82–83.

42. Irving Greenberg, "Toward Jewish Religious Unity," *Judaism* 15, no.2 (spring 1966): 137–38.

43. Irving Greenberg, "The Third Great Cycle of Jewish History," in *Perspectives* (New York: National Jewish Center for Learning and Leadership, 1981), 12.

44. Alan L. Berger, "The Holocaust, Second-Generation Witness, and the Voluntary Covenant in American Judaism," *Religion and American Culture* 5, no. 1 (winter 1995): 23–42, esp. 25–28, 31, 35–36, 40–43.

45. Ibid.

46. Greenberg, "Relationship of Judaism and Christianity," 18.

47. Irving Greenberg, "The New Encounter of Judaism and Christianity," *Barat Review* 3, no. 2 (June 1967): 121.

48. Greenberg, "New Revelations," 259. In addition, as I argued in the introduction to this work, Christian thinkers have exhibited a tension between attraction and repulsion for Jewish culture in their theological constructions of identity throughout history.

49. Ibid., 265.

50. Greenberg, "Cloud of Smoke," 16.

51. Greenberg, "Relationship of Judaism and Christianity," 5.

52. Ibid., 6.

53. Greenberg, "Judaism and History," 149.

54. Ibid., 149–50.

55. Greenberg, "Relationship of Judaism and Christianity," 6–7. This statement does not take into account the apocalyptic as well as the passive-utopian messianism in rabbinic thought expressed in *Sanhedrin*. However, Greenberg will later describe both Judaism and Christianity as denying history in order to protect the absolute validity of their theological positions. Yet this also goes against the historical consciousness of the Jews throughout history as expressed in their legal reasoning. On this, see Funkenstein, *Perceptions*, 1–21.

56. Greenberg, "Judaism and Christianity: Covenants of Redemption," 152.

57. Ibid., 154.

58. Greenberg, "Judaism and History," 150.

59. Ibid.

60. Greenberg, "Relationship of Judaism and Christianity," 13.

61. Greenberg, "New Revelations," 256; In his book *Faith after the Holocaust*, Eliezer Berkovits blames Western civilization and especially Christianity for creating the conditions that led to the Holocaust. In fact, he perceives a straight line leading from Constantine's oppression of Jews in the fourth century to Hitler's extermination of Jews in the twentieth century. See Berkovits, *Faith after the Holocaust* (New York: Ktav, 1973), 38, 41, 94.

62. Greenberg, "New Revelations," 256.

63. Ibid. When discussing Christian origins, Berkovits states, "Christianity did not capture the Roman Empire by the power of a religious idea but by the sword of the emperor" (Berkovits, *Faith after the Holocaust*, 38). See my discussion of Berkovits in relation to Greenberg at the end of chapter 3 in this work.

64. Greenberg, "New Revelations," 253.

65. Ibid., 254.

66. Ibid.

67. Ibid.

68. Ibid., 256–57.

69. Ibid., 257.

70. Ibid.

71. Ibid., 260–61.

72. Ibid., 261.

73. Ibid., 262.

74. Irving Greenberg, "Judaism and Christianity: Their Respective Roles in the Strategy of Redemption," in *Visions of the Other: Jewish and Christian Theologians Assess the Dialogue: Papers Given at the 9th National Workshop on Christian-Jewish Relations, Baltimore, MD 1986*, ed. Eugene J. Fisher (Mahwah, N.J.: Paulist Press, 1994), 19.

75. Irving Greenberg, "Pluralism and Partnership," in ICCJ *Unity without Uniformity: The Challenge of Pluralism*, Martin Buber House Publication, no. 26 (spring 1999): 71.

76. Ibid., 79–80.

77. Greenberg, "New Revelations," 263.

78. Ibid.

79. Ibid., 265–67.

80. Ibid., 264.

81. Greenberg, "Religious Values after the Holocaust," 74.

82. See the introduction to cultural studies by Lawrence Grossberg, "Introduction: Bringin It All Back Home—Pedagogy and Cultural Studies," in *Between Borders: Pedagogy and the Politics of Cultural Studies*, ed. Henry A. Giroux and Peter McLaren (New York: Routledge, 1994), 4–6.

83. Henry A. Giroux discusses Bhabha's portrayal of the "third space" in *Living Dangerously: Multiculturalism and the Politics of Difference* (New York: Peter Lang, 1993), 76. Cf. Homi K. Bhabha, "The Third Space," in *Identity, Community, Culture, Difference*, ed. Jonathan Rutherford (London: Lawrence and Wishart, 1990), 211.

84. Homi K. Bhabha, "Postcolonial Authority and Postmodern Guilt," in *Cultural Studies*, ed. Lawrence Grossberg, Cary Nelson, and Paula A. Treichler (New York: Routledge, 1992), 57–58.

85. James F. Moore, "A Spectrum of Views: Traditional Christian Responses to the Holocaust," *Journal of Ecumenical Studies* 25, no. 2 (spring 1988): 212–24. However, on the whole, contemporary, "mainline" christological thinking has not only ignored the issue of anti-Judaism in Christian theology, but many Protestant and Catholic authorities have also maintained a traditional conversionary attitude toward Judaism and other religions. See Pawlikowski, *Christ in the Light*, 36; Barry Daniel Cytron, "A Rationale and Proposed Curriculum for Jewish-Christian Dialogue" (Ph.D. diss., Iowa State University, 1982), 73–84, esp. 74–75 n. 1; Geoffrey Wigoder, *Jewish-Christian Relations since the Second World War* (Manchester: Manchester University Press, 1988), 29–33. Specifically, contemporary German theologians like Johannes Metz, Walter Kasper, and Karl Rahner have not even addressed the issue of anti-Judaism in Christian theology. On this, see Charlotte

Klein, *Anti-Judaism in Christian Theology* (Philadelphia: Fortress Press, 1978), and Eva Fleischner, *Judaism in German Christian Theology since 1945: Christianity and Israel Considered in Terms of Mission* (Metuchen, N.J.: Scarecrow Press, 1975).

86. Moore, "A Spectrum," 212–13.

87. Greenberg, "Lessens to Be Learned from the Holocaust" (paper presented at the International Conference on the Church Struggle and the Holocaust, Hamburg, 8–11 June 1975). Cf. Alice L. Eckardt and A. Roy Eckardt, *Long Night's Journey into Day: A Revised Retrospective on the Holocaust* (Detroit: Wayne State University Press, 1988), 106.

88. Eckardt and Eckardt, *Long Night's Journey into Day*, 106. Cf. Jürgen Moltmann, *The Crucified God: The Cross of Christ as the Foundation and Criticism of Christian Theology*, trans. R. A. Wilson and John Bowden (New York: Harper and Row, 1974), 175. For an extended discussion of Moltmann's theological response to the Holocaust, see note 124 in this chapter.

89. Van Buren, "Christian Theology and Jewish Reality," 494. Cf. Haynes, *Prospects*, 168.

90. Ibid.

91. Haynes, *Reluctant Witnesses*, 123.

92. Martin S. Jaffee, "The Victim-Community in Myth and History: Holocaust Ritual, the Question of Palestine, and the Rhetoric of Christian Witness," *Journal of Ecumenical Studies* 28, no. 2 (spring 1991): 226.

93. Ibid., 227–28. Cf. Haynes, *Reluctant Witnesses*, 139.

94. Haynes, *Reluctant Witnesses*, 140. It is important to note that when van Buren became aware of Haynes's portrayal of Christian post-Holocaust theologians, he vehemently rejected it. However, as we will see, his Catholic contemporary John Pawlikowski would accuse him of promoting a "Judaism for the Gentiles" in his covenantal portrayal of Judaism and Christianity.

95. Greenberg, "Relationship of Judaism and Christianity," 1–3.

96. Greenberg, "Judaism and Christianity: Their Respective Roles," 11–12.

97. Greenberg, "Religious Values after the Holocaust," 78. Greenberg appears to vacillate in his description of the covenantal relationship between Judaism and Christianity throughout his career. In two articles from 1967, "The New Encounter of Judaism and Christianity," 124, and "The Cultural Revolution and Religious Unity," *Religious Education* 62, no. 2 (March–April, 1967): 103, Greenberg refers to two covenants, yet in his later articles he appears to have switched to a one-covenant position. In "Judaism and Christianity: Their Respective Roles" (1994), Greenberg refers to the divine strategy of using "at least two covenantal communities" to achieve redemption, yet he refers to the "Jewish and Christian covenant" in his essay "Pluralism and Partnership" (1999). Finally, he offers an ambiguous portrayal of the Jewish-Christian relationship with the title of his most recent article, "Judaism and Christianity: Covenants of Redemption," yet in the conclusion of the article, he contrasts Christianity with Islam and other noncovenantal faiths such as Buddhism and forms of Hinduism that strive to fulfill "the universal divine covenant with humanity." He then portrays Christians and possibly Muslims as "members of the people Israel, even as they practice differing religions than Jewry does" (Greenberg, "Judaism and Christianity: Covenants of Redemption," 158). Cf. Paul van Buren, *A*

Theology of the Jewish-Christian Reality: Part III: Christ in Context (San Francisco: Harper and Row, 1988), 69–71, 143–47, 186–202; Eckardt, *Elder and Younger Brothers*, 144–52.

98. John T. Pawlikowski, O.S.M., "The Search for a New Paradigm for the Christian-Jewish Relationship: A Response to Michael Signer," in *Reinterpreting Revelation and Tradition: Jews and Christians in Conversation*, ed. John T. Pawlikowski, O.S.M., and Hayim Goren Perelmuter (Franklin, Wisc.: Sheed and Ward, 2000), 25–27.

99. Ibid., 28.

100. Ibid., 34–35. I agree with Pawlikowski's portrayal of the fluidity of first-century Judaism, yet I would argue that this fluidity lasts much longer. I think that he and those scholars whom he cites are incorrect in portraying an "intense separa-tion" developing between Jewish and Christian communities already by the end of the first century. Moreover, I disagree with the simplistic assumption that the "Church" was no longer composed of any Christian Jews by the second century, except in some areas. Instead, as I have already discussed in the introduction to this work, I agree with Daniel Boyarin's portrayal of a Judeo-Christian circulatory system in which Judaism and Christianity were points on a continuum from the Marcionites who deny the "Jewishness" of Christianity on one end of the spectrum to those Jews who had no affiliation with Jesus on the other. In between, there were arguably many gradations of overlapping and interacting discursive elements or even a blurring of discursive boundaries. This would indicate a flowing, as it were, of discursive elements from one end of the spectrum to the other and back again. Hence, instead of referring to Judaism and Christianity as "quite distinctive faith communities" by the second century, it would be more accurate to speak of rabbinic Judaism and orthodox Christianity. Based on his close analysis of Jewish and Christian intertexts about martyrdom from the second through fourth centuries, Boyarin suggests that while there were areas of complete differentiation between Jews and Christians, there were many areas where it was almost impossible to distinguish between the two identities. Furthermore, he argues that not until the beginning of the fifth century with Theodosius's military imposition of Nicene orthodoxy, did it become legally impossible to be both a Jew and a Christian simulta-neously. See Daniel Boyarin, *Dying for God: Martyrdom and the Making of Christianity and Judaism* (Stanford, Calif.: Stanford University Press, 1999), 8–10. Ultimately, I follow Pawlikowski in rejecting the portrayal of one homogeneous Judeo-Christian covenantal tradition, yet I disagree with the portrayal of parallel but separate Jewish and Christian histories. Instead, with Boyarin, I have suggested the model of intersecting Jewish and Christian historical development and identity construction.

101. Ibid., 40–43.

102. Pawlikowski, *Christ in the Light*, 11–18.

103. James Wallis, "The Theology of Paul M. van Buren and the Jewish-Christian Dialogue" (Ph.D. diss., Claremont Graduate School, 1993), 234–38.

104. Pawlikowski, *Christ in the Light*, 11–18.

105. Pawlikowski, "The Search for a New Paradigm for the Christian-Jewish Relationship," 33.

106. Pawlikowski, *Christ in the Light*, 11–18. Cf. A. Roy Eckardt, "A Response to

Rabbi Olan," *Religion in Life* 42 (fall 1973): 409; Eckardt, *Jews and Christians: The Contemporary Meeting* (Bloomington: Indiana University Press, 1986), 73, 85; Eckardt and Eckardt, *Long Night's Journey into Day*, 136; Wallis, "The Theology of Paul M. van Buren," 108.

107. Pawlikowski, *Christ in the Light*, 11–18. Wallis defends van Buren from the charge that he was portraying Judaism for the Gentiles because of his claim that the Church exists alongside Israel. See Wallis, "The Theology of Paul M. van Buren," 234–38.

108. Haynes, *Reluctant Witnesses*, 135; Haynes, *Prospects*, 167, 210 n. 37.

109. Greenberg, "Relationship of Judaism and Christianity," 13.

110. Greenberg, "Judaism and Christianity: Covenants of Redemption," 142–43.

111. Ibid., 143–44.

112. Ibid., 149.

113. Ibid., 149–50.

114. Ibid., 150.

115. Greenberg, "Judaism and Christianity: Their Respective Roles," 13.

116. Ibid., 21.

117. Ibid., 13; Eckardt, *Elder and Younger Brothers*, 145–52. This reference to "at least two covenantal communities" has prompted Philip Culbertson to describe Greenberg's approach to the Jewish-Christian relationship as a "multi-covenant theory." He claims that according to this theory, God has made a number of covenants with those who have been chosen, Noah, Abraham, Isaac, Jacob, David, and Jesus, but no covenant "precludes or replaces any earlier one." In "Relationship of Judaism and Christianity," Greenberg claims that God actually possesses enough love to have chosen both Judaism and Christianity. He argues that both communities "may yet apply this insight not just to each other but to religions not yet worked in this dialogue" (Greenberg, "Relationship of Judaism and Christianity," 19). Yet, based on his other statements about covenant, one could interpret this as referring to the continuing enfolding and broadening of the one covenant made with Israel. On this issue, see Philip L. Culbertson, "The Seventy Faces of the One God," in *Introduction to Jewish-Christian Relations*, ed. Michael Shermis and Arthur E. Zannoni (New York: Paulist Press, 1991), 148.

118. Greenberg, "Judaism and Christianity: Their Respective Roles," 8; Greenberg, "Religious Values after the Holocaust," 78. This appears to go directly against Wallis's portrayal of Greenberg's covenantal position in which he argues, "Greenberg views the covenant's advancement towards its goal as being assured" (Wallis, "The Theology of Paul M. van Buren," 149 n. 15, 240). The articles from which he gleans Greenberg's position clearly indicate a more providential position than the one to which I have referred. However, in none of Wallis's cited essays does Greenberg state that the covenant's advancement toward its goal is assured. Instead, Greenberg refers to a voluntary divine self-limitation that allows for and requires human participation in the covenant that is not deterministic. Wallis makes this claim in order to contrast Greenberg's and Rosenzweig's covenantal frameworks with that of van Buren, who, influenced by William James, views the world as unfinished and God as a limited agent in the world requiring human cooperation to complete the work of redemption. Because of this position, he argues that many

Jews and Christians will not accept van Buren's views on the Jewish-Christian relationship.

While I agree with this statement, I would argue that Greenberg and van Buren's positions are actually quite similar in the fact that they both are influenced by the pragmatism of William James and describe a more humanistic, this-worldly covenant with a God who is more hidden. Perhaps for the same reason, traditional Jews and Christians may not accept Greenberg's covenantal position, thus illustrating the unique intermediate location that he and van Buren occupy on the boundary of Judaism and Christianity. For the pragmatist influence on Greenberg, see Berger, "The Holocaust," 25–28.

119. Greenberg, "Religious Values after the Holocaust," 78; van Buren, *A Theology of the Jewish-Christian Reality: Part III*, 187.

120. Greenberg, "Religious Values after the Holocaust," 78–79; Greenberg, "Relationship of Judaism and Christianity," 14.

121. Greenberg, "Relationship of Judaism and Christianity," 8–9, 14.

122. Ibid., 18.

123. Greenberg, "Religious Values after the Holocaust," 85–86.

124. Greenberg, "New Revelations," 264. See n. 44.

125. Ibid. Moltmann constructs a type of liberation theology by viewing Auschwitz as one incredible example of the suffering of the contemporary world that his theology of the cross must address. In *The Crucified God*, he finds a reference to the crucified Christ in Wiesel's description of a hanging child whom the latter associated with a suffering God. Moltmann states that this passage is a "shattering expression of the *theologia crucis*" (theology of the cross), and that it is the only "Christian answer" to the question of God's presence in the Holocaust. See Jürgen Moltmann, *The Crucified God: The Cross of Christ as the Foundation and Criticism of Christian Theology*, trans. R.A. Wilson and John Bowden (New York: Harper and Row, 1974), 273–74. Cf. Eckardt and Eckardt, *Long Night's Journey into Day*, 112.

Greenberg's criticism of Moltmann follows directly from that of Alice Eckardt and A. Roy Eckardt. The Eckardts argue that Moltmann understands the Holocaust only as a "partial event," which has an impact on his theology of the cross, but does not see it as a totally unique event that suspends all comprehension. He is also criticized for seeing the cross as a symbol of redemption in light of the Holocaust. Finally, Moltmann is accused of Christianizing or trinitarianizing Jewish suffering. The Eckardts describe this as a veiled triumphalism in the guise of antitriumphalism. See Eckardt and Eckardt, *Long Night's Journey into Day*, 96–97, 102–17, 121; A. Roy Eckardt, "The Recantation of the Covenant," in *Confronting the Holocaust: The Impact of Elie Wiesel*, ed. Alvin H. Rosenfeld and Irving Greenberg (Bloomington: Indiana University Press, 1978), 162–63. Cf. Haynes, *Prospects*, 120–22.

However, Stephen Haynes disagrees with the Eckardts' description of Moltmann as a pre-Holocaust thinker because they ignore his attempt to make the Holocaust a criterion for Christian theology. Haynes argues that Moltmann is caught in a unique dilemma: He knows that a Christian response to the Holocaust is necessary, but he is criticized for interpreting it with Christian symbols. Both Haynes and Pawlikowski admit the validity of many of the Eckardts' criticisms, but they defend Moltmann's Christology as being generally sensitive to Judaism in its biblical expression and contemporary form yet weak in its depiction of the Second Temple period. See Haynes, *Prospects*, 120–22, 146–48; Pawlikowski, *Christ in the Light*, 42–46.

126. Greenberg, "New Revelations," 265 n. 44. One can see this problem occurring in the work of the Christian thinker Franklin Littell and that of the Jewish thinker Ignaz Maybaum, who portray the providential necessity of the Holocaust. Littell portrays a Jewish crucifixion in the Holocaust that is clearly redemptive, and he portrays the Holocaust as a necessary step in the divine plan leading to the Jews' resurrection in the State of Israel. In this instance, he portrays the Jewish people as the collective suffering servant of God, and he draws upon the work of a Jewish thinker, Robert Wolfe, who describes them as "God's perpetually willing instrument." Moore describes this aspect of Franklin Littell's work as an ironic use of Christian categories. See Littell, *The Crucifixion of the Jews* (New York: Harper aned Row, 1975), 114–15.

In his portrayal of the Holocaust, Ignaz Maybaum compares the Holocaust to the crucifixion of Jesus, describing the gas chambers at Auschwitz as the modern manifestation of Jesus' cross at Golgotha. He views the Holocaust as the "third *churban*," following those of the First and Second Temples. God initiated each *churban* for the purpose of "creative destruction." The first *churban* occurred in order to force Jews out into the pagan world to spread God's word. The next one was a destruction of the "primitive" use of sacrifices to enable Jews to move to an advanced relationship with God based on prayer and study. The third *churban* of the Holocaust was a necessary destruction of the vestiges of medieval Europe and its feudal system in order to bring the world into the modern age. He explicitly refers to Hitler as God's instrument used "to cleanse, to purify, to punish a sinful world" through the annihilation of six million innocent Jews. See Ignaz Maybaum, *The Face of God after Auschwitz* (Amsterdam: Polak and Van Gennep, 1965), 36, 61–63, 67. For an analysis of the strengths and weaknesses of Maybaum's approach, see Richard Rubenstein, *After Auschwitz History, Theology, and Contemporary Judaism*, 2d ed., (Baltimore: Johns Hopkins University Press, 1992), 163–68.

127. Greenberg, "New Revelations," 265 n. 44. Cf. A. Roy Eckardt, "Christian Responses to the *Endlosung*," *Religion in Life* 47 (spring 1978): 33–45.

128. Greenberg, "Cloud of Smoke," 32–33.

129. Ibid., 31; Berkovits, *Faith after the Holocaust*, 114–16, 124–27.

130. Greenberg, "Cloud of Smoke," 44.

131. Ibid., 31.

132. Greenberg, "The Third Great Cycle," 8; Berkovits, *Faith after the Holocaust*, 117–18. Cf. Haynes, *Reluctant Witnesses*, 179.

133. Greenberg, "New Revelations," 264.

134. See Jaffee, "The Victim-Community in Myth and History," 227.

135. Greenberg discusses Jewish powerlessness throughout his work. As noted earlier, he refers to medieval Jewish powerlessness as a source for anti-Christian polemics in "New Revelations," 265. In addition, he discusses Jewish powerlessness in "The Third Great Cycle," 13–16; and "The Third Era of Jewish History: Power and Politics," in *Perspectives* (New York: National Jewish Center for Learning and Leadership, 1981), 46. On the construction of the myth of Jewish powerlessness, see

David Biale, *Power and Powerlessness in Jewish History* (New York: Schocken Books, 1987), 112–17.

136. Greenberg, "New Revelations," 262.

137. Marc Ellis, *Toward a Jewish Theology of Liberation* (Maryknoll, N.Y.: Orbis, 1987), 32–36.

138. Rubenstein, *After Auschwitz*, 2d ed., 268.

139. Rosemary Radford Ruether and Herman J. Ruether, *The Wrath of Jonah: The Crisis of Religious Nationalism in the Israeli-Palestinian Conflict* (San Francisco: Harper and Row, 1989), 203.

140. Rubenstein, *After Auschwitz*, 2d ed., 272; Greenberg, "New Revelations," 262; Greenberg, "The Third Great Cycle," 15–16.

141. Greenberg, "The Third Era," 47.

142. See Greenberg, "Judaism and Christianity: Covenants of Redemption," 148.

143. Greenberg, "The Third Great Cycle," 10; Eckardt, "Toward a Secular Theology of Israel," *Religion in Life* 48, no. 4 (winter 1979): 467; Eckardt, *Jews and Christians*, 79; Eckardt and Eckardt, *Long Night's Journey into Day*, 101. Cf. Haynes, *Reluctant Witnesses*, 137–38.

144. Biale, *Power and Powerlessness*, 206–10.

145. Ibid., 163–64.

146. R. Kendall Soulen, "Israel and the Church: A Christian Response to Irving Greenberg's Covenantal Pluralism," in *Christianity in Jewish Terms*, 169.

147. In both the Christian and Jewish camps, there has been a variation of historical perspectives relating to the world. The Catholic Church was always aware of its transformation in history, adhering to a principle of divine accommodation first constructed by Augustine that describes the adjustment of divine revelation according to the capacity of persons to understand it in different ages. The Protestant sense of time is more complex. On the one hand, it has been apocalyptic, based on Luther's rejection of a corrupt history and a desire to withdraw from the world. On the other hand, the liberal Protestants of the eighteenth and nineteenth centuries expressed a world-affirming attitude in their identification of Christianity with cultural progress. See Amos Funkenstein's discussion of this in *Perceptions*, 250–52.

148. Greenberg, "Relationship of Judaism and Christianity," 6–7, 14–16.

149. Greenberg, "Religious Values after the Holocaust," 85.

150. Ibid.; Greenberg, "Relationship of Judaism and Christianity," 18.

151. Greenberg, "Relationship of Judaism and Christianity," 2. For an in-depth discussion of Buber's somewhat ambivalent attitude toward Christianity, see Sandra Lubarsky, *Tolerance and Transformation: Jewish Approaches to Religious Pluralism* (Cincinnati: Hebrew Union College Press, 1990), 73–99; and Novak, *Jewish-Christian Dialogue*, 81–86.

EPILOGUE

1. Miriam Peskowitz observes that in many "Introduction to Judaism" courses, feminist issues and gender considerations are relegated to a section on women in Judaism, while there appears to be a pure form of Judaism unaffected by these questions. She argues that one cannot simply "add women and stir" but rather must

reconstruct the androcentric historical framework from the ground up and take into account "the presence and the constructedness of gender in all aspects of Jewish religion and history" (Miriam Peskowitz, "Engendering Jewish Religious History," in *Judaism since Gender*, ed. Miriam Peskowitz and Laura Levitt [New York: Routledge, 1997], 19–22).

2. Gerd Baumann, *The Multicultural Riddle: Rethinking National, Ethnic, and Religious Identities* (New York: Routledge, 1999), 78–79.

3. Ibid., 138–39.

4. David Biale, Michael Galchinsky, and Susannah Heschel, "Introduction: The Dialectic of Jewish Enlightenment," in *Insider/Outsider: American Jews and Multiculturalism*, ed. David Biale, Michael Galchinsky, and Susannah Heschel, (Berkeley: University of California Press, 1998), 8.

5. Ibid., 5. Cf. David Biale, *Power and Powerlessness in Jewish History* (New York: Schocken Books, 1987).

6. Susannah Heschel, "Jewish Studies as Counterhistory," in *Insider/Outsider*, 102, 108. Cf. Amos Funkenstein, *Perceptions of Jewish History* (Berkeley: University of California Press, 1993), 36, 48.

7. Heschel, "Jewish Studies," 107–8. Cf. Abraham Geiger, *Judaism and Its History*, trans. Charles Newburgh (New York: Bloch, 1911).

8. Heschel, "Jewish Studies," 107–8.

9. Ibid., 109–11.

10. Susannah Heschel describes the formation of modern Jewish thought in this way in ibid., 109.

11. See Heschel's discussion of how Jewish historical figures and the discipline of Jewish studies can contribute to multicultural theory in ibid., 112.

12. See the discussion of this general dialectic between particularism versus universalism in Biale, Galchinsky, and Heschel, "Introduction," 7–8.

13. Kathryn Tanner, *Theories of Culture: A New Agenda for Theology* (Minneapolis, Minn.: Fortress Press, 1997), 112.

14. Ibid., 114.

15. Ibid., 115–16.

Bibliography

Adler, Rachel. "The Jew Who Wasn't There." In *On Being a Jewish Feminist: A Reader*, ed. Susannah Heschel, 12–18. New York: Schocken Books, 1983.

Altmann, Alexander. "Zur Auseinandersetzung mit der 'dialektischen Theologie.'" *Monatschrift für Geschichte und Wissenschaft des Judentums* 79, (1935): 345–61.

———. "Theology in Twentieth-Century German Jewry." *Leo Baeck Institute Yearbook* 1 (1956): 193–216.

Augustine. *The City of God*. Translated by Marcus Dods. New York: Random House Inc., 1950.

Babylonian Talmud. London: Soncino Press, 1961.

Bader-Saye, Scott. "Post-Holocaust Hermeneutics: Scripture, Sacrament, and the Jewish Body of Christ." *Cross Currents* 50, no. 4 (winter 2000/2001): 458–73.

Balibar, Etienne. "Culture and Identity (Working Notes)." Translated by J. Swenson. In *The Identity in Question*, ed. John Rajchman, 173–96. New York: Routledge, 1991.

Barth, Karl. *Church Dogmatics*. Vol. 2:1. *The Doctrine of God*. Edited by G. W. Bromiley and T. F. Torrance. Translated by T. H. C. Parker, W. S. Johnston, Harold Knight and J. L. M. Haire.Edinburgh: T. & T. Clark, 1964.

———. *Church Dogmatics*. Vol. 3:1, *The Doctrine of Creation*. Edited by G. W. Bromiley and T. F. Torrance. Translated by J. W. Edwards, O. Bussey and Harold Knight. Edinburgh: T. & T. Clark, 1958.

———. *Die Christliche Dogmatik in Entwurf, Ferster Band: die three von Worte Gottes*. (Munich, 1927.)

———. *The Epistle to the Romans*. 6th ed. Translated by Edwyn C. Hoskyns. London: Oxford University Press, 1960.

————. "Unsettled Questions for Theology Today." In *Theology and Church*. Translated by Louise Pettibone Smith. London: SCM Press, 1962.

Batnitzky, Leora. *Idolatry and Representation: The Philosophy of Franz Rosenzweig Reconsidered*. Princeton: Princeton, N.J.: University Press, 2000.

Baumann, Gerd. *The Multicultural Riddle: Rethinking National, Ethnic, and Religious Identities*. New York and London: Routledge, 1999.

Bearn, Gordon C. F. "Wittgenstein on the Uncanny," *Soundings* 17, no. 1 (spring 1993): 33.

Berger, Alan L. "The Holocaust, Second-Generation Witness, and the Voluntary Covenant in American Judaism." *Religion and American Culture* 5, no. 1 (winter 1995): 23–47.

Berger, David. "The Jewish-Christian Debate in the High Middle Ages." In *Essential Papers on Judaism and Christianity in Conflict: From Late Antiquity to the Reformation*, ed. Jeremy Cohen, 484–513. New York: New York University Press, 1991.

Berkovits, Eliezer. *Faith after the Holocaust*. New York: Ktav, 1973.

Bhabha, Homi K. "Postcolonial Authority and Postmodern Guilt." In *Cultural Studies*, ed. Lawrence Grossberg, Cary Nelson, and Paula A. Treichler, 56–66. New York: Routledge, 1992.

————. "The Third Space." In *Identity, Community, Culture Difference*, ed. Jonathan Rutherford. London: Lawrence and Wishart, 1990.

Biale, David. *Gershom Scholem: Kabbalah and Counter History*. Cambridge, Mass.: Harvard University Press, 1982.

————. *Power and Powerlessness in Jewish History*. New York: Schocken Books, 1987.

————. *Eros and the Jews from Biblical Israel to Contemporary America*. New York: Basic Books, 1992.

————. "The Perils of Uniqueness." Review of *The Holocaust in Historical Context*, vol. 1, by Steven Katz. *Tikkun* 10, no. 1 (January/February 1995): 79–80, 88.

————. "Between Polemics and Apologetics: Jewish Studies in the Age of Multiculturalism." *Jewish Studies Quarterly* 3, no. 2 (1996): 174–84.

Biale, David, Michael Galchinsky, and Susannah Heschel, eds. *Insider/Outsider: American Jews and Multiculturalism*. Berkeley: University of California Press, 1998.

Blumenthal, David. "Michael Wyschogrod." In *Interpreters of Judaism in the Late Twentieth Century*, ed. Steven T. Katz, 393–405. Washington, D.C.: B'nai B'rith Books, 1993.

Bodenstein, Walter. *Die Theologie Karl Holls im Spiegel des Antiken und Reformatischen Christentums*. Berlin: Walter de Gruyter, 1968.

Boyarin, Daniel. *Carnal Israel: Reading Sex in Talmudic Culture*. Berkeley: University of California Press, 1993.

————. *A Radical Jew: Paul and the Politics of Identity*. Berkeley: University of California Press, 1994.

————. *Dying for God: Martyrdom and the Making of Christianity and Judaism*. Stanford, Calif.: Stanford University Press, 1999.

Boyarin, Jonathan, and Daniel Boyarin. "Introduction/So What's New?" In *Jews and Other Differences: The New Jewish Cultural Studies*, vii–xxii. Minneapolis: University of Minnesota Press, 1997.

Braiterman, Zachary. "'Hitler's Accomplice?': The Tragic Theology of Richard Rubenstein." *Modern Judaism* 17, no. 1 (1997): 75–89.

———. *(God) After Auschwitz: Tradition and Change in Post-Holocaust Jewish Thought.* Princeton, N.J.: Princeton University Press, 1998.

Brown, Colin. "Karl Barth's Doctrine of the Creation." *Churchman* 76 (June 1962): 99–105.

Brown, Peter. *Augustine of Hippo.* Berkeley: University of California Press, 1967.

Buber, Martin. *I and Thou.* Translated by Walter Kaufman. New York: Charles Scribners's Sons, 1970.

Bultmann, Rudolf. *Primitive Christianity in Its Contemporary Setting.* Translated by R. H. Fuller. New York: New American Library, 1974.

Burleigh, John H. S. *The City of God: A Study of St. Augustine's Philosophy.* London: Nisbet, 1949.

Cohen, A. *Everyman's Talmud.* New York: Schocken Books, 1975.

Cohen, Hermann. *A Religion of Reason Out of the Sources of Judaism.* Translated by Simon Kaplan. Atlanta: Scholars Press, 1995.

Cohen, Richard A. *Elevations: The Height of the Good in Rosenzweig and Levinas.* Chicago: University of Chicago Press, 1994.

Culbertson, Philip L. "The Seventy Faces of the One God." In *Introduction to Jewish-Christian Relations,* ed. Michael Shermis and Arthur E. Zannoni, 145–73. New York: Paulist Press, 1991.

Cytron Barry Daniel. "A Rationale and Proposed Curriculum for Jewish-Christian Dialogue." Ph.D. diss., Iowa State University, 1982.

Dalin, David G. "Will Herberg." In *Interpreters of Judaism in the Late Twentieth Century,* ed. Steven T. Katz, 113–30. Washington, D.C.: B'nai B'rith Books, 1993.

Davies, Alan. "The Holocaust and Christian Thought." In *Jewish-Christian Encounters over the Centuries,* ed. Marvin Perry and Frederick M. Schweitzer, 341–67. New York: Peter Lang, 1994.

Dinnerstein, Leonard. *Anti-Semitism in America.* Oxford: Oxford University Press, 1994.

Dippel, John V. H. *Bound upon a Wheel of Fire: Why So Many Jews Made the Tragic Decision to Remain in Nazi Germany.* New York: Basic Books, 1996.

Earley, Glenn. "The Radical Hermeneutical Shift in Post-Holocaust Christian Thought." *Journal of Ecumenical Studies* 18, no. 1 (1981): 16–32.

Eckardt, Alice L., and A. Roy Eckardt. *Long Night's Journey into Day: A Revised Retrospective on the Holocaust.* Detroit: Wayne State University Press, 1988.

Eckardt, A. Roy. *Elder and Younger Brothers: The Encounter of Jews and Christians.* New York: Charles Scribner's Sons, 1967.

———. "A Response to Rabbi Olan." *Religion in Life* 42 (fall 1973): 401–12.

———. "Christian Responses to the *Endlösung.*" *Religion in Life* 47 (spring 1978): 33–45.

———. "The Recantation of the Covenant." In *Confronting the Holocaust: The Impact of Elie Wiesel,* ed. Alvin H. Rosenfeld and Irving Greenberg, 159–68. Bloomington: Indiana University Press, 1978.

———. "Toward a Secular Theology of Israel." *Religion in Life* 48, no. 4 (winter 1979): 462–73.

————. *Jews and Christians: The Contemporary Meeting*. Bloomington: Indiana University Press, 1986.

Eisen, Arnold. *The Chosen People in America: A Study in Jewish Religious Ideology*. Bloomington: Indiana University Press, 1983.

Ellis, Marc. *Toward a Jewish Theology of Liberation*. Maryknoll, N.Y.: Orbis, 1987.

Fackenheim, Emil. *God's Presence in History: Jewish Affirmations and Philosophical Reflections*. New York: New York University Press, 1970.

————. "The Holocaust and the State of Israel: Their Relation." In *Auschwitz: Beginning of a New Era? Reflections on the Holocaust: Papers Given at the International Symposium on the Holocaust held at the Cathedral of Saint John the Divine, New York City, June 3 6, 1974*, ed. Eva Fleischner, 205–15. New York: Ktav Publishing House, Inc., 1974.

————. Preface to *The Jewish Emergence from Powerlessness*, by Yehuda Bauer. Toronto: University of Toronto Press, 1979.

————. *The Jewish Thought of Emil Fackenheim: A Reader*. Edited by Michael L. Morgan. Detroit: Wayne State University Press, 1987.

————. *To Mend the World*. Bloomington: Indiana University Press, 1994.

Flannery, Edward. *The Anguish of the Jews: Twenty-three Centuries of Antisemitism*. New York: Paulist Press, 1985.

Fleischner, Eva. *Judaism in German Christian Theology since 1945: Christianity and Israel Considered in Terms of Mission*. Metuchen, N.J.: Scarecrow Press, 1975.

Frymer-Kensky, Tikva. *In the Wake of the Goddesses: Women, Culture and the Biblical Transformation of Pagan Myth*. New York: Free Press, 1992.

Frymer-Kensky, Tikva, David Novak, Peter Ochs, David Fox Sandmel, and Michael Signer, eds. *Christianity in Jewish Terms*. Boulder, Colo.: Westview Press, 2000.

Frymer-Kensky, Tikva, David Novak, Peter Ochs, and Michael Signer. "Dabru Emet: A Jewish Statement on Christians and Christianity." *New York Times*, 10 September 2000, sec. 1, p. 23.

Fulkerson, Mary McClintock. *Changing the Subject: Women's Discourses and Feminist Theology*. Minneapolis, Minn.: Fortress Press, 1994.

Funkenstein, Amos. *Signonot Be-Parshanut Ha-Mikra Biyme Ha-Benayim*. [Styles in Medieval Biblical Exegesis: An Introduction]. Tel Aviv: Ministry of Defense, 1990.

————. *Perceptions of Jewish History*. Berkeley: University of California Press, 1993.

Geiger, Abraham. *Judaism and Its History*. Translated by Charles Newburgh. New York: Bloch, 1911.

Gertel, Elliot B. "Because of Our Sins." *Tradition* 15, no. 4 (spring 1976): 68–82.

Gibbs, Robert. *Correlations in Rosenzweig and Levinas*. Princeton, N.J.: Princeton University Press, 1992.

Giroux, Henry A. *Border Crossings: Cultural Workers and the Politics of Education*. New York: Routledge, 1992.

————. "Resisting Difference: Cultural Studies and the Discourse of Critical Pedagogy." In *Cultural Studies*, ed. Lawrence Grossberg, Cary Nelson, and Paula A. Treichler, 199–212. New York: Routledge, 1992.

————. *Living Dangerously: Multiculturalism and the Politics of Difference*. New York: Peter Lang, 1993.

Glatzer, Nahum N. *Franz Rosenzweig: His Life and Thought*. New York: Schocken Books, 1961.

Goldenberg, Robert, and Judith Plaskow. "Rabbi's Odyssey." Review of *Power Struggle*, by Richard Rubenstein. *New Republic*, 5 October 1974, 26–27.

Green, Arthur E. "A Response to Richard Rubenstein." *Conservative Judaism* 28, no. 4 (summer 1974): 26–32.

Greenberg, Cheryl. "Pluralism and Its Discontents: The Case of Blacks and Jews." In *Insider/Outsider: American Jews and Multiculturalism*, ed. David Biale, Michael Galchinsky, and Susannah Heschel, 55–87. Berkeley: University of California Press, 1998.

Greenberg, Irving. "Toward Jewish Religious Unity: A Symposium." *Judaism* 15, no. 2 (spring 1966): 129–63.

———. "The Cultural Revolution and Religious Unity." *Religious Education* 62, no. 2 (March–April 1967): 98–103, 224.

———. "The New Encounter of Judaism and Christianity." *Barat Review* 3, no. 2 (June 1967): 113–25.

———. "Cloud of Smoke, Pillar of Fire: Judaism, Christianity, and Modernity after the Holocaust." In *Auschwitz: Beginning of a New Era? Reflections on the Holocaust: Papers Given at the International Symposium on the Holocaust Held at the Cathedral of Saint John the Divine, New York City, June 3–6, 1974*, ed. Eva Fleischner, 7–55. New York: Ktav, 1974.

———. "Lessons to Be Learned from the Holocaust." Paper presented at the International Conference on the Church Struggle and the Holocaust, Hamburg, 8–11 June 1975.

———. "Judaism and History: Historical Events and Religious Change." In *Ancient Roots and Modern Meanings: A Contemporary Reader in Jewish Identity*, ed. Jerry V. Diller, 139–62. New York: Bloch, 1978.

———. "New Revelations and New Patterns in the Relationship of Judaism and Christianity." *Journal of Ecumenical Studies* 16, no. 2 (spring 1979): 249–67.

———. "The Third Era of Jewish History: Power and Politics." In *Perspectives*, 45–55. New York: National Jewish Center for Learning and Leadership, 1981.

———. "The Third Great Cycle of Jewish History." In *Perspectives*, 1–26. New York: National Jewish Center for Learning and Leadership, 1981.

———. "Religious Values after the Holocaust: A Jewish View." In *Jews and Christians after the Holocaust*, ed. Abraham J. Peck, 63–86. Philadelphia: Fortress Press, 1982.

———. "The Relationship of Judaism and Christianity: Toward a New Organic Model." *Perspectives/Quarterly Review* 4, no. 4 (winter 1984): 1–19.

———. "Voluntary Covenant." In *Contemporary Jewish Religious Responses to the Shoah*, ed. Steven L. Jacobs, 78–105. Lanham, Md.: University Press of America, 1993.

———. "Judaism and Christianity: Their Respective Roles in the Strategy of Redemption." In *Visions of the Other: Jewish and Christian Theologians Assess the Dialogue: Papers Given at the 9th National Workshop on Christian-Jewish Relations, Baltimore, MD 1986*, ed. Eugene J. Fisher, 7–27. Mahwah, N.J.: Paulist Press, 1994.

———. "Pluralism and Partnership." *ICCJ Unity without Uniformity: The Challenge of Pluralism.* Martin Buber House Publication, no. 26 (spring 1999): 68–81.

———. "Judaism and Christianity: Covenants of Redemption." In *Christianity in Jewish Terms*, ed. Tikva Frymer-Kensky, David Novak, Peter Ochs, David Fox Sandmel, and Michael A. Signer, 141–58. Boulder, Colo.: Westview Press, 2000.

Grossberg, Lawrence. "Introduction: Bringin It All Back Home—Pedagogy and Cultural Studies." In *Between Borders: Pedagogy and the Politics of Cultural Studies*, ed. Henry A. Giroux and Peter McLaren, 1–25. New York: Routledge, 1994.

———. "Cultural Studies: What's in a Name? (One More Time)." In *Bringing It All Back Home: Essays on Cultural Studies*, 245–71. Durham, N.C.: Duke University Press, 1997.

Halevi, Yehuda. *The Kuzari: An Argument for the Faith of Israel.* Translated by Hartwig Hirschfeld. New York: Schocken Books, 1964.

Haynes, Stephen R. "'Between the Times': German Theology and the Weimar Zeitgeist." *Soundings* 74, nos. 1–2 (spring/summer 1991): 9–44.

———. *Prospects for Post-Holocaust Theology.* Atlanta: Scholars Press, 1991.

———. *Reluctant Witnesses: Jews and the Christian Imagination.* Louisville, Ky.: Westminster John Knox Press, 1995.

Hellig, Jocelyn. "Richard L. Rubenstein." In *Interpreters of Judaism in the Late Twentieth Century*, ed. Steven T. Katz, 59–89. Washington, D.C.: B'nai B'rith Books, 1993.

———. "Rabbinic Powerlessness and the Power of Women." In *What Kind of God? Essays in Honor of Richard L. Rubenstein*, ed. Betty Rogers Ruberstein and Michael Berenbaum, 113–31. Lanham, Md.: University Press of America, 1995.

Herberg, Will. "Judaism and Christianity: Their Unity and Difference." In *Jewish Perspectives on Christianity*, ed. Fritz Rothschild, 240–55. New York: Continuum, 1996.

Heron, Alasdair I. C. *A Century of Protestant Theology.* Philadelphia: Westminster Press, 1980.

Heschel, Abraham Joshua. "No Religion Is an Island." In *Jewish Perspectives on Christianity: Leo Baeck, Martin Buber, Franz Rosenzweig, Will Herberg, and Abraham Joshua Heschel*, ed. Fritz Rothschild, 309–24. New York: Continuum, 1996.

Heschel, Susannah. "Anti-Judaism in Christian Feminist Theology." *Tikkun* 5, no. 3 (May/June 1990): 25–28, 95–97.

———. "Jewish Studies as Counterhistory." In *Insider/Outsider: American Jews and Multiculturalism*, ed. David Biale, Michale Galchinsky, and Susannah Heschel, 101–15. Berkeley: University of California Press, 1998.

Holl, Karl. *What Did Luther Understand by Religion?* Edited by James Luther Adams and Walter F. Bense. Translated by Fred W. Meuser and Walter R. Wietzke. Philadelphia: Fortress Press, 1977.

Horowitz, Sara R. "The Paradox of Jewish Studies in the New Academy." In *Insider/Outsider: American Jews and Multiculturalism*, ed. David Biale, Michael Galchinsky, and Susannah Heschel, 116–30. Berkeley: University of California Press, 1998.

Hunsiger, George. *How to Read Karl Barth: The Shape of His Theology*. Oxford: Oxford University Press, 1991.

Isaac, Jules. *Jésus et Israël*. Paris: Editions Albin Michel, 1948.

Jackson, Samuel Macauley, ed. *The New Schaff-Herzog Encyclopedia of Religious Knowledge*. Grand Rapids, Mich.: Baker Book House, 1964. S.v. "Unitarians," by Francis A. Christie.

Jaffee, Martin S. "The Victim-Community in Myth and History: Holocaust Ritual, the Question of Palestine, and the Rhetoric of Christian Witness." *Journal of Ecumenical Studies* 28, no. 2 (spring 1991): 223–38.

Jameson, Frederic. "On Cultural Studies." In *The Identity in Question*, ed. John Rajchman, 251–95. New York: Routledge, 1995.

Kaplan, Edward K. "Abraham Joshua Heschel." In *Interpreters of Judaism in the Late Twentieth Century*, ed. Steven T. Katz, 140–50. Washington, D.C.: B'nai B'rith Books, 1993.

Katz, Steven T. *Post-Holocaust Dialogues: Critical Studies in Modern Jewish Thought*. New York: New York University Press, 1983.

———. "On Historicism and Eternity: Reflections on the 100th Birthday of Franz Rosenzweig." In *Der Philosoph Franz Rosenzweig: Internationaler Kongress-Kassel 1986*. Vol. 2, *Das neue Denken und seine Dimensionen*, ed. Wolfdietrich Schmied-Kowarzik, 745–69. Munich: Verlag Karl Alber Freiburg, 1988.

———. "Irving (Yitzchak) Greenberg." In *Interpreters of Judaism in the Late Twentieth Century*, ed. Steven T. Katz, 59–89. Washington, D.C.: B'nai B'rith Books, 1993.

———. *The Holocaust in Historical Context*. Vol. 1, *The Holocaust and Mass Death before the Modern Age*. New York: Oxford University Press, 1994.

Kaufman, William E. *Contemporary Jewish Philosophies*. New York: Reconstructionist Press and Behrman House, 1976.

Klein, Charlotte. *Anti-Judaism in Christian Theology*. Philadelphia: Fortress Press, 1978.

Knoll, Joachim H. "In memoriam Hans-Joachim Schoeps: Der Mensch, sein Werk und sein Zeit." In *Deutsch-jüdische Geschichte im 19 und 20. Jahrhundert*, edited by Ludger Heid and Joachim H. Knoll, 231–48. *Studien zur Geistesgeschichte*, vol. 15. Stuttgart: Burg, 1992.

Koester, Helmut. *History and Literature of Early Christianity*. Vol. 2, *Introduction to the New Testament*. New York: Walter de Gruyter, 1987.

Kraut, Benny. "The Ambivalent Relations of American Reform Judaism with Unitarianism in the Last Third of the Nineteenth Century." *Journal of Ecumenical Studies* 23, no. 1 (winter 1986): 58–68.

———. "A Unitarian Rabbi? The Case of Solomon H. Sonneschein." In *Jewish Apostasy in the Modern World*, ed. Todd M. Endelman, 272–308. New York: Holmes and Meier, 1987.

Krell, Marc A. "Decentering Judaism and Christianity: Using Feminist Theory to Construct a Postmodern Jewish-Christian Theology." *Cross Currents* 50, no. 4 (winter 2000/2001): 474–87.

———. "Eliezer Berkovits's Post-Holocaust Theology: A Dialectic between Polemics and Reception." *Journal of Ecumenical Studies* 37, no. 1 (winter 2000): 28–45.

———. "Schoeps vs. Rosenzweig: Transcending Religious Borders." *Zeitschrift für Religions-und Geistesgeschichte* 52, no. 1 (2000): 25–37.

Lease, Gary, ed. "Der Briefwechsel zwischen Karl Barth und Hans-Joachim Schoeps." In *Menora*, 105–40. Munich: Piper, 1991.

———. *"Odd Fellows" in the Politics of Religion: Modernism, National Socialism, and German Judaism.* Berlin: Mouton de Gruyter, 1995.

Leibig, James E. "Post-Conciliar Initiatives toward Recognition of the Salvific Reality of Judaism: A Theological Challenge of 'Nostra Aetate.'" Ph.D. diss., Catholic University of America, 1993.

Levy, Felix. "The Uniqueness of Israel." In *His Own Torah: Felix A. Levy Memorial Volume*, ed. Sefton D. Temkin, 161–73. New York: Jonathan David, 1969.

Lewin, Kurt. "Self-Hatred among Jews." *Contemporary Jewish Record* 4, no. 3 (June 1941): 219–32.

Littell, Franklin. *The Crucifixion of the Jews.* New York: Harper and Row, 1975.

Loew, ben Bezalel, Yehuda. *Netzah Yisrael.* Tel Aviv, 1964.

———. *Sefer Tifferet Yisrael.* Jerusalem, 1970.

———. *Sefer Gevurot Hashem.* Jerusalem, 1971.

Löwith, Karl. *From Hegel to Nietzsche: The Revolution in Nineteenth-Century Thought.* Translated by David E. Green. New York: Holt, Rinehart and Winston, 1964. Reprint, New York: Columbia University Press, 1991.

Lubarsky, Sandra. *Tolerance and Transformation: Jewish Approaches to Religious Pluralism.* Cincinnati: Hebrew Union College Press, 1990.

Marcus, Ivan G. "Jews and Christians Imagining the Other in Medieval Europe." *Prooftexts* 15 (1995): 209–26.

———. *Rituals of Childhood: Jewish Acculturation in Medieval Europe.* New Haven, Conn.: Yale University Press, 1996.

Maybaum, Ignaz. *The Face of God after Auschwitz.* Amsterdam: Polak and Van Gennep, 1965.

McClintock Fulkerson, Mary. *Changing the Subject: Women's Discourses and Feminist Theology.* Minneapolis, Minn.: Fortress Press, 1994.

McCormack, Bruce L. *Karl Barth's Critically Realistic Dialectical Theology: Its Genesis and Development, 1909–1936.* Oxford: Clarendon Press, 1995.

McLaren, Peter. "Multiculturalism and the Postmodern Critique: Toward a Pedagogy of Resistance and Transformation." In *Between Borders: Pedagogy and the Politics of Cultural Studies*, ed. Henry A. Giroux and Peter McLaren, 192–222. New York: Routledge, 1994.

Mendelssohn, Moses. *Jerusalem or on Religious Power and Judaism.* Translated by Allan Arkush. Hanover and London: University Press of New England, 1983.

Mendes-Flohr, Paul. "Rosenzweig and the Crisis of Historicism." In *The Philosophy of Franz Rosenzweig*, 138–61. Hanover, N.H.: University Press of New England, 1988.

———. *From Mysticism to Dialogue: Martin Buber's Transformation of German Social Thought.* Detroit: Wayne State University Press, 1989.

———. *German Jews: A Dual Identity.* New Haven, Conn.: Yale University Press, 1999.

Merkle, John C. "Introduction." In *Jewish Perspectives on Christianity: Leo Baeck, Martin Buber, Franz Rosenzweig, Will Herberg, and Abraham Joshua Heschel*, ed. Fritz Rothschild, 267–77. New York: Continuum, 1996.

Miller, Ronald. *Dialogue and Disagreement: Franz Rosenzweig's Relevance to Contempo-*

rary Jewish-Christian Understanding. Lanham, Md.: University Press of America, 1989.

Minh-Ha, Trinh T. *When the Moon Waxes Red: Representation, Gender and Cultural Politics*. New York: Routledge, 1991.

Moltmann, Jürgen. *The Crucified God: The Cross of Christ as the Foundation and Criticism of Christian Theology*. Translated by R. A. Wilson and John Bowden. New York: Harper and Row, 1974.

Moore, James F. "A Spectrum of Views: Traditional Christian Responses to the Holocaust." *Journal of Ecumenical Studies* 25, no. 2 (spring 1988): 212–24.

Moore, Robert L. Review of *My Brother Paul*, by Richard L. Rubenstein. *Psychohistory Review* 5 (December 1976): 47–48.

———. "Pauline Theology and the Return of the Repressed: Depth Psychology and Early Christian Thought." *Zygon* 13 (June 1978): 158–68.

Morgan, Michael L. *Dilemmas in Modern Jewish Thought: The Dialectics of Revelation and History*. Bloomington: Indiana University Press, 1992.

Moses, Stephane. "Franz Rosenzweig in Perspective: Reflections on His Last Diaries." In *The Philosophy of Franz Rosenzweig*, ed. Paul Mendes-Flohr, 185–201. Hanover, N.H.: University Press of New England, 1988.

———. *System and Revelation: The Philosophy of Franz Rosenzweig*. Translated by Catherine Tihanyi. Detroit: Wayne State University Press, 1992.

Mosse, George. "The Influence of the Völkish Idea on German Jewry." In *Germans and Jews: The Right, the Left, and the Search for a "Third Force" in Pre-Nazi Germany*. New York: Howard Fertig, 1970.

Novak, David. *Jewish-Christian Dialogue: A Jewish Justification*. Oxford: Oxford University Press, 1989.

Ochs, Peter, and David Fox Sandmel, "Christianity in Jewish Terms: A Project to Redefine the Relationship." *Cross Currents* 50, n. 4 (winter 2000/2001): 448–57.

Oppenheim, Michael. "Irving Greenberg and a Jewish Dialectic of Hope." *Judaism* 49, no. 194 (spring 2000): 189–203.

Overbeck, Franz. *Christentum und Kultur: Gedanken und Anmerkungen zur modernen Theologie*. Edited by Carl Albrecht Bernoulli. Basel: Benno Schwabe, 1919.

Oxford Dictionary of the Christian Church, 3rd ed. S.v. "Unitarianism."

Pardes, Ilana. *Counter-traditions in the Bible: A Feminist Approach*. Cambridge, Mass.: Harvard University Press, 1992.

Parkes, James. *The Conflict of the Church and Synagogue: A Study in the Origins of Antisemitism*. London: Soncino Press, 1934.

———. *Judaism and Christianity*. Chicago: University of Chicago Press, 1948.

———. *Antisemitism*. Chicago: Quadrangle Books, 1964.

Pawlikowski, John T., O.S.M. *What Are They Saying about Christian-Jewish Relations?* New York: Paulist Press, 1980.

———. *Christ in the Light of the Christian-Jewish Dialogue*. New York: Paulist Press, 1982.

———. "The Search for a New Paradigm for the Christian-Jewish Relationship: A Response to Michael Signer." In *Reinterpreting Revelation and Tradition: Jews and Christians in Conversation*, ed. John T. Pawlikowski, O.S.M. and Hayim Goren Perelmuter, 25–48. Franklin, Wisc.: Sheed and Ward, 2000.

Peskowitz, Miriam. "Engendering Jewish Religious History." In *Judaism since Gender*, ed. Miriam Peskowitz and Laura Levitt, 17–39. New York: Routledge, 1997.

Plaskow, Judith. "Christian Feminism and Anti-Judaism." *Cross Currents* 33 (fall 1978): 306–9.

———. "Feminist Anti-Judaism and the Christian God." *Journal of Feminist Studies in Religion* 7, no. 2 (fall 1991): 99–109.

Rashkover, Randi. "Jewish Responses to Jewish-Christian Dialogue." *Cross Currents* 50, nos. 1–2 (spring/summer 2000): 211–20.

Robbins, Jill. *Prodigal Son/Elder Brother: Interpretations and Alterity in Augustine, Petrarch, Kafka, Levinas.* Chicago: University of Chicago Press, 1991.

Rohman, Klaus. "Radical Theology in the Making: Richard L. Rubenstein Reshaped Jewish Theology from Its Beginnings." In *What Kind of God? Essays in Honor of Richard L. Rubenstein*, ed. by Betty Rogers and Michael Berenbaum, 3–23. Lanham, Md.: University Press of America, 1995.

Rosenstock-Huessy, Eugen, ed. *Judaism Despite Christianity: The "Letters on Christianity and Judaism" between Eugen Rosenstock-Huessy and Franz Rosenzweig.* University: Alabama: University of Alabama Press, 1969.

Rosenzweig, Franz. *Brief.* Edited by Edith Rosenzweig. Berlin: Schocken Verlag, 1935.

———. "Apologetisches Denke." In *Kleinere Schriften*, 31–42. Berlin: Schocken, 1937.

———. *On Jewish Learning.* Translated by Nahum N. Glatzer. New York: Schocken Books, 1965.

———. *Franz Rosenzweig: Der Mensch und sein Werk: Gessammelte Schriften.* Vol. 2, *Brief und Tagebucher*, part 1: 1918–1929, ed. by R. Rosenzweig and E. Rosenzweig Scheinmann. The Hague: Martinus Nijhoff, 1979.

———. *Franz Rosenzweig: Der Mensch und sein Werk: Gessammelte Schriften.* Vol. 3, *Zweistromland: Kleinere Schriften zu Glauben und Denken*, ed. Reinhold Mayer and Annemarie Mayer. Dordrecht: Martinus Nijhoff, 1984.

———. *The Star of Redemption.* 2d ed. Translated by William W. Hallo. Notre Dame, Ind.: Notre Dame University Press, 1985.

———. *Ninety-two Poems and Hymns of Yehuda Halevi.* Edited by Richard A. Cohen. Translated by Thomas Kovach, Eva Jospe, and Gilya Gerda Schmidt. Albany: State University of New York Press, 2000.

Rothschild, Fritz, ed. *Jewish Perspectives on Christianity: Leo Baeck, Martin Buber, Franz Rosenzweig, Will Herberg, and Abraham Joshua Heschel.* New York: Continuum, 1996.

Rubenstein, Richard. *After Auschwitz: Radical Theology and Contemporary Judaism.* Indianapolis: Bobbs-Merrill, 1966.

———. "'The Nothingness' of God." *The Christian Century*, 21 February 1968, 230–32.

———. *The Religious Imagination: A Study in Psychoanalysis and Jewish Theology.* Indianapolis: Bobbs-Merrill, 1968.

———. "Varieties of God in the Psychologist's Frame of Reference." In *Psychology and Religion: A Contemporary Dialogue*, ed. Joseph Havens, 5–14. Princeton, N.J.: D. Van Nostrand, 1968.

———. *Morality and Eros.* New York: McGraw-Hill, 1970.

———. *My Brother Paul.* New York: Harper and Row, 1972.

———. "Jewish Theology and the Current World Situation." *Conservative Judaism* 28, no. 4 (summer 1974): 3–25.

———. *Power Struggle.* New York: Charles Scribner's Sons, 1974.

———. "Response to the Issue on Judaism and Psycho-History of *The Journal of Psycho-History*." *Journal of Psycho-History* 7 (spring 1979): 543–55.

———. "Luther and the Roots of the Holocaust." In *Persistent Prejudice: Perspectives on Anti-Semitism,* ed. Herbert Hirsch and Jack D. Spiro, 31–41. Fairfax, Va.: George Mason University Press, 1988.

———. *After Auschwitz: History, Theology, and Contemporary Judaism.* 2d ed. Baltimore: Johns Hopkins University Press, 1992.

———. Interview by author, 21 May 1997, Bridgeport, Connecticut. Tape recording.

———. "A Twentieth-Century Journey." In *From the Unthinkable to the Unavoidable: American Christian and Jewish Scholars Encounter the Holocaust,* ed. Carol Rittner and John K. Roth, 157–72. Westport Conn.: Greenwood Press, 1997.

Ruether, Rosemary Radford, and Herman J. Ruether. *The Wrath of Jonah: The Crisis of Religious Nationalism in the Israeli-Palestinian Conflict.* San Francisco: Harper and Row, 1989.

Sanders, E. P. *Paul and Palestinian Judaism: A Comparison of Patterns of Religion.* Minneapolis, Minn.: Fortress Press, 1977.

Saperstein, Marc. "Christian Doctrine and the State of the Question." Paper presented at the Remembering for the Future 2000 Conference on the Holocaust, Oxford, 19 July 2000.

Schelling, Friedrich Wilhelm Joseph. *Philosophy of Art.* Translated by Douglas W. Stott. Minneapolis:Univesity of Minnesota Press, 1989.

Schoeps, Hans-Joachim. "Zur freideutschen Fahre." *Die Weginante* (October 1926): 13–15.

———. "American Made in Germany—*Is gibt eine freideutsche position,*" *Die Freideutsche Position. Rundbenef an Jugendführer zur Besinnung und Stellungnahme* 1 (spring 1929): 1–6.

———. "Der Nationalsozialismus als verkappte Religion," *Eltheto* 93 (March 1939): 93–98.

———. *Philosemitismus im Barock: Religions-und geistgeschichtliche Untersuchungen.* Tübingen: Mohr, 1952.

———. *Die letzten dreissig Jahre: Rückblicke.* Stuttgart: Ernst Klett Verlag, 1956.

———. *Paul: The Theology of the Apostle in the Light of Jewish Religious History.* Translated by Harold Knight. Philadelphia: Westminster Press, 1961.

———. *The Jewish Christian Argument: A History of Theologies in Conflict.* 3d ed. Translated by David E. Green. London: Faber and Faber, 1963.

———. *Jewish Christianity: Factional Disputes in the Early Church.* Translated by Douglas R. A. Hare. Philadelphia: Fortress Press, 1969.

———. "Secessio Judaica-Israel in Ewigkeit." In *Bereit für Deutschland. Der Patriotismus deutscher Juden und der Nationalsozialismus,* 277–88. Berlin: Haude and Spencer, 1970.

———. *Ja-Nein-Und Trotzdem Erinnerungen. Begegnungen, Erfahrungen.* Mainz: Hase & Koehler Verlag, 1974.

———. *Jüdischer Glaube in dieser Zeit: Prolegomena zur Grundlegung einer systematischen Theologie des Judentums*. In *Gesammelte Schriften*, ed. Julius H. Schoeps, 1–90. Hildescheim: Georg Olms, 1990.

———, ed. *Salomon Ludwig Steinheim zum Gedenken*. Leiden: E. J. Brill, 1966.

Schoeps, Hans Joachim, and Hans Blüher. *Streit um Israel: Ein jüdisch-christliches Gespräch*. Hamburg: Hanseatische Verlagsanstalt, 1933.

Scholem, Gershom. "Offener Brief an den Verfasser der Schrift, 'Jüdischer Glaube in dieser Zeit.'" *Bayerische Israelitische Gemeindezeitung*, 15 August 1932, 241–44.

———. *Major Trends in Jewish Mysticism*. 3d ed. New York: Schocken Books, 1971.

———. "Revelation and Tradition as Religious Categories in Judaism." In *The Messianic Idea in Judaism and Other Essays on Jewish Spirituality*. New York: Schocken Books, 1971.

———. *Briefe I: 1914–1947*. Edited by Itta Shedletzky. Munich: Verlag C. H. Beck, 1994.

Silberstein, Laurence J. "Others Within and Others Without." In *The Other in Jewish Thought and History: Constructions of Jewish Culture and Identity*, ed. Laurence J. Silberstein and Robert L. Cohn, 1–34. New York: New York University Press, 1994.

———. "Mapping, Not Tracing: Opening Reflection." In *Mapping Jewish Identities*, 1–36. New York: New York University Press, 2000.

Smith, Mark S. *The Early History of God: Yahweh and Other Deities in Ancient Israel*. San Francisco: Harper and Row, 1990.

Soulen, R. Kendall. "Israel and the Church: A Christian Response to Irving Greenberg's Covenantal Pluralism." In *Christianity in Jewish Terms*, ed. Tikva Frymer-Kensky, David Novak, Peter Ochs, David Fox Sandmel, and Michael A. Signer, 167–74. Boulder, Colo.: Westview Press, 2000.

Stein, Howard F. "Judaism and the Group Fantasy of Martyrdom: The Psychodynamic Paradox of Survival through Persecution." *Journal of Psycho-History* 6, no. 2 (fall 1978): 151–210.

Steinheim, Salomon Ludwig. *Die Offenbarung nach dem Lehrbegriffe der Synagogue*. Vol. 1, *Ein Schiboleth*. Frankfurt am Main: Schmerber, 1835.

———. *Die Politik nach dem Begriffe der Offenbarung als Theokratie*. Leipzig: Teubner, 1845.

Tanner, Kathryn. *Theories of Culture: A New Agenda for Theology*. Minneapolis, Minn.: Fortress Press, 1997.

Tracy, David. *Plurality and Ambiguity: Hermeneutics, Religion, Hope*. San Francisco: Harper and Row, 1987.

Tyson, Joseph B. *The New Testament and Early Christianity*. New York: Macmillan, 1984.

Van Buren, Paul. "Christian Theology and Jewish Reality: An Essay-Review." *Journal of the American Academy of Religion* 45, no. 4 (1977): 491–95.

———. *A Theology of the Jewish-Christian Reality. Part III: Christ in Context*. San Francisco: Harper and Row, 1988.

Von Balthazar, *Karl Barth: Darstellung und Deutung seiner Theologie* [The Theology of Karl Barth] New York: Rinehart and Winston, 1971.

Von Kellenbach, Katherina. *Anti-Judaism in Feminist Religious Writings*. Atlanta: Scholars Press, 1994.

Wacker, Marie-Theres. "Feminist Theology and Anti-Judaism: The Status of the Discussion and the Context of the Problem in the Federal Republic of Germany." *Journal of Feminist Studies in Religion* 7, no. 2 (fall 1991): 109–16.

Wagner, Richard. "Judaism and Music." In *Judaism in Music and Other Essays.* Translated by W. Ashton Ellis. Lincoln: University of Nebraska Press, 1995.

Wallis, James. "The Theology of Paul M. van Buren and the Jewish-Christian Dialogue." Ph.D. diss., Claremont Graduate School, 1993.

Wasserstrom, Steven. *Between Muslim and Jew: The Problem of Symbiosis under Early Islam.* Princeton, N.J.: Princeton University Press, 1995.

Wiesel, Elie. "Jewish Values in the Post-Holocaust Future." *Judaism* 16, no. 3 (summer 1967): 266–99.

Wigoder, Geoffrey. *Jewish-Christian Relations since the Second World War.* Manchester: Manchester University Press, 1988.

Wyschogrod, Michael. *The Body of Faith: God in the People Israel.* San Francisco: Harper and Row, 1983.

Index